Reel to Real by Reel

First Edition Design Publishing

Reel to Real by Reel
Copyright ©2015 Chris Callaway

ISBN 978-1622-878-08-6 PRINT
ISBN 978-1622-878-09-3 EBOOK

LCCN 2015932582

January 2015

Published and Distributed by
First Edition Design Publishing, Inc.
P.O. Box 20217, Sarasota, FL 34276-3217
www.firsteditiondesignpublishing.com

Interior Illustration Credit – Todd Muller

A special thank you to my parents,

Tom and Boni Callaway,

for their love and encouragement.

Thank you to Greg Glasgow for the countless

hours spent editing the manuscript.

Thank you to Erin O'Grady (I love you), Doug

Van Pelt, Bruce Brown, Dave Flomberg,

Stewart Sallo and all at *Boulder Weekly* (past

and present), *HM*, Dave Herrera, Kiernan

Maletsky and all at *Westword*, Mark

Bliesener, Nic Brown, Betsy Pearce, and all

the artists in this book.

Reel to Real by Reel

By Chris Callaway

André,

Thank you for the always liking the better bands and musicians. And thank you for your friendship.

Interviews

Introduction: Questions and More Questions

I ask lots of questions. This has been the pattern of my life since I was old enough to utter words that, to this day, often make little sense. On my best days, my verbal skills amount to a few good sentences, usually after several cups of coffee or a beer. I've never been a sugar hound and cannot imagine what would result if my tastes catered to corn-syrup-laden beverages and food items. Hopefully, the world (or at least my circle of friends and acquaintances) will never know.

The first question of significance I remember uttering was when I was a four-year-old cauldron of curiosity. I had been hanging out at our neighbor's house, and their sons, roughly one and three years older than me, were discussing a word of interest. The utterance in question was "fudge." Well, the word wasn't really "fudge," but it did start with the same consonant and rhymed with "truck." How interesting the word sounded. I had no idea what it meant, but I was told that it was a bad word and that I'd get in trouble with my parents if I used it. I simply said, "Yeah, well, I'm going to ask my mom." The older brother smiled and shook his head. The younger brother looked at me and said, "No you won't." I replied, "Yes I wiiiillll!" I stomped off, ran back across the thin strip of wooded area to my house, went up to my mom, who was probably watching *Guiding Light* or polishing a piece of furniture, and said, without any sort of reservation, "Mom, is (the acronym for "for unlawful carnal knowledge") a bad word?"

I have to hand it to my mom. She did not get upset. She simply replied, "Chris, yes, never use that word." Of course, when I knew what I was doing and used that type of language, my mom would become angry and disappointed. I once had the privilege of having my mouth washed out with soap and was sometimes spanked when neighborhood moms would report on my filthy mouth. I don't harbor any bitterness.

But the questions continued after my young and innocent f-word inquiry. Things like "How does electricity work?" would exit my mouth in a Southern drawl. I was always into finding out for myself with most things, and electricity was no different. This involved plugging in cords with a key ring attached to the prongs until my dad realized what I was doing and bought me scientific project kits that involved batteries instead of an electrical outlet, along with some other "electricity-free" options—including a piece of plywood with multiple three-prong outlets on it expertly constructed by my grandfather. This way I could plug whatever I wanted into the sockets without the shock value, and my dad didn't have to sit at his desk at work wondering if I was in the process of electrocuting myself or setting the house on fire. It also prevented my mom from having a heart attack when she would round the corner as I was pushing in another key-ring loaded plug into an electrical outlet.

There were more questions: What poisons can't I drink? What's poisonous? How can I warn other kids about poisons? Apparently I saw a news broadcast where a child of similar age had consumed poison, not knowing what he or she was drinking, and this experience, according to my mom, took the shape of a letter she "helped" me write at four years old to Ralph Nader. He was the head of a task force or something like it that involved "Mr. Yuck" stickers. These could be affixed to poisonous items to ward off childhood consumption. I plastered those suckers on every conceivable bottle containing anything even remotely harmful.

Guns. That was another category of interest that resulted in a litany of questions. I asked my dad about different pistols, rifles, machine guns and shotguns—he had a military background and knew a lot about weapons. I'd ask my grandfather too. It seemed I had an elevated interest in things that could kill me. My mom had a friend who worked at Colt Firearms and sent me press photos of guns. I plastered those all over my room at the age of eight. I wrote to gun manufacturers like Ruger and received catalogs and stickers. I collected toy guns and could tell you what model various toy guys were replicated after.

Cars were also a fascination, and I had tons of questions on those too—my dad would take me to shows and I could identify classic cars and new vehicles alike. At one time I had car pricing guides and could tell you what a 1985 Cadillac Eldorado would run you or what a 1983 Jaguar XJS would cost. This started at the age of eight as well. I'm still trying to figure out the classic Jaguar coupe with a thirteen-cylinder engine I saw once. How would that work? Don't cylinders have to be an even number to function?

Given my sense of curiosity and penchant for endless streams of questions, it's no surprise that I would go into journalism, at least on a freelance basis. Here, in the journalism forum, I get to ask lots of questions. I am able to try and get at the heart of things. And it's no shock that I would chase music journalism. I was a huge music fan. My dad started me off on that path when I was an infant, playing Beatles tunes and old Chicago songs on a big Sony reel-to-reel tape player. Then there was *The Dukes of Hazzard* television show, with the addictive theme song performed by Waylon Jennings. My mom took me to the record store at the mall in Blacksburg and bought me the 99-cent single. I thought the "B" side was pretty good too. I was really into that show. My classmates Elliot and Chris and I would play *The Dukes of Hazzard* at recess during our first-grade year. They had Bo and Luke Duke shirts and I had a Boss Hogg shirt. Unfortunately it was based on your shirt, so I was always stuck playing Boss Hogg.

Later on, musical love came from additional places: there were my Aunt Diane and Uncle Rick, younger than my parents, who, in the mid-'80s turned me on to Tears for Fears and Simple Minds. (My uncle gave me his collection of pristine Kinks singles about twenty-nine years later—I can't thank him enough.) Rock radio only furthered my enjoyment of pop music. There were also books, magazines, friends— like André Salles, who always seemed to have a more developed musical taste—and the continued influence of my dad, who, beyond the Sony reel-to-reel machine, often played rock radio, cassettes and a old 1960s wood-grain radio in the garage while working on projects. Often friends would give him mix tapes or burn classic rock records for him. The inspiration was endless.

It did get rocky at one point. Somewhere in the mid-'80s, I became serious about my Christian faith and was told that rock was "of the devil" (especially "secular" rock). Even though there was nothing in the Bible to support this assumption, I went with it. I would listen to the words of some very conservative but well-meaning people who didn't really understand what they were restricting in their speeches and admonitions.

Due to this influence, I even wrote a song called "Worldly People" in 1986. It was about the "evils" of heavy metal, and part of it went "don't take drugs, don't grow your hair long" and "worldly people throw away pornographic pictures and throw away heavy metal." It was very judgmental. There was no grace, no attempt to understand other people and where they were coming from.

During my "rock is evil" period, I happened to see a television program on gospel music, and there was my answer: "gospel music." I kind of liked the way it sounded, even though it was far from rock. I asked my parents for some gospel music cassettes or albums. I woke up Christmas morning to a plethora of wrapped goodies—several of these were in my stocking. Those were always the most interesting. My dad had a way of using toilet paper tubes, etc. to disguise the item. I wound up with four cassettes: Rick Cua's *You're My Road*, Steve Camp's *Shake Me to Wake Me*, Steve Green's *He Holds the Keys* and Glad's *Live at the Kennedy Center*. Rick was rock, but with Christian lyrics. I was safe. Steve Camp wasn't bad either—he wasn't as hard-edged as Rick. Steve Green sounded too "safe" and wimpy for a guy who liked rock—it was something my mom or her friends would enjoy. They would borrow each other's Sandi Patty records—it was horrible. Glad—well, they were more of an a cappella group, and I just couldn't develop a taste.

All of these records, unless I am mistaken, used the same distributor, so each cassette had a little sticker attached to the shrink-wrap—"Buy 3 Get One Free" or something like that. Pretty soon a trip to Logos, the Christian bookstore in

Framingham, was necessary, and I discovered Swedish rockers Jerusalem and also that U2 was considered "kind of a Christian" band. My foray into U2 and Christian hard rock had begun. Later I would dive into Christian metal but would maintain an interest in U2 and, to a much greater degree, the Alarm—another band with Christian ties.

In high school, I went back to listening to secular music while still enjoying Christian rock. I couldn't avoid Rush—I was a bass player, after all! In college I would gradually shed most of the Christian rock, except for a few bands and artists.

My first foray into writing, however, started in elementary school around the time I was listening to '80s rock radio. While I had a long way to go before entering the world of entertainment journalism, music still figured prominently in my life. I'd bring in cassettes to play during art class. Surprisingly, our art teacher couldn't stand the Boston *Don't Look Back* cassette I brought in once. We were living outside Boston, she was middle-aged—how could she not know them? She asked, "Who is this?" and then asked if I could promptly remove said cassette from the mono cassette player on the counter.

There was a writing assignment—we had to author a "book." I took the task seriously. The tale I created was called *The Double Bass Guitar,* and the covers were constructed out of white poster board that had an eye-blindingly bright color on the reverse side—this is probably why I started losing my vision. The "book" itself had everything you would want if you were twelve years old and watched *The Karate Kid* one too many times. The story took place in Japan during the "16000 century" and involved the theft of a priceless double-bass guitar that, if found today, "would be worth about $1,500,000,000 U.S. dollars."

Surely my historical knowledge was not on par with my topic, but my parents took a glance at my project and made the comment, "You should be a writer. Maybe that's what you'll do in life."

This was certainly not what a young rock 'n' roll guitarist wanted to hear. Writing? That wasn't cool. I was too busy fashioning drum sets out of holiday cookie tins and bass drums out of big cardboard barrels with metal rims on them. I would take my dad's Sony reel-to-reel tape machine, a phone recording microphone with a suction cup and some super strong magnets and make an acoustic guitar into an electric, with the tape machine functioning as the amp. This was the closest I could come to an actual electric. The acoustic belonged to my dad's friend, and when he got it back, it was in pretty sorry shape.

I also frustrated the crap out of my chubby music teacher at Walpole Music in Walpole, Massachusetts. I would never practice. I always wanted to play by ear. I could have cared less about the staffs, notes and chords on a sheet of paper. Later on, I would have a bass teacher at the same music store throw my music book across the room because I wouldn't practice and would try to pick up stuff by ear—even complicated pieces by bands like King's X and Rush. He looked at me and almost yelled as he tossed it, "Fine, we'll have it your way."

My parents' comment about writing made me retreat into playing music more—I was a rebellious pre-teen and teen, and authoring anything beyond lyrics didn't interest me. Things at my house could get interesting and headache-inducing for my parents, though they seldom complained. My friend Jason would bang on the "drum set" we had created, and I would sing (well, make sounds with my vocal cords) and play guitar. We eventually invited my friend André Salles to play with us, but I don't think he ever came to a rehearsal. You see, André was the only one of us who could actually play. Jason and I, however, did name the band—"Methuselah"—and recorded a lousy cassette called *969 Years*. We were both very into the Christian heavy metal scene and wanted to give our band a biblical name. I went as far as creating a costume of sorts—I tore up a white T-shirt and tried to emulate Les Carlsen, lead singer of Christian metal band Bloodgood.

Plenty of bands came and went (André was in a couple of them), and we got progressively better. There was even a rap/hard rock mix concoction called Glimpse of Reality with my close friend Chris on drums and, eventually, my buddy

Tony on guitar. Chris' vintage Ludwig set could have financed an entire album had he been able to sell it for what it would be worth today, but we were kids and had no sense of what the future would hold. I can say this—our music was horrible, but we played out a bit and put out two cassettes worth of material.

After the rap/hard rock band folded and college got underway, I thought about music journalism again. I had briefly authored and edited a horrible music newsletter years before, when I became enamored with the Christian music magazines I was reading. It was quickly shelved as music performance was continuously calling my name. I don't know that the five people on the mailing list ever missed my "publication." However, that same itch I had to start the newsletter presented itself again early on in college, and I started scratching. I realized I could combine my love of music and possibly write professionally about music and musicians. After briefly writing for a friend's music newsletter, the real experience began.

I had never been all that fearful of approaching people, and I did just that to get my foot in the door with writing. Doug Van Pelt, founder of *Heaven's Metal* (later *HM*), gave me my first real article, and Bruce A. Brown, a writer for *CCM Magazine*, gave me the chance to write an album review. I met both of these gentlemen at a music conference in 1994 during my freshman year of college, and a relationship ensued. Soon, I was writing a plethora of articles for Doug. After college I moved to Nashville, where I continued to write, although to a lesser degree. At that point, I was doing marketing for a record label and did not have much time. After two years, however, I moved back to Denver and started authoring pieces for the *Boulder Weekly*. My first editor there, Dave Flomberg, gave me the room I needed to write and often would let me go with my own ideas. If someone was coming to Boulder or Denver to play, then an interview was probably fair game.

I was still pursuing music pretty heavily, and during my early years writing for the *Weekly*, I was performing in a modern rock band that kept receiving more and more accolades. That band had its demise three years after I joined due to some internal issues. In a matter of months after it ended, we had label interest—go figure. I would go on to form another band with three of the same members, still thinking that rock stardom was in my future—it just never happened.

While all this was going on, music editors came and went with the *Weekly* and I was writing less and less. I eventually switched gears and started authoring pieces for Denver's *Westword*. At this point in time I was in yet another local band—this time I actually knew the potential was there, as we had an extremely gifted vocalist and songwriter fronting the group who had plenty of major label and touring experience. But after four years, I didn't feel that much had changed, so I left the band with friendships still intact, put my bass in the closet and decided to concentrate on writing. It wasn't anyone's fault—the combination, situation and/or timing just didn't work out.

In late 2011, my good friend Greg Glasgow, who spent years as the books and entertainment editor at Boulder's *Daily Camera*, said to me, "You have all these interviews. Why don't you publish them?" It sounded like a crazy idea at first. I had almost tossed most of the recordings about six months prior to that conversation, but for some reason, kept them and actually transferred many of them from microcassette to CD. Throughout most of my life I had been a packrat, but the reverse had been the norm for quite some time.

The more I thought about Greg's suggestion, the more I liked the idea. What happens when you set out to write an article based on an interview is this: the artist's publicist sets up the interview, the artist calls you (usually through his publicist), then you ask permission to record the interview for possible use. The artist agrees and you wind up—at least in my experience—with fifteen to twenty minutes of recorded conversation. When you develop your story (unless you decide to run the whole transcription), you only use a few quotes. So there's a lot of material left over that never gets used but that fans may find interesting.

For the book, I took the liberty of removing questions and answers that could potentially cause a legal issue or just didn't make logical sense to include. In some cases, I've also removed parts of interviews where I asked questions that were just plain stupid or laughably uninformed. Also, wherever it seems like there was laughter, there probably was, but indicating those instances often doesn't read very well.

In the end, these are real conversations with creative types, talking about their craft, their lives and everything in between. There's also a good bit of my life in this book, which shows how music has irrevocably woven itself into who I am.

Thank you for taking the time to read this book. I hope you enjoy what is contained on the pages herein.

ROBYN HITCHCOCK

Thursday, July 22, 1999
Article: *Boulder Weekly* (July 29, 1999)

This was the interview that started it all. As I mentioned a few pages earlier, I had written for other publications for several years, but this was the first interview with a known mainstream pop star—someone who actually had CDs in the regular record store bins, not in the Christian music section—and whose name was known to serious pop music fans.

I spent several years authoring articles for Christian music magazines, and when I started writing for the *Boulder Weekly* in May of 1999 (the same month I moved back to the Denver area from Nashville), I briefly covered artists and events that, honestly, did not pump any blood through my pop-loving veins. However, I refused to moan in bitterness, because I was gaining work experience writing for a local newspaper and, hopefully, getting my name established among those who read local papers.

I also liked the fact that the publication was in Boulder— while in Nashville, I had dreamed of moving there. The bohemian lifestyle, great microbrewed beer and laid-back atmosphere appealed to me. I had spent a good deal of time in Boulder while in high school and during summers away from college and had fond memories of times spent there. Those hopes were quickly squashed like a caterpillar under a steel-toed boot when I saw how much rent was required in the areas in which I wanted to live. My mom casually said one day, "I just saw this two-bedroom upstairs apartment and it's twenty-four hundred dollars a month. It's near Pearl Street Mall. Isn't that where you'd want to live? Wow, that's expensive." Yes, affirmative, Mom.

Pearl Street was one of my two preferred areas of town—it had great nightlife and good eateries, not to mention bookstores and whatnot. My second area of choice was the University Hill area—fondly known as "the Hill"—which touched the University of Colorado campus and invited its reputed partiers. That area, also, was terribly expensive.

So my beer-loving, culture-seeking, adventure-craving self would have to settle somewhere else. At first, it was a spare bedroom at my parents' place. After a few months, it was an apartment complex near the Denver Tech Center with two former college roommates with whom I was still good friends. Two years later, it was a move to the suburb of Highlands Ranch. This was certainly an area to avoid if you were single and liked nightlife. My buddy Tim and I (he now lives near Seattle with his wife and daughter) were always making truly tasteless jokes about Highlands Ranch while we lived there—we still do when we see each other.

And a full-time writing job? That never happened. Neither did a job working for W.A.R.? or any of the other labels or entertainment companies in town. Instead, I started doing cell phone activations for Nextel, courtesy of my former college roommate, Jeff.

But I did get to start interviewing pop musicians for the *Boulder Weekly,* and this kept me somewhat sane, along with playing bass in local band Breathing Eve. A story on British artist Robyn Hitchcock was my first real foray into rock journalism. It was a long way from one of my early articles for the *Weekly,* when my editor assigned me a piece on a local group I had never heard of. I was bored to tears working on that article—the music just didn't resonate with me. The band members I interviewed were incredibly nice, but it was still a struggle. I drove out to a woman's house near the foothills in Boulder and did one of my only in-person interviews. She was breastfeeding her baby almost the entire time I was going through my list of questions and trying to concentrate on asking them. It was extremely uncomfortable. I think my posterior sweat like a river and my armpits oozed like a sieve from the moment the infant latched onto the breast. It was hot too, being summer and all. I couldn't wait to leave.

As I got into my car and drove off, I remember thinking, "How am I going to write something interesting, since I'm not really into this? And, wow, that breast thing was weird." I struggled through writing the article, eventually stopped having nipple nightmares and continued on with the *Weekly*—and that's where Mr. Hitchcock eventually came into play with his fine British sense of humour.

Warner Bros. sent me an advance copy of Robyn's newest disc, *Jewels for Sophia*. This started a relationship with a publicist there that eventually led to my being able to interview Alex Lifeson of Rush. I did like the disc—it arrived in a pink plastic clamshell case back when these were hard to find. The music was interesting. It wasn't typical pop, but it did have some great elements and catchiness to it, especially the first tune, "Mexican God." Robyn's comment during the interview where he compared his music to a baby crying still makes me chuckle, and he proved himself to be an excellent conversationalist.

We discussed *Storefront Hitchcock*, a movie that the legendary Jonathan Demme had undertaken. It featured Robyn himself performing in front of a storefront window. We also discussed floating pens—the gimmicky writing utensils that sometimes have a magnet on the tip and a base so they in essence, stand on their own.

The interview with the well-spoken Mr. Hitchcock went extremely well and was made even better by his great British accent and lounge-chair laidbackedness. I laughed a lot and received some great quotes and loads of good information. The article, surprisingly, didn't take long to write, and to this day, I feel it is one of my strongest efforts. Dave Flomberg, my editor, called me and said, "Hey, that was probably your best piece yet. [Can't remember who] and I were just discussing how great it turned out. Good job." It seems like from then on, I was able to make more and more suggestions on what I wanted to write and often was able to do interviews with those musicians I truly enjoyed.

Thanks, Robyn.

****

You have been doing music for at least a couple of decades—what is your opinion of popular music as it stands now in the 1990s?
That is a pretty big question. Well, it's an industry. Perhaps it's a bigger industry than it was when I started. It's certainly a bigger industry than when Elvis Presley started. Popular music is about money, first and foremost, and that mustn't be forgotten. Artists are valued by the industry not on the quality of their work, but on how much money they generate for the business. Nonetheless, they're all referred to as artists. The same principle applied when I started making records more than twenty years ago. It hasn't really changed. People say bubblegum sucked in the 1960s. You can now say, "Well I don't like Britney Spears or Boyz II Men, Boys to Boys—whatever it is." Pop music was disposable. It's always been disposable. Perhaps there is just so much now that is disposable that we are beginning to choke on it a bit. So much popcorn comes out of the machine, as it were, that I can't really be bothered to open my mouth and swallow all of it. There were points like in the late '60s and the time of punk ten years later when people would go out and buy every new album with a gatefold sleeve or every sexy new independent seven-inch simply because it was there. You can't really do that now. The old stuff won't go away and the new stuff keeps pouring in. I think we are reaching saturation of disposability, really. There's probably lots of good stuff around, but I really don't know. I haven't really got the time or the inclination to assess it. I actually watch movies now, you know.

You have always put a lot into your music. Have you run into problems in the music industry because you haven't just done whatever? I mean, you haven't done the bubblegum thing. You've had a lot of integrity to what you are doing. Has that caused a lot of problems for you?
Well, in some ways. I don't know. The stuff that's gone out—the innovative stuff was never really done there to please people. It did wind up pleasing people, but it wasn't what

people expected. Nobody manufactured Elvis Presley or the Beatles, Dylan or the Stones or the Who or, you know—and I don't quite know where you move up to from there. The Clash were kind of manufactured. Were Madness great innovators? I don't know, but they're fun, you know. The industry keeps a seat warm for me somewhere in the corner of the room because I make it look good. And they can look like, "Well, we have credible artists in here, like Robyn Hitchcock." To be less cynical, there are people in the business who do like my stuff. Like if you like quality, old-time crafted songs and that sort of thing. They'll enjoy my stuff like they might enjoy a vintage car. They don't expect to go very far in it, but they realize that it's well made. Then they will get on with the next super project. So I haven't been driven into extinction by the business. I have done quite well, I suppose.

That's good, because I know a lot of artists who have tried to make credible art and have often run into the problem of not having a record contract anymore. That seems to be the case today especially with the—you heard about the recent [large corporate music takeover]?
Well they were getting rid of only the acts, but they got rid of the company itself. They [just] bring it back to capitalism—just how much could be justified in the pursuit of increased profits. The argument that having fewer acts enables them to concentrate more on those acts may be true, but it means the fewer acts they have are all safer bets. People tell me that even Sheryl Crow will be introduced as a new artist every time she does an album, because the public will have forgotten her last album. Maybe lots of people think Cher has just started. Maybe there's people who think *Do You Believe in Love After Love* [sic, *Believe*] is her first record. Who knows? America has sadly always been about the erasing of its own history. Although in the course of the disposable culture, classic Americana sprang up with all these fantastic things like Elvis and the jukebox and diners and bobby socks

and rock 'n' roll and things. That's all been eradicated and replaced by strip malls, skateboards and oblivion.

That's true. Speaking of capitalism—your new record has to do with that a little bit. What do you hope to accomplish with the new record?
Only to release it. It's there. It was the most recent thing I've done. I hope people enjoy it. What I wanted to accomplish by making it was to make a record that was quite informally done with different groups of musicians with a little less of a rehearsal—where the musicians were discovering as they recorded new parts. They were making things up on tape, so you catch things at their freshest. Very often in the studio, people have worked things out in demos and they're just trying to re-create or add to their re-creation or something.

What was it like recording that way?
Fantastic. I haven't done that for a long time. I'd either work solo or with the same band for the whole record. In this case, I had sort of three different congregations of musicians. We would go in quite fast with the minimum of rehearsals and record stuff.

In your bio it mentioned that Peter Buck was involved in the record. To what capacity was he involved?
Well there are three songs on the album—"Viva! Sea-Tac," "Jewels for Sophia" and "Elizabeth Jade"—[that] feature the Young Fresh Fellows and Tim Keegan and Peter Buck. They were recorded in Seattle. I think we rehearsed around Peter's house one afternoon. I and Peter and Scott (McCaughey), who's playing bass.

With the tour that you are doing right now, what can people expect?
Well, where are you calling from? Boulder. So Colorado. I am on my own in Colorado. Tim Keegan's joining me for this week of gigs down the West Coast, but he's flying back from L.A. So what's happening? Well, it's Sonic Boom with his sort of—I don't know the best way of describing it really. Just

various pulsing thickets of sound. It's quite dark, sort of stomach-clinching stuff, but quite rhythmic in a way. It really builds up the sense of expectation. Then there's me playing acoustic guitar, then a bit of electric at the end of the set. Toward the end of the set, I become a rock band if you like. I get louder. And then there's Sebadoh doing what they do. And then the Flaming Lips with the film of the drummer playing drums while he's actually on stage playing keyboards.

Have you tried the headphones concert yet?
I haven't really put them on myself, but I know a lot of people wear them.

I know it was mentioned that on this tour the Flaming Lips were going to hand out headphones.
I think it has the effect of internalizing everybody slightly. It takes people into their own world. They're less likely to sit there talking to each other. They should get more absorbed by the music.

It sounded interesting. I never heard of anyone doing that. What has been your most interesting tour experience in the twenty-plus years that you've been a performer?
Well, probably the most interesting one was—I can't really mention it, unfortunately.

Anything humorous that sticks out in your mind?
Oh boy. There have been things that have been a real pleasure and sort of been a real pain. So much of it is forgotten. I have been around and I haven't kept notes and I really have lost so much time on the road. I just don't remember a gig until I come back there seven years later and I go, "Oh, yeah. I know where the dressing room is." It's the thing of revisiting hundreds of spots that you've forgotten about. It's sort of timed amnesia or something like that. I think what's interesting about touring in the end is that the momentum is the object in itself. You're not really getting

anywhere. The important thing is to keep going. That especially works well in America because America isn't a place to come to rest, really. America is a place—you get to one coast and then it's time to set off back. Get to California [and] you have to find a way of getting back to New York. Get to New Orleans [and] you've got to set off for Seattle. It's just designed to be crossed.

Do you find that touring is grueling these days?
Yeah it is. Especially, you know, a lot of this we are doing in vans and I haven't really done that for a while. So I'm doing a bit of flying, but we are doing so many dates [that I] can't really fly between every show. We are playing many more places than I would normally play. Normally I would do about fifteen gigs on the tour. I am going around America one and a half times.

Are there shows scheduled in one part of the country and then you are turning right around and going back?
It's not too bad. We're going up from L.A. to Denver, but I'm going to fly that bit, and then we go down to Oklahoma and I will fly that bit, and then we set off down through Texas, come up through Atlanta and Chapel Hill, D.C., New York, the stuff on the Eastern seaboard. That's not too bad. We've already been up [to] St. Louis. We started in St. Louis. Now we are up in Seattle.

That's a long haul. Going back to the record—I know you worked with Jon Brion on this record. What was it like working with him?
Oh, great, because Jon, in a nice way, is quite impatient. He doesn't like to hang around much. So we had more trouble finishing things than starting things. He is always happy to just get out another roll of tape and get going. He can fill things up with tracks very fast and then just discard them again. He's not someone who sits there for hours trying to craft a bass part or work out an arrangement. He also liked to play on the songs not having heard them before. So particularly working with someone like Jon, there are a lot of

REEL TO REAL BY REEL

things he's discovering and they're on tape—something like "Dark Princess," there's all these little sort of noises he's making, which he's made before.

One thing I noticed about *Jewels for Sophia* is that it's very thick. There is different instrumentation that pops out in different places and you almost need a pair of headphones to grab it all. It's really engaging.
It's not painstakingly crafted note for note, but there is a lot. It's quite saturated music and you're right about headphones. My stuff isn't stuff to have on in the background. It's just annoying like a baby crying. It's there to listen to—to provide its own world for you to get into. It probably is very much a headphone record.

It is a great record. Are there plans to do things with radio with this? "Mexican God," that is a great ...
If you call out the Warner people in front of me and tell them "Mexican God" would be good on the radio, I would love to see them respond. I think "Viva! Sea-Tac" is getting played a bit because it's rocking and it's about Seattle. They're certainly playing it up here. I hope people catch on to it one way or another.

This is on a different note. Tell me about your involvement with Jonathan Demme's movie. [The film is called *Storefront Hitchcock* and was released to theaters in 1998 -Ed.]
Oh, you mean the one about me, with me in it? Well, he came along to a gig that I was doing, and I had Deni Bonet playing violin for me, and he came along to a show. He and his wife turned up in the dressing room afterward. [They] came in through the trap door and introduced themselves, and he said, "Do you want to make a movie?" So about eighteen months later I found myself in this storefront window in New York—four cameras pointing at me, the street behind my back, running through a bunch of songs. That was it, really. It will show at various art house [theaters].

18 | P a g e

Have you seen it yourself?
Oh yeah, I have seen it a few times.

What do you think?
It's very difficult seeing yourself—your head that big and your guitar that big. It was a bit of a shock. But I think now it's basically filmed and recorded and I think I sing very well. Maybe I am a bit uptight, but that's not surprising given the circumstances of his work. [It's] not very natural. Four cameras and running through the same show four times with the identical song sequence. I think I should have been able to vary the songs, but it's a very flattering document. It will remain young and beautiful as I get older and more decrepit. It's very nice. I'm really touched that Jonathan did it. I think there are some great moments in it. I like the way he holds camera angles for twenty seconds. Nobody in a rock video would dare do that. It's very much [an] anti-video film. It's the reverse of what music television has been all about. It sort of cuts away when he feels like [it], but he's really not frightened just staying with the camera on the same thing for a while and letting the fingers do the talking.

That sounds like it will be an interesting movie.
It's going to be. It's an art house sort of thing where you have coffee. There must be some place like that in Boulder where you can [get] coffee and real oatcakes.

Yeah, there are lots of places like that here. Next question, when will the Robyn Hitchcock action figure be available?
Well with the steadily expanding stomach, it gets bigger every nine months. I don't know. We're now selling floating pens.

With a little magnet on it?
No it's not a magnet. It's got a tomato that floats up and down the fluid. It starts on the top of the candlestick and it winds up in the black hand.

Is that for the new record?
No, that's just stuff we do. My girlfriend, Michele, she also designed the image on the cover of the album. She helps me out with a lot of things. She came up with the idea of the floating pen. So I designed that. We discuss a lot of visual ideas together.

How's the floating pen selling?
Well, not bad actually. People seem to like buying it on the road. It's cheaper than buying a T-shirt. So maybe there will be an action figure eventually, but we'd have to customize it. And also the trouble with that is people can stick pins in them, and I don't want to leave a slew of voodoo dolls around the United States.

If you had a bad performance one night or something?
No, I fear it will be worse than that. You know, you get some strange people coming along.

What was it like sorting through all the tracks you recorded and deciding what to put on this record? Was that a hard process for you?
Yes, it was a hard process, which is why it's good to have some help. But it wasn't like I sat down and listened to all twenty-four songs in a row. I knew certain songs were definites, but I didn't know what order to put it in. I swapped three of the songs around at the last minute. There wasn't any logical sequence for any of these things. There wasn't an obvious song that been going to start the album all along. In the beginning of the year the album was going to start with "Elizabeth Jade" and "Antwoman," which is now right down toward the end of the record. So it kept moving. "Mexican God," I think it was actually on the outtakes album. It was written off completely until three months ago.

Is the outtakes album available now?
No, it's coming out in November or so. But Warner is letting me release that myself in exchange for a small override, which is nice. It will be available through the museum of me

at RobynHitchcock.com or through live shows. I don't think we're selling it in shops as such.

Is the floating pen also available on your webpage?
Yeah, and the T-shirts will be available. There's lots of [old] stuff as well, like overstock from the 1980s and early '90s. I think there's some old Soft Boys CDs, which is probably good because I think they are out of print. I am sort of interested in getting new things in there.

That's great. I hope the tour continues to go well.
Well I hope we make it as far as Denver.

Is there anything else you want to add?
I wanted to add—is this Boulder? Boy, Boulder, Colorado—I hope everybody can breathe. It's a hard place to play harmonica in. You [were] very short of air last time I was singing in Boulder.

I can imagine that would be hard. Is singing also a problem or just harmonica?
Playing the harmonica for some reason. I just remember having to breathe a bit more and sing a bit less. I had a good gig, but this time I think we are playing in Denver. I don't know if that is as high up.

I think Boulder is a little higher.
Yeah, I am happy to be just playing in Denver.

I appreciate it, Robyn.
It's a pleasure, Chris. I must go and have a feed. Are you coming along to the Denver show?

Yes.
Well, maybe I will bump into you there.

SQUEEZE
(GLENN TILBROOK)

Sometime in September 1999
Article: *Boulder Weekly* (September 30, 1999)

My cousins were always gracious in listening to the horrible bands I was in during my formative years. The yearly trips to Syracuse, New York, were probably horrific for my extended family. I'm still not sure why they just didn't hide their boom boxes when they knew I was paying a visit and would have horrible cassette recordings with me that I would want them to hear. Maybe it was love—or maybe it was the fear my aunt could instill with a single glance.

The bands themselves sometimes featured drums fashioned from Christmas cookie tins (requisitioned from my mom) and a big cardboard shipping canister that acted as a bass drum. There were the signature off-pitch vocals (most of the time) and really basic bass parts (if there were any to begin with, and if there were, they *may* have been in time). We'd often record with a Realistic (RadioShack brand) thirty-dollar four-channel mixer into a boom box with a "mix mic" input. This allowed us to record one set of instruments and then go back and record other parts on top of it, while retaining what we had already recorded. It was multitrack recording, so to speak, and even though the quality wasn't professional, it was worlds cheaper than going into a studio (which none of us could have afforded at age fourteen). The results are still fun to listen to at times. It wasn't all that bad.

But my cousins were patient, and my cousin Bill and I sometimes discussed music. He knew I loved the Huey Lewis and the News song "I Want a New Drug," and he gave me a workaround with my mom, who could not stand the tune. "Chris, maybe he's saying he's done with the bad drugs and is looking for something more like aspirin." He was brilliant. When I tried that line of logic with my mom, I just received a dirty look in return.

Bill was a big Prince fan, so we'd discuss Prince and the Revolution. He was also a big fan of the British band Squeeze. I wasn't a fan of Squeeze at the time, as their music sounded too fake to my uninitiated ears—in reality, however, it was anything but. Also, Squeeze wasn't a metal band. Bill had the *Singles 45's and Under* cassette, which, of course, had the classic pop hit "Tempted" on it—but still it didn't do anything for me.

Strangely enough, Bill and I both liked the Outfield, and he left my cassette copy of *Play Deep* on the grill while working his shift at McDonald's. He brought back the case and it looked like a waffle fry. That was the end of "All the Love" for me.

Things would change, however, and I would grow to appreciate Squeeze, along with Prince and some other artists Bill enjoyed. It went way beyond the Outfield.

My friend André really liked Squeeze, but he didn't like me when he was almost kicked out of our junior high sex-ed class taught by our pastor—I would crack the jokes and he would get blamed.

I didn't get André's love for Squeeze. He also liked Crowded House, another band I avoided at the time. It would be a while before I would grow up in my musical tastes.

Later the professionals stepped in and helped with the maturation of my listening ears, proving that Bill and André had more refined tastes. While I was living in Nashville after college, Jade Hanson, of the band Believable Picnic, gave me both albums by legendary pop band Jellyfish. He swore by Jellyfish, and soon I was hooked, like an out-of-state pothead at his or her first puff of legal Colorado weed. Soon, I became a power-pop aficionado. That's all I would listen to. Squeeze was a part of that musical world, and I soon took the dive into another sweet ear-candy ocean by purchasing *The Piccadilly Collection*, a best-of Squeeze album. It was full of earnest vocals and well-crafted songs. Glenn Tilbrook and Chris Difford proved themselves to be two of the finest songwriters to my emerging ears. Tilbrook's singing took me—and still brings me—to a place of relaxation. Only Neil Finn gets the job done faster.

When I arrived back in Denver from my stint in Nashville and had been pursuing music journalism for a bit, I saw that Squeeze would be playing the Ogden Theatre. I was able to arrange a phone interview for the *Boulder Weekly* and promptly received the act's new album, *Domino*. The album cover made me chuckle with the glee that only comes from someone who truly loves dogs—it was a picture of an adorable boxer with his head cocked to one side. (Was its name Domino?) The songs were decent—there were a couple of gems, but nothing like the band's past work. The performances were fantastic, however.

Soon, Glenn Tilbrook and I got on the phone and we had a lot of fun racking up a forty-dollar international phone call charge that the *Boulder Weekly* was kind enough to pay. He was with his family in Australia, and I could hear his kids making a commotion in the background. He was conversational and, at times, very funny. I asked him about a former Squeeze drummer, Kevin Wilkinson, who had recently passed away—Glenn was uncomfortable with the question and indicated so. I quickly moved on to another question—one of the only times I've encountered that sort of thing during an interview. I've learned to avoid that sort of question unless it's somewhat foundational to what I am trying to accomplish in a written piece.

Squeeze's show at the Ogden remains one of the best I've ever seen. They played a slew of great songs and were incredibly tight. Glenn's voice was unbelievably strong, and his guitar playing was exquisite. I never imagined him to be such an accomplished player. There were probably only a hundred people or so in the audience, but for those who used their time wisely and came out, they experienced a stellar rock show that most bands only dream about playing. Too bad Chris Difford wasn't on the tour—that addition would have taken it over the top of the next hill.

****

Is *Domino* a continuation of the traditional Squeeze sound? Are you trying to go in a different direction on this record?

No, I am not trying to go in a different direction—we were not trying to go in a different direction. I think Squeeze has sort of evolved. Chris and I had made one drastic decision to jump off in a different direction, and it felt the material at that point was my least favorite, looking back over our career. So we have learned to be more instinctual about it rather than to make a decision to do this or that. I think it works better that way.

You've been doing music for a long time—since the '70s with Squeeze. What have you learned from the past twenty years? Is there anything that sticks out in your mind?

No, because I suppose I don't think in terms like that. I would say that the music, like life, is something that you acquire bits and pieces of every day, and the whole picture of it goes into forming what you are. With music, the thing is that half of the stuff that makes me write the way I do was picked up when I was nine, ten, eleven, twelve years old—that sort of period of listening to stuff. I guess it carries into my teenage years, but it was very formative to me—the sort of pop music of that time. I think that has always stayed with me. The other half of it is whatever you listen to and whatever you have listened to at any point. So I have learned to keep my ears open—not dismiss anything.

Back when you were nine, ten, eleven—were you listening to British pop bands like Badfinger and the Beatles and people like that?

Well, I was listening to the Beatles, but I was also listening to the Monkees quite a lot. They had a great team of songwriters working behind them, and then they wrote some great songs themselves. There [was] a lot of stuff around, both British and American, that was [an] incredible influence on me then. I think it was a great age for pop songwriting, and that stayed with me. One of my big influences is just that

25 | P a g e

time. The funny thing, I very rarely have to listen to that sort of stuff now. But it's always there for me.

In the '80s you went through a period when Squeeze wasn't a band. Why did you decide to reform the band?
Well, we broke up Squeeze in 1982. That was at the end of doing an album a year for five years, touring behind that—generally doing everything that we were asked to do. At the end of that period, we didn't enjoy it anymore. It was a horrible feeling. I didn't like it. We were our most successful then, probably, but none of it was fun. No one was guiding us properly, really. So we thought, "Well, this is not fun anymore," this is our band, this is what we did. And we had a couple years not doing anything in particular. That was a nice period to sort of just drift back down to Earth again. We did a little benefit gig—a little charity gig in a local pub with Squeeze for the fun of it. And it was fun. It was like, "Oh yeah, that is what it was meant to be." So that is why we got the band back together. I always swore that we would never get it together again. It just shows how wrong I was because I really enjoyed it. What we learned was to not pile on the work like we had been doing, to give ourselves some space every now and then because everyone needs that.

Is Squeeze currently something that you enjoy and that is rewarding to you now?
Yeah, I enjoy it very much. The thing is with Squeeze now—we are touring as a four-piece and we did the album as a five-piece, and I feel great about touring with the band. The band is terrific—we sound terrific as a four-piece. [However], I don't feel like beyond this record that I really want to carry Squeeze on without Chris because it doesn't feel right to me. So to sum that up—next year I am going to be doing a record on my own, and I want to use the same band. But it won't be called Squeeze.

I was going to say I saw the concert that you did for MTV—that was incredible. Do you feel that until people see Squeeze live they kind of categorize you as just

another pop band? I didn't know what you guys could dish out until I saw the concert and saw how good the material translated live. It was incredible.
People say all sorts of things about us, and that is really not my position to try and second-guess what people say. I suppose some people think we disappeared about 1982 and never came back again, although a much smaller group of people will be aware that we've been releasing records every couple of years. You can get yourself into all sorts of corners by thinking about that. What I concentrate on is what I am onto now and the fact that Squeeze as a band, our output of this decade, I have been very proud of. I can't say that about any other decade that we worked in. That is a good track record.

This is as far as the '90s?
Yes, that is right. We have had four albums out, and each one of them I am really proud of. So that is a good vantage point for me and that is really all I can think about.

The concert you did for MTV—was it *Hard Rock Live*?
Yeah, that's right.

Do you feel that did a lot to show people in the States that you were still around?
I hope so, because we have got a good, vibrant band at the moment. I am very proud of it, and I am very proud of the fact that it keeps on evolving. I am very proud of the fact that we come up with songs and Chris comes up with lyrics that continually I think are brilliant. We are promoting *Domino* now, but I can look back over our last four albums and think, "Yeah, well, I'm pleased with those too." It's a good position to be in. I like that. I enjoy it as well. That is the other thing that I haven't said. That's the most important thing.

You are handling the vocals for this tour. Does that put additional pressure on you that Chris would normally be handling? What are your feelings on being in that position on this tour, being the front man? [Glenn is

generally the lead vocalist. I was lacking in my Squeeze knowledge at the time. –Ed.]

I am absolutely fine with it. I miss Chris. I miss Chris' contribution. I don't want to say anything other than that because it's the truth. I would rather he was here, but the fact that he is not here, I don't feel like some additional burden [is] on me. I sing most of the songs anyway, but the thing that we do great is that sort of octave thing which now isn't there, but, you know, we get by.

I am sure it all sounds great. Have you done any shows on the tour yet?
No, not yet. Our first show is in San Francisco and it's Wednesday.

I know that there was a drummer (Kevin Wilkinson) that used to tour with you who passed away recently—how did that affect you guys?
Oh terribly, awfully. I find it very difficult to talk about somebody's life who is not there, who was a part of our band. He wasn't part of our band at that point, but yes, he was a lovely bloke and I miss him very much.

Since you have been involved in music, have you seen that happen to a lot of people you know?
No, fortunately, I haven't. No. I would say one other person that I know has ended up a similar way, but—you know, I don't know—I can't really talk about it.

Sure. I understand that. As far as Chris not touring, are you going to be working with him again?
I think so, yes. I don't think that Chris and I will ever stop working. I think the frequency that we work together will probably diminish from now. And I think we have to do some other things before we work together again, but, yes, I definitely think we will work together. I am in Australia at the moment, as you may or may not know, but I saw Chris a couple days before I left England, and it was great to see him.

Lovely to sit down and chat as friends. It's not like it's going to go away.

Sure. Obviously, his reason for not touring is definitely honorable and I am sure it took a lot for him to make the decision.
Yes, I think so. I completely respect his decision.

What was it like working with Elvis Costello? I know that you worked with him on a record.
Very good, actually. It gave us a boost of confidence. It gave us the confidence to try some other things. Another direction that I think we wouldn't have had the confidence to do before that. So I think Elvis opened a lot of doors for us in a very positive way.

Over your career, what is an instance or a moment that stands out? Something humorous.
The one that springs to mind is actually [from the] last time we played in San Francisco, which [was] February of this year. This woman came up to me and said—which made me laugh—that I was her Elvis. Which I wasn't quite sure how to take. And then she lifted up the sleeve of her shirt. The previous time I had been there she had asked me to sign her arm, and she had my signature tattooed onto her arm, which is quite shocking. I told her I thought she might be a bit of a nut, but actually she was very funny and an interesting person—not just a nutter.

You haven't had much experience with stalkers, have you?
No. Thankfully not.

Anything else you wanted to mention? I want to do a nice promotional piece.
That's lovely. Just say that we are the world's number-one band in my mind. In the security of my own home, we're the world's number-one band.

29 | P a g e

Will you guys be playing "Pulling Mussels (From the Shell)" on this tour?
Yes, we will.

Well, I appreciate it Glenn. Thanks a lot.
Thanks very much. Cheers. Bye.

MIKE PETERS

Sometime in late October 1999
Article: *Boulder Weekly* (October 28, 1999)

My addiction to music knew no bounds when I was growing up just forty-five minutes south of Boston in a little town called Norfolk. Really, as a youngster, I would easily become addicted to almost anything—crime dramas like *Wonder Woman* and *Charlie's Angels* (I had a huge crush on Cheryl Ladd—I've always loved blondes), Hardy Boys books, frozen pizza and French fries—there's a long list I could compile.

Prior to New England, our family lived in Virginia. Between the ages of six and eight, I thought that anyone driving a Ford Econoline van was a kidnapper. That meant that older vans, like the Dodge Tradesman, were also suspect, if not more so. I once meandered around our neighborhood, riding my red Ross Convertible cruiser bike and jotting down license plate numbers from "questionable" vehicles into a little spiral notebook.

After we moved to New England in 1982, I told my new classmates I was in the FBI (unfortunately I did have a real police badge, courtesy of a family friend, so some of these kids believed me—one kid, David, actually said, "Chris really is an FBI!"). Maybe it was a form of adjustment. I was eight, had a Southern accent and moved to an area outside Boston—I was the butt of jokes.

My addiction to crime dramas and detective books also developed into a situation where I consistently thought someone was breaking into our house. I would hear the wind rustle some leaves or a tree branch sway (we had almost an acre of land) and think it was the Lindbergh kidnapper coming to take me away. Never mind that we lived in a very safe area, with professional football players in the neighborhood, in a town where nothing really ever happened. We didn't even have a fast-food restaurant.

The problem was that I would hear these things at about 1 a.m., after reading a Hardy Boys or an Alfred Hitchcock and the Three Investigators novel. My mind would be filled with Jupiter Jones and friends or Frank and Joe Hardy investigating sinister events, so my noggin was primed and ready. I would go running into my parents' room in the comfort of my foot-padded superhero pajamas saying nervously, "Dad, there's someone breaking into our house. I hear the ladder. Can you come look?" Now the problem was this: I had not had sex-ed yet, and let's just say that my parents were probably enjoying a little adult time together. It's probably why I only have one brother.

But music—that was something I gravitated toward more than children's detective books, television crime dramas, recording "suspicious" vehicle license plates and unknowingly breaking up my parents' adult fun.

Relatively early in my rock 'n' roll addiction, I discovered Welsh band the Alarm, courtesy of a mention in the late, great, New England-based *NewSound Magazine*. The well-written publication covered Christian rock and mainstream bands in equal fashion, as long as the "secular" act had some sort of Christian influence. I discovered Alarm frontman Mike Peters courtesy of a *NewSound* blurb, and soon after, found myself at the Walpole Mall with my mom. I made a beeline for the record store where I would often go while my mom went off to other stores. It was one of those older malls that had a fountain or two in the middle, their bottoms riddled with pennies, and it also had a Carvel ice cream store—you can still buy their ice cream cakes. If you've never had one, you do not know what you are missing. The mall also had Bradlees, a now-defunct chain department store—I always had to take a leak when we visited that store and they charged twenty-five cents to use the restroom.

Anyway, upon entering the record store, there was a new-releases wall off to the left where they had records and cassettes posted at sale prices. Compact discs were still in long cardboard boxes at the time and were more or less relegated to bins. The long boxes, I've heard, were designed so that the CDs were harder to steal.

I scanned the new-releases wall and saw the Kinks live record *The Road* and then came across the Alarm's *Eye of the Hurricane*. I instantly recalled reading about the band in *NewSound*. I paid the six ninety-nine for the cassette, took it home and devoured it with more gusto than the Ellio's frozen pizzas I used to eat as an after-school snack. I remember often thinking, while listening to *Eye of the Hurricane*, "Why is this band not as big, or bigger, than U2?" I mean, they had great songs, they had the similar chiming guitars and anthemic choruses and the same level of spiritual intensity. It's something I'll never understand.

I soon discovered a couple of Alarm fans at my church. Liz and Mike were a few years older than I was, but our love for the band was equal. Mike, whose dad ran sound for the church, told me one day that he had gone to see the band open for Bob Dylan in Boston. I was jealous—really jealous. Almost as jealous as I had been when I could hear U2 playing Foxboro Stadium from my house during the *Joshua Tree* tour and I wasn't in attendance. I'm not sure why—my dad had said he'd buy tickets. Maybe it was because I thought U2 had turned their back on Christianity—how I could determine that when I had never spoken to any of the band members I'll never know. I've realized over the years that missing that show was one of my biggest entertainment regrets.

Unfortunately, I didn't get to see the Alarm play until 2000 (for U2 it was 1997) at a classic rock/country bar in Golden, Colorado, called the Buffalo Rose. A metal band opened, strangely enough.

The crowd, no more than forty or fifty people, showed Mike Peters and company an arena-level amount of support and, in return, they received an incredibly passionate rock 'n' roll show. By this point in time, the band's lineup had completely changed—Peters left the original group in the early '90s and had reformed it in recent times with new members. The sound was different as well—it was much louder and power chord-filled than the old Alarm. While

33 | P a g e

there were still some comparisons to U2, those had almost abated completely.

I had met Mike several months earlier, when he came through Denver with his wife, Jules. He was part of an acoustic tour with some other musicians from the Alarm's era. I was able to secure an interview a few weeks prior to the show and had a great phone conversation with Mike. He was incredibly well-spoken and paused when he was done answering a question, so I wound up with some great quotes.

Regrettably, I didn't get to see the acoustic performance, but, thankfully, was able to come down to Denver's Soiled Dove (at the time located on the corner of Market and 20th) and hang out with Mike after he had finished playing. He and Jules were both incredibly appreciative, kind people.

Mike, regardless of his cancer battles, remembers a name and where you live. His humor and soft approach with people further my appreciation for his art. Still going strong, he continues to record with the Alarm and holds the annual Gathering festival in his native Wales. He also co-founded nonprofit, the Love Hope Strength Foundation, an international organization that vigilantly fights cancer and labors diligently in providing opportunities for people to sign up as bone marrow donors. The group also holds fundraising events, such as a hike in Vail, Colorado, in June of 2013 that featured four-hundred participants and raised over a hundred thousand dollars. Mike, himself, was at the Vail event.

****

After all these years, how does it feel to still be performing?
Well, I've probably had more fun now than I ever had in my life doing it. I think you are able to take a lot of strength from all the times that you've been through a city. [I've] made a lot of good friends in the time that I came through with the Alarm. Last night we played Columbus, and after the show you just chat with lots of people who saw us playing in 1986 with Pat Benatar. It's great because you meet people and

they still ask you, "When are you coming back?" It's like a [group] of old friends in places, and we are a bit like a little family. We've all gone through so much together. The songs have a lot of meaning to people, especially some of the older ones. [They are] maybe more meaningful to people than when they first came out. So, in a way, the songs are a lot more diverse now. I have been playing for about forty-five minutes, but I can pack a lot into it.

Have you been doing medleys of old songs?
No. I sort of vary it. I have been playing a couple of brand new things, a few songs from the Alarm era, and the rest is a mixture of the solo material I've put together since the band. So there's something for everybody, I think.

What has been your favorite time period in your career?
Well, to be quite honest, I don't know how it sounds, but the last year has been the most amazing time I have ever had musically. I've been able to go from making *Rise* [last year] and working with Billy (Duffy), which led into making the *Coloursound* album. It just came out in Britain a week ago, and it's been received brilliantly in the UK. [It] charted at number twelve in the indie charts. I'm here doing this tour with the Mission and Gene Loves Jezebel. I've written the music for a play, which I'm going to record in December in the BBC studio in Cardiff, and Eddie (MacDonald) from the Alarm is going to come and play on it with me. I'm playing some dates with Big Country in December, and I'm taking the electric band out on that as well, and then [I've] got the Gathering to look forward to. So the last year has been absolutely amazing because it's been very diverse. I've been able to make new connections, like Billy, and take that on to a whole other level and also reestablish some musical connections from the past as well.

Tell me a little bit about the play that you wrote the music for. Did you actually write the play or just the music?

No, just the music. The play was written by a Welsh writer named Helen Griffin. I was playing a gig with James Dean Bradfield, the singer of the Manic Street Preachers. We were playing a Kosovo benefit. We were both approached by Phil Clark, who's the artistic director of the Sherman Theatre in Cardiff, Wales, and he asked us both to write music for separate plays. The script I was given was by Helen called *Flesh and Blood*. It's a real sort of family drama. It deals with a lot of family topics in a very confrontational way, and it's a very hard-hitting play. It was quite challenging to write the music for it. I actually performed at the opening of the Welsh assembly this year. The Queen was there, and Tony Blair and all the major Welsh artists played—you know, Tom Jones, Mike Peters.

Did he do "What's New, Pussy Cat?"
He sang—I have to think about it—"The Green, Green Grass of Home." Everyone got to sing one song, and I sang "A New South Wales" with Mark Taylor and Dave (Sharp) from the Alarm came and played piano.

And he [Mark Taylor] actually played on the recording of that song that's on *Change*.
That's right. It was the same choir, Mark Taylor, myself, and we performed the song and I actually rewrote the lyrics to "A New Wales." The choir is going to play on the album that we're recording next month. Mark's going to come and play piano. Eddie MacDonald's written string arrangements. I tried to involve Tony Visconti, but he is making another album. He has other commitments. I actually invited Dave [Sharp] and Nigel [Twist] from the Alarm to come and play if they would like to, as well.

Do you know how many people would love that if it actually happened?
I've thrown the whole sessions open to the fans in the UK. We're allowing a certain amount to come and sit as we're doing it. We're recording the album in two days. We want to record it live. And so we're having an audience there for the

whole two days, from morning 'til night. And then on the last night, myself, Eddie, Mark and the choir are going to hold a sort of concert—play some old songs as well as recording a whole new album.

Is it going to be intimidating having all the fans there while you are recording?
Nope. Well, again, something I've learned since the Alarm is to be less precious about stuff like that. It might be a bit more difficult for Eddie than me because he's not really been making that kind of record since the Alarm. But I have made records in lots of kinds of situations since I left the band. It's been really beneficial. I have made three solo albums that have been released. Two of them have been released in America, but I've actually put three out, including *Breathe*, which came out in Britain.

And then *Feel Free* came after *Breathe*?
Feel Free came after *Breathe,* and then *Rise* came after that, but in between all those records I have made another eight albums that have just come out through the [Internet] or mail order, through the shows.

I saw those on your website. It looks like you have been really busy.
I get a lot of insight because I've been able to do things like make records based around—say I made one album of ten rare Alarm songs that we'd recorded in a certain way. But when we recorded them, say a song like "Pavilion Steps," for instance. We recorded that during the *Declaration* album, and Alan Shacklock, the producer, really changed the whole song around. He changed the arrangement, and it didn't work, and that's why it became a B-side. There were some great recordings of an arrangement we used to play. It was bootlegged and the fans loved the way we played it in 1982, opposed to the way it came out in 1984. But there were no really good recordings of it in that arrangement. So I actually took all my original equipment—the old amps and the old guitars I still keep out of storage, took them into the studio,

REEL TO REAL BY REEL

made an album of ten songs on all the original equipment. And I literally went in with a sort of filmmaker's eye and re-created sounds and tried to copy the tone of my voice at the time and the same tone that we used on the guitars, played all the instruments myself. It fooled a lot of people. *The Album Network* in America got a copy of the album and they even put it on their sampler CDs that they send out in their magazine. They attributed it to the Alarm. And it was just me.

That's a big magazine, too.
Well, it picked up a bit of airplay over here, actually, and certain people are starved for the Alarm, I suppose. Quite a lot of people have picked up on it. And I've recut a new version of "Majority" for that album, and that got added to quite a few radio stations.

I have *The Best of the Alarm and Mike Peters* that came out in England and I know that has "Majority" on it. That had a really good selection of songs.
Yeah, well I sort of had a hand in that. So I was able to make sure there were some goodies in there. Not just the standard fare. I put important tracks on it that were big for the fans, like "One Step Closer to Home" and "Walk Forever by My Side" and "Majority," that were as big as any of the singles we had when we played them live. I didn't want it to just be [a] singles record.

And the solo stuff you chose to put on there fit really well too.
Yeah, I chose stuff that was written immediately after the Alarm or something I was maybe working on during the Alarm that carried on after that. I didn't want to put songs that were set too far away from the work I had done with the Alarm, so that maybe it had some kind of follow-on to it and was a natural progression from it.

I didn't even know this was out—it's sometimes hard to hear about stuff in America. But, yeah, I worked for a

company in Nashville and my boss was actually over in the UK and he picked up the album.
Well, that's good. It's done really well in the UK—the album.

After you left the Alarm—did you have a period where you didn't want to make music?
No, it wasn't that. It's just I didn't know what kind of music I wanted to make. I wasn't really prepared for leaving the Alarm. It wasn't something I really thought about. It was a very spur-of-the-moment thing on one level. It was very confusing at first, because one side of me experienced a great sense of loss but another part of me experienced a great sense of freedom as well. I think for the first few years after the Alarm, I was being quite eclectic and making lots of different kinds of music and not really quite sure which direction to take. I also think when you leave a band like the Alarm, initially you react to that musically and you maybe try to justify certain things or try to overcompensate and try to overexpress yourself. You try to express those kinds of things you don't need to do. I feel that with the *Rise* album, that was the first record that I made as a Mike Peters record, where I wasn't trying to sort of carry on work I had maybe started while I was in the Alarm or try to prove things. I felt like after *Feel Free*, I was able to put a lot of things behind me after that period. And then *Rise* is a record from a new quality period in my life, hopefully the beginning of a whole new period, which I think has been expressed. I've made a lot of music and a lot of big steps since the *Rise* album. So it does feel good to be at this point, but again I think you have to go through confusing musical periods of times in your life, and nothing can prepare you for when they are going to happen. They can happen when you are at the top and you've got a number-one album. Or they can happen when you left the band that you've built and dreamt of and loved and still love all your life. And nothing can prepare you for what will happen, and you've just got to work your way through it. I left the Alarm and basically slipped into a musical underground again. The media, generally they're looking for the newer artists on the block—people who've got the clean slate—and they write

about them. But I think it's no bad thing to actually go underground again and be able to sort of work out your mistakes and make some songs. The more interesting music is not in the charts.

Has it been frustrating with your solo career, not necessarily having the same kind of push as you did with the Alarm?
I wouldn't say frustrating, but it's something that you hope is going to happen. The music industry has changed so much, and I understand it a lot more. I didn't actually enjoy the periods when we were being pushed and people were investing millions of dollars into trying to get us on the radio and all that sort of stuff. I prefer it to be a lot simpler. Maybe I'm a bit naïve, but I still believe that the old values can apply—that you make a great record, people start talking about it, and people want to play it on the air because it's a great record, but that doesn't really happen that much these days. A lot of money is spent on music that we're hearing today on the radio and on TV; everything we hear has a huge marketing slush fund behind it. And that's frustrating when you make a record and you come up against that. But actually what happens to my own music, in a way, it's worked. I don't find that frustrating, because I have been fortunate enough to work with good people who've really believed in what I do, and they're trying to do their best for you all the time and push for you to get into places and to compete, and it's all been on a very honest level, and that's been great. You can't be having that sort of personal endeavor behind your music when people are putting big money behind it. They want a big return, and that takes a big toll on you mentally. I didn't really enjoy that side of it with the Alarm too much. I don't think any of us did. I think we all reacted differently to fame and success in our own different ways. It's quite a divisive beast to deal with, fame.

You mentioned *Rise* a second ago. It seems like a rebirth for you. What were you feeling as you sat down and listened to the whole CD for the first time?

The first time we played it all back in one go was actually in the studio before we mixed the album. I knew it was a good record because we actually finished ahead of schedule, which I had never done in my life. I'd got fourteen days to make the album, and we actually completed it in twelve. Billy came along for the sessions, and Eddie from the Alarm came along, and we had a big game of football outside and came in and played all the tracks back, and it just worked. I could tell it was working with my new musical partners like Billy and the band that I was working with, and I knew it worked on another level with Eddie MacDonald. Eddie was really blown away. He said some really nice things about the record straight away. And I knew it was working on a lot of levels. But I also knew it was good even up to the writing stage. I had written a lot of the songs in a burst in '98—either '97 or '98. I can't quite remember. I actually road-tested the songs. I played them all acoustically. I went on the European tour and took all the songs out just on my acoustic guitar. And I knew they were working. My criteria for every song on the *Rise* album was that I had to be able to perform it as an acoustic piece with just the lyric and the guitar chords. And it had to speak on that level. I felt with all the songs on *Rise,* I could play them in that context with completely unknown songs. In Europe I was playing some of my known songs and then slipping in all these songs from the *Rise* album. And after the shows, people were coming up and saying to me, "What's that song that goes, 'let it go, let it go, let it go?' ["Burnout Syndrome," one of the best tunes on the disc. - Ed] What's that one that goes, 'come together?'" And it was a great feeling because people were actually stopping me and saying, "Loved the song 'High on the Hill' that you played tonight," and they went on about how "Spirit of '76" meant something to them ten years ago. It meant that everyone has been able to move on. It felt that we had all grown up, not just me but my audience as well, and we were all moving together in sync with it.

Tell me about Coloursound. What are your plans for Coloursound? [This is the band that Mike formed with Billy Duffy of the Cult. - Ed.]

Well, the plans are to slot in as much as we can within the framework of Mike Peters making a lot of records and the Cult making records again. It means that we can't work in the traditional sense and flock around the world, but we can play special events and we can do things on the Internet. We have got an album out in the UK which is doing really well. Great reviews on it. It will come out here next year. We actually recorded an acoustic album that will come out next year. We recorded in London last weekend, oh wait, last Saturday, and we played a show in London. It was filmed. It was an amazing gig. Eddie [MacDonald] was there, and Ian Astbury (the Cult) was there, and Billy and I were on stage, and our former band members were all in the audience. We will do other work when the album comes [out] in America. Hopefully we will be able to find a slot where we can come in and maybe play half a dozen shows and we'll just take it as it comes. We feel we are coming into a new decade, a new millennium. We both feel that we can take on a lot of work. We are experienced. We've experienced bands breaking up, getting back together again, reconnecting, forging our own musical path, dealing with working without our past and working on the future, and we feel that we're able to deal with it all now. But we can't just deal with it in the way we used to, like with kids, and get in the van and flock it around the world. We're trying to elevate it on much more of a creative level, rather than spend a lot of time being a sort of reproductive organ and going out on the road and re-gigging the old songs all the time. Coloursound gives us a chance to work on new things all the time. We will go out on tour and celebrate it and play shows, but it won't be masses of them. We might steal one off of the Internet or something like that, or use the technology to be able to be in a group at the same time as being of the group as well.

It is confusing to be able to talk about it over the phone like this. You're going to write it up, and this was always the hardest thing about being in the Alarm, is you would spend twelve months making a record off the road. Nobody knew what was going on. And then you come back and you'd be able to talk to your fans through someone like yourself, and you'd have this third-party dialogue with the audience. Now, with the Internet, we've been able to develop this whole thing where we can communicate with our audience on a daily basis. People can actually log onto the site and phone into our office in Wales and find where we are, what's happening, and that way you can communicate things a lot faster and a lot clearer. So it's not confusing to the fans that Mike Peters is in Coloursound, Mike Peters is on tour as a solo artist, Mike Peters is making music for a play and an album that's going to come out, Mike Peters tours in December with his solo band that's playing with Big Country. All this is going on. And it's not confusing because they can actually physically see it all laid out in front of them on the Internet page. But to actually convey this through the media to someone who's going to pick and read a story and doesn't know all the background and for you to floss it in, to fit it in with your editorial—it's going to be difficult.

You mentioned about communicating with your fans— your music has always seemed very personal, like a conversation with a close friend. You know, songs like "Dawn Chorus," "Eye of the Hurricane," "Feel Free"— what do you hope people take away from your songs?
Well, I just hope people gain some form of inspiration to be able to come to a show, or play a record and hear a song I've written and be able to draw from that strength to be able to apply the same commitment to getting through life that I put into my own life. I've faced a lot of traumatic situations as well as happy occasions, and I have written about them all and everything in between. Hopefully people can gain some—just some form of strength and encouragement to deal with the situations that they are faced with in a positive way. I have always been a person who's tried to see the glass as being half full, as opposed to half empty, and I try to pass that on through my music. I have always tried to write about

things in a positive way. Even on the darkest songs I've written, say like a "Dawn Chorus," there's always a light at the end of the tunnel of a Mike Peters song. I'm a believer in that, and I think that that's something that people can look for in their own lives.

A song like "Dawn Chorus," is that about a personal experience that you had or is it about a friend?
I always try and write from some form of personal experience. I actually just did a couple of weeks on the Internet just before this tour started. I decided to go on and be part of the Internet community and answer questions, sort of permanently online for about two weeks. People talk about the *Strength* album a lot, and I always say that *Declaration* was an album that changed a lot of people's lives, and the *Strength* album completely saved a lot of people's lives. I've got a lot of letters from people who've faced the most incredibly difficult life situations. I've got an amazing collection of letters from people who've said, "I was turned back from a suicide because I put that record on as the last record I wanted to hear on this planet, and then the lyrics made me stop doing it, and I'm still here, and thanks to you, Dave, Eddie and Nigel for making that music." They're much better to have than your gold discs. I think people can relate to [the songs] even though sometimes they might not be specifically about something I've been through, but it is maybe something that I have seen, or friends have gone through, or I've experienced—something like that. But rather than write it up, you try to make it work as a song with a piece of music that goes with the chord sequences that you're working on. I try to work as close as possible to what I am writing instinctively. I try to put words to the music that go hand in hand. Sometimes the music's darker; I try to make sure I go that way lyrically as well.

Is it hard for you to be as personal as you are in your songs, or is it just something that comes naturally?
I'm not sure. I don't try to overanalyze it very much. I think if I learned to write music, for instance, I think it would stop a

certain instinctive thing that you do because you don't understand the mechanics of making music. You just make music because you enjoy it, and it's what comes out naturally. Sometimes if you understand it as a formula, it can be a limiting thing all of a sudden. From working with Billy, for instance, on the Coloursound album, I learned a lot because he was very keen that we create something that was a result of the two of us working together and it wasn't just a whole series of Billy Duffy guitar tracks with my vocals on them. On one of my songs, Billy had to come up with a guitar riff to go with it. We actually created the music from the ground up, working on every aspect of it together, and lyrically I didn't feel I needed to write autobiographically to Coloursound, but I could write based around the pictures I was being sent through Billy's guitar playing. The only thing I wanted to do with the music was make it positive and make it celebratory of life, but I created different kinds of lyrics with Coloursound, which I think was important in that context. In my own work, I do tend to be quite egocentric in writing about myself, about how life's impacted me or if I see friends in a certain situation, people I know, whatever. Then I tend to think, "Well, what would I do in that situation?" then write it on that level, but when I was working with Coloursound, I wanted to be a little bit more ambiguous. I don't know how it's going to impact my future work, but it's definitely had an effect on me as a writer and helped me to understand the way it works.

You probably get this question a lot, but all these years you always seemed adept at mixing your faith and rock 'n' roll. Has that been a hard or an easy thing for you?
Well, no, it's never easy, because there are certain things that you can't be that overt about. I don't like being totally overt about my politics or my faith. I think those are things that if you slam them down on the table for people, they're very divisive things. Families and countries split up arguing over religion and politics. I prefer to see those things being things that bring people together, and so to do that, you have to write about them in a very personal way. When you are

making a record, people from all walks of life are going to come in contact with your music. And I try to have it so that it's something that pulls people in and doesn't just put them off straight away because they can't relate to the lyrics. It's very difficult when you go through certain life situations and you feel you want to communicate something. But I think it's better to be subtle than to blast you in your face.

The reason I asked that is because songs like "The Stand" and "Walk Forever By My Side"—"Walk Forever By My Side" is like a beautiful praise song, and it's just always amazed me—like, "Wow, how did he get away with that?" I just want to congratulate you for being able to do that, because the meaning is inherent in the songs, and it has to be hard to articulate that and not turn people off to your music.

Well, yeah, thanks, Chris, but I think that it is something that I made a conscious effort to not be allowed to be pulled into certain things where people expect you to do that. I have played at Greenbelt—a big sort of Christian festival in Britain—many times, and a lot of people there are always encouraging you: "Will you go make a full Christian record?" or do things like that, and I think then you become typecast, then people begin to switch off.

How have the Greenbelt performances been?

It's been quite a festival for me, because I've played there in many forms. The first time I went was 1986. That was the first time I had ever done an acoustic show on my own, and it was amazing. The year after, I brought the band back and we played on the main stage and it was great. And I've played some of my first solo shows there. I took Coloursound to play there last year, which was amazing. We played at the last open air Greenbelt Festival. It's changed into a new sort of form now for the millennium, responding to the fact that there are so many festivals. When Greenbelt started it was the only real festival—there was that and Reading—and now there are twenty festivals in Britain.

Then there's yours, the Gathering.
That's right, yeah.

How has that been going? I have some friends that have put on some festivals here in the States, and they always wind up losing a lot of money. Is it pretty hard to put on something like that and not risk losing your shirt?
Yeah, but it's not like a festival for fifty thousand. It's a festival for like two thousand people who come in and who all have a common love for an artist's music.

Mainly yours.
Yeah. But it's great for the ego. People come in, our whole family gets involved and we arrange all the hotels in [Unclear. - Ed.] the venue. It's a role reversal. I get to stay at home and all the fans have to go on tour. They do all the traveling and the flying, and they're getting on the buses, and they turn up at the gig, and they know what it feels like. But because they do the traveling, I am then able to put a lot more detail into the concert. When you go out and tour, you tend to want to present a similar body of material so that people around the world are feeling the same sort of communication that you are trying to put out. You are trying to say, "This is how I've moved on as an artist," and "These are the songs that are relevant today from yesterday." But at the Gathering, you open the doors and all that. You say "Right, play a lot now." And even the most obscure B-side is a big hit with those two thousand people. Because they're the two thousand people who have got every record you have ever made in their collections, and they know every word. So it's an amazing concert to take part in, and I'm going to have to be on my toes because people do know the music probably as well if not better than myself.

Do you ever forget words?
Occasionally. Like at last year's Gathering, I think, someone brought up the number of songs I played on the Internet. I think it was sixty-eight songs over the whole weekend. So that is a lot of songs to play in a short period of time. And I

also don't like to repeat any songs during that weekend. So I juggle them around so that I can make more work. Last year, on the Friday night concert, I actually did three separate sets. The first set I played with two acoustic guitars, a bass and a drum kit, and we played songs like "For Freedom" and "The Deceiver" and "How the Mighty Fall" and some of the more acoustic-based [Unclear - Ed.] of Alarm rock songs. And then I did a solo set in the round on my own. I came off of the main stage into the center of the hall, did a solo acoustic set. Then I came back on, and I added an electric guitarist into the equation. We did "Majority" and "Deeside," finished up with a lot of big Alarm songs. Then on the Saturday, I did a solo set based around all the solo work I've done. Then we finished up with a whole Coloursound set. Billy and I played a couple of Cult songs and some Alarm songs as well as [Unclear. - Ed.] with "68 Guns." And so it's an amazing weekend and then we have parties afterwards. I went on stage and we did a whole set of glam rock songs. And we're all in makeup and platforms and high heels and all that stuff.

No black and yellow spandex?
No, no, no. I mean Glitter. [Gary] Glitter, Sweet songs and David Bowie and T. Rex numbers were allowed.

Oh, Ziggy Stardust stuff.
That's it. Yeah. So, it's great. People see you for who you are, really. They see you in [your] local hometown. People come from Peru, America, Japan, Australia, all over Europe to be there. And then there'll be friends and local people as well. People that they have met on the Internet chat lines, and it's such a strong-feeling event and everyone's had their lives changed by an Alarm song, or a Mike Peters song or whatever. And they're there sharing their experiences with people who feel the same way. The Alarm is not the most current band in the world today, but its music is still very valid. That's why I can still go out on tour and people still will write about it. There'll definitely be a point in the future where the spotlight will fall on the Alarm again. The records will come out again, or I'll be able to make a certain kind of

record that takes it to another level and make people come back and reevaluate and re-listen to the Alarm records.

Or you guys will reunite? Tour the world?
You never know. You never say never to those things. I have tried to put the band together on a number of occasions, but for whatever reason it has not come together. I did invite the band to play at the Welsh Assembly a few months ago with the BBC putting it all together, but it didn't happen. But you never know. That's why I thought with the album *Flesh and Blood*, I'd invite the band members to come and play, because it's not the Alarm, it's not an Alarm-related project. So I thought, "Well if I get them all in the same room together playing and enjoying it, then you never know where it might lead."

What is the funniest or most interesting thing that has happened to you over the years you have been a performer?
We talked about that one the other night. When I was on the Pretenders tour with the Alarm, we'd done three nights in San Diego. In the middle of "68 Guns," I always go, "I want to hear you singing '68 Guns'" and all this sort of stuff. It's always great—it worked out brilliantly. And the fourth night we went to Santa Barbara. I came on stage and go, "Hello, Santa Barbara, good to be here. Blah, blah blah." And then by the time we got to the end of "68 Guns," I forgot where I was and I'm in the middle going, "San Diego, I want to hear you singing!" There's not a word coming back. I do it again and again. I virtually stood on top of the entire stadium, screaming, "San Diego, I want to hear you singing!" I finally spot this guy in the front row and he's waving at me and he's going, "Santa Barbara." I got off stage pretty quick that night.

You didn't have anything thrown in your direction, did you?
No, I think everyone was just thinking, "Oh, this is great. How's he going to get out of this? He's digging a big grave here."

But see, you've got the option of just running backstage.
I know. You can't, though. I've still got two choruses to go.

What's next for Mike Peters? What do you see the future holding for you?
Well, it's going to be really intense now for the next couple of years—because I've got the *Flesh and Blood* album to make in December, a Big Country tour to do in December, the Gathering in January, and then I am actually going to be in the play *Flesh and Blood* touring around Britain. I am going to perform the music live in the play. I've got a new solo record to make—Coloursound acoustic album to come out— Coloursound album to come out in America that will involve playing a few dates. So it's fairly intense at the moment.

What can people expect from the next solo record?
The follow-up to *Rise* will be—it's going to be interesting because I am actually playing a couple of songs that I have in mind for the record on this tour. But it's still being formed at the moment, so I think when you come to the show you will hear a couple of songs and you will sort of get some idea, but it could all change within the next few months. It's just in that process of development at the moment. Eddie and I might write a couple songs for it, or I might work on a couple with Billy for it as well. It's still coming. It'll have its roots in *Rise*. It'll be a development of that, I think, really.

Well thanks a lot for doing this, Mike. I really appreciate it.
All right, Chris, no problem.

Counting Crows (Charlie Gillingham)

Sometime in late November 1999
Article: *Boulder Weekly* (December 2, 1999)

Everyone who grew up with radio in and around his/her life has a soundtrack for specific points in their formative years. My dad would play FM radio on road trips to and from Baldwinsville, New York, to see my relatives; to Florida for sun-and-sea drenched vacations; and, later, to South Carolina for yet another beach. I remember hearing Jimmy Buffett's "Margaritaville" at age four or five while sitting with my parents and late Grandma Frisone (and my infant brother, Andy) in one of those dark-paneled '70s restaurants—replete with padded captain's chairs and the smell of heavy soup in the air—somewhere in Chambersburg, Pennsylvania, while staying overnight on our way to Florida. The song preserved the memory. I also remember hearing Hall & Oates's "I Can't Go for That (No Can Do)" while heading to or from Florida one year—I was probably six at the time.

1984 proved to be a year with a soundtrack all its own. I was in the fourth grade, had a fantastic teacher by the name of Mrs. Thibedeau, and had my first crush. This girl, March, was beautiful to my nine-year-old eyes. But of course, I couldn't admit I liked her. That would have been school suicide—girls were still gross. I remember she had a friend, Tracy, and Tracy would tell me that March liked me while we'd be out playing on the school jungle gym. The news felt good but awkward—everybody wants to be liked. But still, I was afraid of girls. My buddy Jeff and I launched some sort of stupid plan so she'd know I didn't like her. I don't remember the details, but I'm sure it was no different than something Larry and Beaver would have done on *Leave It to Beaver*.

During this whole period of fourth-grade stupidity, radio was blowing up and throwing shards of light in my direction. There were so many good pop songs that year and into 1985.

They may not all sound so good now, but back then it was magical. Van Halen's *MCMLXXXIV* (1984) came out during that time and rocked my world. My aunt bought the cassette for me at an upstate New York mall during a visit, and soon "Panama," "Hot for Teacher" and "Jump" were frequently played in the room of Christopher A. Callaway.

I later moved on from Van Halen. Similar scenarios, however, continued as I got into U2, Christian heavy metal and then, eventually, Americana/roots rock in college.

I think for most people, college probably presents the biggest deluge of music and memory association. Post-high school education is often the first time you are away from home and starting out on your own—my transition was rocky at first. I've never been good with change, but I eventually settled in like most everyone else. And music provided a great soundtrack.

There were a couple of bands during my first two years of college that really signified the whole time period for me—Counting Crows and Gin Blossoms. Both wrote excellent, radio-friendly pop songs, but there was an earnestness in the vocals and an emotionality in the way the material was played that stood out. Of the two bands, I gravitated more toward Counting Crows.

Bill Mallonee of Vigilantes of Love helped solidify my interest in Counting Crows a few years later. I was a big V.O.L. fan by then, and Bill's music was sometimes very similar. Perhaps that's why I liked Counting Crows so much in the first place. In college, I interviewed Bill for a paper I was writing and he mentioned how he and his wife (at the time) Brenda had seen the Crows live recently, and how amazingly the band performed. Of course Bill liked Adam Duritz and Co.—why wouldn't he? It was heart-on-sleeve Americana rock with catchy hooks, honest lyrics and a tinge of folk flavoring delivered in a raw fashion—very familiar territory for him.

I dove deep into the Crows my final year of school, even more so after interviewing Bill, and I couldn't stop listening to *August and Everything After*. That, and Gin Blossoms' *New Miserable Experience*, fueled my senior year (along with a steady dose of the Samples and, of course, Vigilantes of Love). *August and Everything After* was *that* record. It spoke to the heart. It examined the emotions and wasn't afraid of vulnerability regardless of the pain involved. Producer T-Bone Burnett knew what he was doing and helped craft what remains a rock masterpiece. The follow-up, *Recovering the Satellites*, purchased a week or so after college graduation and before I moved to Nashville, was as emotionally honest as *August* but with the decibel level raised a few notches. I was hooked, and as with *August and Everything After*, played the disc over and over again. Its contents helped me maneuver yet another transition—moving from college life to my first foray into the workplace in a city far from home.

It wasn't until after I moved back to Denver from Nashville a couple years later that I had a chance to interview the Crows. The band had just released their third full-length, *This Desert Life*, and I pursued my first "big" interview for the *Boulder Weekly* with my editor's blessing. I think the band's publicist asked me about the *Weekly's* circulation and I gave them what I thought was an accurate number. It took me no time to get the interview, and, later on, I realized I had greatly exaggerated the publication's circulation. I chuckled once I found out. It never had a negative repercussion, however, and my relationships with publicists have always remained strong. After all, the *Weekly* was and is a strong paper and has continued year after year despite the continuous financial failings of print media.

I didn't get to interview frontman Adam Duritz, but I was given an opportunity with Charlie Gillingham, the Crows' keyboardist/pianist/organist/accordionist. During the phone interview, he was considerate and took the time to answer my questions, making a joke every now and then. He answered a lot of questions about Duritz—probably more than he cared to answer—but he was still very professional and gave me a lot of good information and, interestingly, spoke a bit about being a new father. Unfortunately, the interview was plagued by calls from other people coming in on my landline phone and creating a "beep" sound in the middle of meaningful dialogue. I had a cell phone, but technology (at least that I knew about) had not become available to record off a mobile device.

The band performed at the University of Denver's Magness Arena on December 2, 1999, as part of the *This Desert Life* tour, and Gigolo Aunts opened. While I didn't enjoy the Gigolo Aunts' set, I became a fan when they released the brilliant *Pacific Ocean Blues* later on. There's a song on that album, "Once in a While," that is one of the most beautiful love songs I've ever heard.

The Crows played a solid show, but I do remember wishing that their live performance had been rawer—there were just too many people on stage to play the tunes. My roommate Tim, also a huge Counting Crows fan at the time, agreed.

I would see the band again ten years later—July 29, 2009—this time at Red Rocks with my good friend Will. It was pouring rain, and we kept ourselves warm by drinking overpriced eight-dollar Coors Lights. Neither one of us could stomach the opener—the songs just weren't there, and there was something missing. The rain would come in sheets throughout the concert and then dissipate in a continuous, revolving pattern. Throughout the inclement weather, however, Duritz's intensity did not disappoint, even though the opening band joined the Crows on several songs.

Soon after the show, Will and I would see our friendship flicker and fade due to a young lady. It was one of the most painful six months I've encountered, especially due to the length of my friendship and closeness with Will. Eventually forgiveness came into play, and we are once again close friends.

****

The album sounds great. You guys always re-create yourself with every record from a sonic perspective. What was it like recording *This Desert Life*?
I think we were a little bit more relaxed about it. We didn't go in with any songs in mind. We started out with almost nothing written, whereas on the previous record we had

written everything and over-rehearsed it, you know, fretted over it for months. On this record, we just went in and tried things. It was easier in the sense that it was more playful and we could try things and have fun.

I know that you always choose to record in houses.
Right.

I guess you rent a house and record in it. Was this one in the Hollywood Hills?
Yeah, it was right up over Hollywood Bowl.

Why do you choose to do that? Is it the energy? Or what causes you to choose houses?
We have always done it in houses, probably because studios are such a pain in the ass. Our first producer said, "Studios stink of despair." It's really good because you can relax, and it can be more of a party because there's more room to hang out. Also, you live there, and so every minute, every thought is devoted to the record. You can never come in and treat it like a job. It becomes your life.

Do you find that it allows you to record at odd times and things that you normally wouldn't do? Like a spur-of-the-moment idea or something?
Right. Some of the songs on this record, like "Four Days" and "Mrs. Potter's Lullaby," were recorded in the middle of the night minutes after they were written, the basic tracks. "Four Days," pretty much the whole song, I think was …

One thing I noticed about that song is it has a really cool guitar texture to it. It sounds really lo-fi. How did you guys wind up coming up with that guitar sound?
Actually that wacky guitar sound was played by Clay [Jones], a friend of the band. You mean the big snarly …

Yeah, the one that sounds like it's coming out of one of Ray Davies' old punctured cabinets.

It is. It's coming out of a little tiny amp. The guitar players can tell you, but I can't. A little tiny amp like about a foot wide—they were laying on the floor and mic-ing from the back, completely distorted.

One of the other things I noticed about this record is it has a lot more piano on it than previous records, and it seems to have a real melodic structure to it. Is it hard to continuously come up with parts like that? I also noticed that you co-wrote "I Wish I Was a Girl," which is one of the strongest melodic songs on the record. Is it hard to continuously come up with melodic pieces?
I don't know. We tend to wind up with too much stuff, rather than too little—or at least I do over in keyboard land. A lot of stuff gets thrown out. "I Wish I Was a Girl" started as a recording that I did at my house. I played all the parts and I had this version of that song that was just me, and then we re-recorded it with everybody. And Adam [Duritz] wrote a lyric and a melody to it.

It's a great song. I am sure you have been asked this question a lot, but why wait three years before this record?
Well, it's not entirely all our fault, although we are kind of slow. We did take a long time to record. I've been in other bands that were much quicker. We tend to second-guess ourselves a lot. All the songs go through a lot of revisions. Sometimes getting the simplest part on record [Faint recording, unclear. -Ed.]. And it just keeps going around and around and around. So some of it's our fault, some of it is that. But mostly it's the way the record business is, man.

The whole [large corporate music takeover] thing?
Well, they want you touring as long as possible. They kind of want you to take a long time. We actually finished—I think the last track for this record was recorded in February and it wasn't released until November. That's not really us—that was us going back and forth with the record company. We did take about a half a year—more than that—nine months,

ten months to record the record. That slowed it down, but also before that we toured for a year and a half. After that, we messed around with the record company.

With touring—that's a long time to be on the road. Do you come to a place where you honestly don't want to do it anymore? Have you ever come to that place and just kept on going?
Well, you know, I like being on the road. It suits me. It's harder on some of the other guys. Usually when a tour starts, I'm really happy for about four or five months. I just like being out on the road. The only times we've ever had to give up was because of Adam's voice. You'd never guess it from our songs, but we are pretty happy on the road. We have a lot of laughs and play a lot of poker.

What do you hope people take away from *This Desert Life* after listening to it and living with it for a while? What do you hope they get out of it?
Well, I think it's our best record. I think it's got some of our best lyrics. I think there are some stories there that are true, that are very touching. And I think what people like about Counting Crows is the way Adam is honest about a lot of the feelings that he has and when he tells stories about people who are in pain. All the music stays so drenched in irony and distance. Our music tends to be a lot closer. I think that's what people are looking for with Counting Crows.
[Short discussion about Adam's honesty in songwriting. -Ed.]

T-Bone Burnett's career has been all about that [honest songwriting]. Is that one of the reasons why you decided to work with him?
T-Bone? I think mostly it was because we respected him as a songwriter. And he'd done a really good job on [Unclear. – Ed.] So that was why we picked him. The second producer, Gil Norton, we picked him because we love the Pixies and we wondered if we could do some of that edge. And on this last record, the producers were Dave Lowery, who was the lead singer of Camper Van Beethoven and later in Cracker, and his

longtime partner Dennis Herring. The two of them produced this record. I think they were a really good team. David Lowery was extremely creative. When we wanted to go a crazy direction, he would help us to be able to go in a crazy direction and run with it. And Dennis was great at keeping it melodic and keeping it in line and keeping it true. I think Dennis and David did a really good job of capturing the essence of the band.

It sounds like a great record. I haven't heard it too much since it's only been out for a couple weeks. I know that people have said that you are a band that you have to see live. [Bill Mallonee of Vigilantes of Love stated this during an interview I did with him back in 1996 or '97— that's probably where I'm pulling this reference. -Ed.] If performing live wasn't a part of the whole picture, would you even want to do this whole thing?
Oh geez. You know what, I wouldn't mind being a studio band either. I have a little one-year-old boy. This is my first tour with a one-year-old boy far away and it's different. Now, I wouldn't really mind having a job where [Unclear. -Ed.]

If you have a family, it probably gets difficult at times just constantly being on the road.
Yeah, well you know, you deal with it.

What was it like seven or eight years ago when "Mr. Jones" got really big? What was that like?
It was a surprise. It was a welcome surprise. As you just said, in our live shows we had always taken a lot of risks and improvised a little bit, and we would take really deep emotional risks from time to time. And when "Jones" got to be a hit, instead of being real music fans [at the shows], we used to just get a lot of dates, you know, just people on a date. They just wanted to hear the hit. It was strange for us, because we do something that we do, and this is what we get back, just play a club and the normal sort of reaction, but we played the first two chords of "Mr. Jones," and they'd scream

and scream and scream. And if we changed a line they just looked confused and horrified.

I know Adam does that.
Yeah, he changes lines and stuff. For the fans, for the people who are real music fans, real fans of the band, if Adam changes the line, they'll remember that and go, "Wow, what's he going to say next?" So it was weird for us, because it became hard to fit into those shoes, just being entertainment when we had always been so personal. And so for a while, we changed that. But, nowadays, we're just lucky to be able to do what we do. And Adam—he was sort of unhappy for a while because everything was out of his control. And now he's used to it. He's been leader of the band for the long time. He knows what he's doing and the whole [Unclear. –Ed.].

What has been the most humorous thing that has happened to yourself or the band since you've been doing this?
Let me think. I don't know. There was the time Adam's luggage fell off the side of the bus in Paris. It got strewn all up and down the highway. I can't think of anything that's printable or that isn't an inside joke.

What can people expect from this tour?
Well, we are going to be playing a lot of songs from the new record. We will play "Mr. Jones" pretty much every night.

Does it get to the point where you play that song over and over and you just hate it?
Well no, not for us because we skipped it so many times. But now we're just at the point where all that's way over and done with and, in essence, at the end of the day it's just kind of a good pop song, pop/rock [thing]. As we've always done, we improvise every night. Play different songs every night. [Unclear. -Ed]. If you've never seen Adam, Adam is a pretty dynamic performer.

I've heard that he is incredibly intense live, which always makes for a good show. I have heard rumors—is Adam's hair real?
No. They're hair extensions.

Hair extensions?
Yeah.

I know there have been rumors floating around.
Well, it's not really a secret.

I had never heard anybody address it.
And I use Jax Wax [A popular car wax. –Ed.] for my hair.

Adam also mentions Elizabeth a lot in his lyrics. Is that an actual person?
Yes, Betsy is a real person. Anna is a real person. Maria is a fictional character. Many of the songs are true stories. "Mrs. Potter's Lullaby" is kind of a true story.

Is Elizabeth an old girlfriend?
Yeah, Adam and Betsy, they were going out around the time we were recording the first record. When we went on tour the first time, they had never had a—she wasn't ready for a commitment and I guess she got kind of jealous. But anyway, they broke up. And then "I Wish I Was a Girl," that lyric is just about how hard it is sometimes for two people in a relationship to be honest with each other because there's a certain means of trust between the genders; you know, "men are like this" or "women are like that." So the song is just, "You'd believe me if I was your girlfriend."

The lyrics are always deep. The thing that's cool about the lyrics is you can examine them and figure out what the intended meaning is, which is really good because so much pop today is just so spoon-fed, so clichéd. It's probably hard to come up with something that is not that way because that's so much of what is out there. And it's

a risky thing I would think. But you guys seem to be pretty successful doing it.
[Bits of this were unclear, but it was all in praise of Adam. -Ed.] All the people I played with were saying, "This guy is writing about the truth. He's writing about what's going on." The second verse of "Round Here" made me join the band.

That first record [*August and Everything After*]—there wasn't really anything like it that came out at that time.
I couldn't listen to it for a long time because I was sort of in denial about it. I kept thinking about the record we could have made, the record I wished we'd made. But then just when we were starting to make this newest record, I went back and [listened to the record] and I like it now.

Is it hard to listen to your own stuff? Do you wind up being super-critical?
Yes for me, because I think of things that might have been. But this new record is the first record where I wouldn't change very much. I like it. I think it's good. [Discussion of the first album, how structured it was, how the musicians didn't show off—much of the recording was unclear for this section, so I did not try to transcribe it. -Ed.]

On the second record [*Recovering the Satellites*], it seems like you guys just said, "To hell with it. We are going to have some fun."
Yeah, we're going to have some fun, we're going to have some guitar solos and stuff. We kind of dressed it all up and that, but I think it wasn't until this record that we actually had it all [together].

And one of the cool things about the new record—there's little things in the production that really stand out. Like in "Four Days," when Matt is just doing the sixteenth notes on his bass, when they raise the [volume] level a little bit.
Yeah, let the instruments shine through without comprom-iseing [the song].

I appreciate it, Charlie. You guys are busy and I appreciate you taking the time to do this.
Okay. Where are you at again?

I am in Boulder, Colorado.
We played there not too long ago.

Oh yeah for the Gavin thing, the radio summit—was it fun just playing in a small club setting?
It is and it isn't. It can be really fun or, you know, there's a lot of technical hassles. But the shows were definitely a lot of fun.

A lot more intimate.
Yeah. We are going to play Denver in about …

December 2nd, I think.
It's coming right up.

I definitely appreciate it, Charlie and I hope you guys have a great tour. I look forward to seeing the tour when you come through Denver.

STIR FRIED
(BUDDY CAGE)

Late January or early February 2000
Article: *Boulder Weekly* **(February 10, 2000)**

An adoration of classic rock was instilled in me from my earliest memories. I've mentioned already how the magical, hypnotizing motion of reel-to-reel tapes and the sounds they produced on my dad's behemoth Sony machine were formative to what I like to hear in a musical artist. The Beatles' "White Album" and Chicago's propulsive "25 or 6 to 4," from their self-titled disc—these two recordings were foundational to the ingredients I looked for in good rock tunes. The melodies of the Beatles and the driving nature of "25 or 6 to 4"—especially the out-of-this world drumming by Danny Seraphine—somehow entered into my mind in a place from which they were never able to escape, and that's a good thing.

Later on I would hear the muted bass tones on classic Eric Clapton solo material and various ensemble groupings, like Derek & the Dominos and Blind Faith. As a young bass player hearing those sounds for the first time, I was taken aback. I spent years and various amounts of money trying to replicate those sounds, and I spent hours of research trying to determine what those players were using. Was it flat-wound bass strings, vintage Ampeg SVT eight-by-ten cabinets and amp heads, the famous Ampeg Portaflex bass amp, old Fender basses (the Jazz or Precision)? Was it the analog method of recording? The questions were endless. I came to a place where I thought that the bass tone I wanted could be achieved by analog recording and went out and spent seven hundred and fifty dollars on a used eight-track Otari multi-track machine and a sixteen-channel Soundcraft mixing board. The board alone was probably worth seven hundred and fifty-dollars, but I was able to get a good deal as I purchased both from my college, where I had taken a studio class a few years prior using the very same equipment. The school had decided to depart with the old gear, and since I asked about it, they sold it to me.

A few years later I parted with the Otari reel-to-reel machine and Soundcraft mixing board, unsuccessful at figuring out how to effectively use them. Chad, the guitarist in Crash Orchid (the band I was in at the time) and I discovered digital recording via his computer and some nice microphones. The ease-of-use won us over. We were also living in a house off Broadway in the southern part of Denver that doubled as our own recording studio. The simpler setup, using less space and requiring less work, was better.

Back before I had ever picked up a bass, and before I ever thought about purchasing studio equipment, I was the kid mentioned earlier, enamored with Beatlesque pop melodies and driving rhythm sections. As I grew out of my Incredible Hulk pajamas and started wearing jeans and shirts and attending elementary school, I was again drawn to the reel-to-reel machine and fascinated with my dad's invitingly smelly reel-to-reel tape collection, along with his fantastic stack of dust-covered LPs.

During this formative time period, I would sometimes spend time with my neighborhood friend James. I had recently started liking metal (I think AC/DC's "What Do You Do for Money Honey," heard through a jukebox at a swimming pool, solidified that newfound love). But my parents wouldn't let me near any metal albums of my own. My dad had a BASF chrome cassette copy of the "White Album," procured from his reel-to-reel tape recording. One day, James and I went along on a ride to the hardware store in the town center of Norfolk, and I brought along a Panasonic tape recorder and blasted the "White Album" while my dad was in the store. I had just rediscovered "Everybody's Got Something to Hide Except Me and My Monkey," and it was loud and abrasive and as close to metal as I was allowed! I was proud of loudness and wanted to play that song over and over. I couldn't buy Motley Crue's *Shout at the Devil* or Ratt's *Out of the Cellar*. Those cassettes would have never passed the discerning eyes (and ears) of my mom, so it was the Beatles.

During the Panasonic listening experience, James and I were sitting in my parents' Ram custom minivan waiting for my dad. I turned up the tape recorder in all its mono glory, and James was probably discussing the Pontiac Parisienne station wagon his father had purchased. All of a sudden we see two teenage guys walk toward the van. For some reason we figured they were going to kidnap us. They were probably just trying to have a little fun. We locked the doors pretty quickly!

My knowledge of classic rock would soon grow exponentially. Every summer my mom would send my brother and me to a Christian camp in upstate New York. The people there meant well, but while they preached the gospel, it had a certain amount of legalism added to it. I remember going to a bonfire one night where a guy got up and spoke about how he was at a mall, sharing his faith with a couple of long-haired men. The two men grew frustrated and apparently commented, in an irritated manner, "We are Christians!" The speaker talked about how Christian men should not have long hair and should repent of rock 'n' roll. I was pissed off. I've come to realize that this point of view has many flaws and that Jesus could care less about the length of someone's hair or his or her preference for a particular music style.

While visiting this camp, I picked up a book called *Pop Goes the Gospel* at the onsite store. This "masterpiece" went into full detail about how rock music was basically of the devil, and it contained a list of mainstream bands and what made each one of them evil. It even contained reports of "backwards masking," when a musician supposedly goes into a song and records a vocal line that is placed in reverse within the confines of the composition. The book discussed some of these supposed messages. The author argued that these backward messages could be unscrambled by the brain and influence the listener. I was fascinated by this and tried playing different songs backward to see if I could hear anything, even going so far as to use my dad's oft-mentioned

Sony reel-to-reel machine as I could manually feed the tape backward across the playback heads.

Since the certain reality of it had already been suggested by *Pop Goes the Gospel*, and the power of suggestion is very strong, I thought I heard things. André, a personage mentioned throughout this book, and I would discuss this, especially after we had a speaker come to our church who claimed he had worked in the music industry and had run into Satanism first hand. He talked about backwards masking too.

While this speaker, if I remember correctly, didn't ask his audience to throw away rock altogether, *Pop Goes the Gospel* seemed to aim for that goal. Rather than embracing culture and using discernment based on one's convictions, this book seemed to propagate the removal of oneself from any type of involvement in popular culture. It even attacked Christian rock. I believe the author, John Blanchard (along with Peter Anderson and Derek Cleave), was well-meaning. The problem, I would argue, lies in isolating oneself from culture and spending all your time with likeminded people. The funny thing is that Jesus didn't do this. He was out and about, hanging out with the neglected, the needy and the hurting.

Perhaps these authors, unbeknownst to themselves, had a well-disguised need for control. Maybe they were, without realizing it, scared of what would happen if they left the area as a gray one—open to interpretation and the individual's discretion. Ken Mansfield, who worked extensively with the Beatles, speaks in churches and is very affectionate when he reminisces in his books about his work with the group. This is a man who takes his faith very seriously but realizes that culture is something to be embraced while armed with discernment.

While *Pop Goes the Gospel* had its weaknesses, it did, as I mentioned earlier, contain a detailed listing of a number of "evil" rock artists. This mini encyclopedia of sorts gave me knowledge of much of classic rock. From that point on, I would look through albums from my dad's collection, at record stores and in the public library and mentally record what I read. I got to know producers, session musicians, songwriters, record labels and the years different recordings were issued, and I started to develop a large mental encyclopedia that still serves me well when I play bar trivia.

And my musical education continued. My parents had friends named Dale and Dale. They were a fantastic married couple, always friendly and full of personality. Once when we were invited over for dinner, I was asked to say the blessing. So we held hands. I closed my eyes and bowed my head in prayer. Somewhere in that brief time period, Mr. Dale directed my hand into the butter dish.

Mr. Dale subscribed to *Rolling Stone*. So while I was nose-deep in *Pop Goes the Gospel*, my dad's record collection, albums at the Walpole Public Library, plastic-bagged cassettes at the Norfolk Public Library, the "Nice Price" closeout albums at Bradlees and the record store at the Walpole Mall, I would now leaf through *Rolling Stone* whenever we went to the Dales' house for dinner. I especially devoured the November 16, 1989 issue of the magazine, which was devoted to the one hundred best rock albums. The huge page size, the articles, the reviews—it was life-changing.

At the same time I was reading and listening, I was also visually experiencing rock 'n' roll. My first concert—by a Christian artist named John Fischer—was held in the gym at Medway High School in Medway, Massachusetts. My first "secular" concert (except for seeing Poison-like band Hurricane open for Stryper a couple years prior) was Heart at Great Woods, an outdoor amphitheater in Mansfield, Mass., on July 13, 1990. I was in awe. I probably gazed around at the people and surroundings for the entirety of the two-band experience like an aspiring painter going to the Louvre for the first time, or going to Munich and seeing the true brilliance of Van Gogh's *Sunflowers*.

Skip ahead to years later when, due to my parents' encouragement, I became a music journalist and, because of my time spent studying rock 'n' roll and listening to its ominous legends, was naturally drawn to those artists who were more road-worn. The years spent living the rock star life appealed to me, and I would interview those individuals whenever I could. There was just something about interviewing a veteran rocker versus the "flavor of the week."

Early in my days with the *Boulder Weekly*, I spoke on the phone with a guy named Buddy Cage. I didn't know much about Buddy other than the fact he was coming to Boulder as part of a band called Stir Fried. The name alone described the band to me—I knew it was somehow jam rock-oriented, perhaps Cajun, reggae, zydeco—something along those lines. But once Buddy and I started chatting, I discovered there was much more to him. He had played pedal steel for Bob Dylan and Jerry Garcia and counted some of rock's father figures as friends. The interview went on to encompass much more than Stir Fried, and I discovered a man grateful for the gift of life and still excited to be expressing his musical gifts.

Buddy started our interview mentioning a funny instance with Bob Dylan. I tried to get him to talk about it over the phone, but he wouldn't due to the fact that he would have to play himself and Dylan, and most of the humor was physical. At the end of the interview, he said he'd show me his Dylan story if I came down to the Stir Fried show. I never made it, but I wish I had. The story alone would have been well worth the trip. Perhaps Buddy's book covers the Dylan event in detail—if you have the chance, I encourage you to invest in a copy.

****

You have a pretty vast history with what you've done. What is your most memorable or funniest instance in your relationship with either Bob Dylan or Jerry Garcia?
Oh man, you couldn't even cover that in a day's article. There is one in particular of Bob Dylan that is really heavy. It's a neat one, but I'd have to be in front of you. I'd have to do the bit, I'd have to do Dylan, I'd have to do me. It's inside the studio, which is like a monster. But I couldn't do it over the phone. It just wouldn't translate. But, Jerry, I mean, we were always laughing. I don't know what was funny. We'd walk in the room and fucking keel over.

It's always been fun. I could never recall work that we did together that wasn't fun. I can't imagine either of us looking at each other and going, "Aw, fuck." It was all fun. It was all about music.

Is there any instance that you can recall?
No, that doesn't do any good for me to give out something just on the phone like that. I can tell you how I came into the Riders and that kind of stuff. The famous train trip across Canada. I was playing with Ian and Sylvia at the time.

That was with Janis Joplin, right?
Well yeah, but there was the Band, Joplin, the Dead. It was insane who was on that. Buddy Guy. It was just nuts. At one point, one of the bar cars with Garcia playing rhythm guitar and him and Joplin—at least Joplin and he and Sylvia and Delaney and Bonnie Bramlett and Rick Danko singing "No More Cane On the Brazos"—I mean, you had to hear it. Some of the best singers in the nation—in the world—going at it. Garcia wouldn't even touch it. All he did was play rhythm because they were just hauling ass.

What was that like for you? Do you think about that a lot?
Well it certainly it comes up a lot. Let's put it that way. A lot of people ask about it and it's one of those "Wish I was there and you were and what was it like?" It was really the first time we all got to pay our peace and love to each other and our respect personally instead of through another person or something. Everybody thinks that we all go out on these major tours and we all see each other. It's not like that. And it can be—if you are not suited for it—a very lonely life. But we were just crazy. There were about two hundred freaks, man. I mean, it was the bands. Think of the bands, right? All the wives, the kids, the whole disaster. We were a tripped-out bunch of just fun—everybody wanted to play their best for each other. Look their best. So everybody was on top and it was insane. It was a drunken fiasco. But it was—the music—I guess everybody's young enough at the time [and] should be

able to shake that shit off, you know? But Janis just loved it. That was her favorite gig in the whole world.

Was that '68?
No, that was in '70.

That was in '70, OK. And that was across pretty much all of Canada, wasn't it?
Yup, pretty much.

You went through the wilderness and just stopped at different places?
Yeah, we stopped in major cities. The crews would all go out and unload all the shit off the boxcars and drive them to these major football stadiums in Canada, you know, CFL and stuff. And we would do these open-air deals—they were huge, man, and were just so much fun. Just a billion hippies all freaked out and having fun and great music and fine playing. The trips between the gigs were wonderful because we all got to hang out together or sip some wine or you know—just hang out and bullshit. And play. Garcia one time sent a crew guy over to me and he said, "Hey, Jerry would like to have you play your steel [pedal steel]." And I went, "Yeah, well I [Unclear. –Ed.]. I didn't feel like I wanted to be singled out. And he came over and said, "Oh man, do it! We'll have the other crew set both of them if you will agree to it; we will play together and my crew will set all your shit up." "Oh, OK." And so they did, and we played on the train while the train was moving. It was a wonderful deal.

Do you have a favorite memory from that trip?
I have many, many, many! I have so many it would just knock you down. We ran out of booze somewhere around midnight—somewhere around eleven o'clock or so one night going to Saskatchewan. Where is that? Saskatchewan—well, no, that is the name of the province—some big town. We're going anywhere—anyway they keep their liquor stores for one reason or another—their package stores open until two a.m.!

Are they all government run up there?
Yeah! Apparently. And so the entrepreneurs—the two guys that were running this deal—they told us, "Yeah, man." So they went around and took a private collection. Everybody put in about, I don't know, three, four hundred bucks and they went and got this massive amount of booze and shit. First time Garcia really ever got drunk. The whole train was unconscious at the end, except for the engineer, I guess. Maybe he was. I don't know. But it was that, and Buddy Guy getting up on the staging. He decided to climb the stage with a guitar. You had to see that stuff. Janis—she was running up to convince the conductors. "I want to see the fucking engine, man!" "Oh well, ma'am, we can't do that." "You can't? Why can't you, man?" So she just enabled them. She got them stoned. Canadian conductors. It's never heard of, right? They didn't even know what they were doing. They finally got her up to the engine and she actually got the engineers stoned, which was really funny. It was just a hilarious time.

Since you have been in music so long, how is the life of a musician different today than it was back then?
It's no different as far as the way I conduct myself and what I do and how I do it, you know, my usual habits and stuff. It's a good job where you don't have to punch a time card or do a nine-to-five thing. You can go away when you want. You can sit down when you want. And it's all music, which if you don't love music, get another job. It's a lot of fun. It's always been for me. I got a big kick out of it, always have, playing with guys—we got a new bass player we are working in now. He's working into us and doing a pretty good job. We are just having fun with that.

Is it hard to bring somebody new on board?
No, not of that quality. Because the guy's got different stuff to bring in, to bring to the table, and you bring the stuff up and we are laughing and just—nobody's too serious in this thing. After all, we are not Leonard Bernstein. But then, he has a humorous side, so I don't know. I have been doing this professionally [for] thirty-eight going on thirty-nine years. I

was fifteen [when I started]. So it's been a long, long, long, long time. And the first years were a real struggle with a pedal steel guitar with a rock 'n' roll brain trying to find a place to hang my hat. Here I was with this country-western instrument and just couldn't—I got bored of the country music business. I just thought that was too confining, so stifling, such crap. And where do I get to play this? And then I heard Dylan—I was on the road somewhere and I was a young kid and I heard Dylan—and they first played his "Like a Rolling Stone." It was like somebody took a big key and put it into this big door and opened the door and on the other side was a whole other galaxy and said, "There you go, man." And I knew there was a place to go. And when the Band put out *Music from Big Pink*, I was positive that I had a place to live. So I was free to do whatever I wanted, pretty much. I have been swimming uphill all my life with this instrument.

It seems to have made a resurgence in recent years. I think the guy's name is Greg Leisz—I think he lives in California somewhere. It seems like a lot more rock bands these days have pedal steel on them.

Aw, neat, man. That's neat because I didn't know what I was doing in the beginning when I started with this stuff and nobody else was. I was the only unconventional guy in the world, basically. Maybe there was a couple, three of us, but we were all screwing around with it and I certainly wasn't going to play by Nashville rules or any of that stuff.

So did you initially start by playing country?

I had to. I was forced to. I hated country music, [or] what I thought was country music. I hated it passionately, like most rock 'n' roll guys do with that kind of background. But then I was forced into playing it and then I ran into, very fortunately, a lot of kind, kind of hip guys, and particularly one guy, Mickey McGivern. I'll never forget him. He is still living, as a matter of fact. I was talking to him about two or three months ago. He was so kind to me and a tough bastard, but really showed me a lot of shit, and he didn't freak out when I started playing off-the-wall stuff. He'd kind of look at me sideways—"Pass me that thing you're smoking." So I really got a lot of help from a lot of really great people. Then I ran into Ronnie Hawkins, played for him, and then I played for Ian and Sylvia and the Band and some Grateful Dead and so and so and so. It just fell in that way.

How did Stir Fried come about?
Well, I don't really know. It actually started about six years ago or so, and those guys were all revolving around playing in a thing that we're—you know, you always need a tune to start anything with, and it started with Johnny's [Markowski] tunes. A lot of that was his dad's [Tommy Kaye's] tunes. He was one of those guys that sat in an office and rolled off all these pop hits and stuff. But he was a great writer in his own right, and he kind of passed it on to Johnny. So they started with that, and then I guess about three years ago, I was playing this festival up near Woodstock, New York. I played with this other band, and I was pulling my steel out, and these guys were setting up and they were saying, "Would you mind playing with us?" "No. No, I don't mind at all." So I sat down and we played and I liked their stuff instantly. When I come into any group, I try to bring them up a couple of levels if I can—that is a part of my job or my responsibility, you know, add my portfolio to yours and see what we can do with it.

How would you describe the style?
Phew. Man, I'm the worst in the world to ask that question. A lot of people call it "jam groove" and I wouldn't say it's so much of a jam band as more of a groove band. And the songs, the lyrics—I'm finally hearing some of the lyrics after three years. I'm that way. I'm just slow at picking up lyrics. Somebody'll sing "Birthday" [The "Happy Birthday to You" song? –Ed.] to me and, I'll go, "Oh, is that what that is? No shit. Oh I know that. What those words—oh!" And the same with Johnny's tunes. I'm co-producing this third CD of theirs in the studio, and I've been offered the opportunity of hearing a lot of his words. And [Unclear –Ed.] oh down! I am

very pleased about it. There was something good that I liked after all. And it's really kind of nice, but ...

Are you officially a member of the band?
No, not really. I have never been officially a member of anything in my own world. I've always been independent. Although I would attach myself—I was a New Rider—took over from Garcia in '71—so I was a New Rider for eleven years. And I guess I will be a Stir Fried for as long as that goes on, but I also do all sorts of other things, you know, projects and stuff. But I play with Stir Fried all the time, and they're finally getting the recognition that they've deserved for a long time. They've upgraded their band in certain areas and they really have done a lot of work and now they're far less suicidal. Still a little on the homicidal side. People are starting to return phone calls and they've got an agent friend—a guy that works out of Evergreen—at Fraser actually. Candy Store Productions, and he is terrific. He's booking them like a motherfucker.

That's great. It keeps you guys busy.
Absolutely. And that is the whole name of it as far as I am concerned. The more you play, the better you get.

What is it like for you to still be able to do what you love after all these years?
I am very lucky. I went through an extreme bout at the end of my alcoholism in the late '80s, mid to late '80s. It really turned—that went right down the shit chute and I was lucky enough to have some friends that I stumbled into that threw me into an A.A. room in '89 and I didn't look back. I have stayed with it ever since, and I am in good shape and I feel great. Every day is a gift that I can go out and play my guitar. You'd be surprised at how many guys—I guess you wouldn't. You'd be surprised how many guys I get to help along the way in this business.

Sure, I mean even a lot of the people you grew up playing with. A lot of people have gone through those things. Every time I turn on VH1's *Behind the Music* ...
Oh yeah. I tried a couple of different confrontations with Garcia over the years, and he never made it. And [Rick] Danko, I tried to work with him. Sent him letters from me to Garcia and a hundred to me and all this kind of, "What can we do?" I mean this that and the other. "Jerry, you dumb motherfucker!" And Danko never got it. Look at where he's at now. We just buried him about a month ago.

What was that like for you? That had to be really difficult.
Well it wasn't as difficult as you'd think, because I said goodbye to Rick in my heart a year and a half ago. We played our last date together. We ended up playing a Labor Day weekend up near Watertown, New York—a big festival—and he asked me to play, just him and me and nobody else. We hadn't done that for years, just the two of us, and I said, "Sure, man." This was subsequent to the confrontation letters I had written him, and he wasn't even cognizant at all. I said, "Sure, I'll play with you." We did a whole raft of numbers and the last number we did together was "Stage Fright." How appropriate, right, or how apropos to the occasion. I knew he was sick and I knew he was dying. And that's just what that was. I have to keep my own nose clean.

There's only so much you can do.
That's it. So that's what that was all about. I just can't take responsibility that he wouldn't take for his own life. And it goes with so many of them. There's a lot of them [that are] broken.

It's good that there are people like you that were part of that scene that were able to get all the negative things that went along with it ...
Yeah, I was really lucky, man. Really lucky.

I appreciate it, Buddy.
Oh, Chris, my pleasure.

I saw a story on, I think it was VH1 or MTV, about the train tour.
Yeah.

So that's really interesting.
It is. It was a great deal. When I meet you, I will run you through the Dylan one.

I would love to hear that. I was in a studio in Nashville, I can't remember which one, I think it was Emerald, and they told me Dylan was just in there recording and how he liked to have all the lights down and he'd crouch in a corner and do his thing.
Oh yeah, man. I didn't find him so obscure, but he is definitely focused. And believe me, he gets what he wants. He knows how to work the deal.

BRUCE COCKBURN

Friday, February 18, 2000
Article: *Boulder Weekly* (February 24, 2000)

During March of 1998, I made a big decision. While the two years I had just spent in Nashville were interesting, and I had experiences I will never forget, I missed Colorado. In the Southern city known for music—mostly country and Christian—I had what I thought was a significant romantic relationship and had a great job in the music business, but I failed to put down roots. Developing friendships that weren't work-related was difficult. I avoided going to the church I had grown to appreciate because my ex-girlfriend went there. When I'd attend, I couldn't help looking around the parking lot to see if her car was there. If I saw the familiar sedan, my stomach would clench. The thought of going inside, sitting in a pew and looking out to see if I could find her was unavoidable; my biggest fear was that she would be there with some guy's arm wrapped around her shoulder.

There was at least one time when I drove the twenty minutes to get to church, saw that my ex's car was there, turned around and went home. I was miserable. It was a hard relationship to get over. I felt like I had finally met someone who was attractive, intelligent, understood me, had similar interests, was a Christian, and pursued me before I even knew what was happening.

I tried going to another church, but by that time I didn't have the desire to plug in. I even invested my time in an intense co-ed church small group (I think this may have been yet another church). It was a small group of small groups. We were all dedicated to changing, and the goal was to hone in on personal items we wanted God to transform in our lives— mostly areas where we felt we were failing or needed to improve. Perhaps it was issues relating to a divorce, patience, or maybe an anger issue. The leader of the group, a great pastor, actually sent out forms—with our permission, of course—to two or three of each person's closest friends, asking them to "rate" and review us. It was all to make us better people. However, after a while I dropped out—it was too much for me at the time. I probably could have used a counselor instead. I was already my own harshest critic.

Work was the most interesting aspect of my time in Nashville. I loved my co-workers and the professionals and musicians I worked with, but outside of the office it was a different story. I met other women, went out on dates, but nothing seemed to click. While my roommate and I were friendly, we never grew close. I had a few guys I would spend time with, but those relationships never really developed past a surface friendship.

I also remember having my loneliest New Year's Eve on record so far in 1998. There was an invite that went out to attend a church singles group celebration at someone's apartment. I had no other options and went, but I knew absolutely no one in the room. There were a few people I had met and spoken to a few times, but out of the ten or so people present, I knew maybe two names. I tried to make the time bearable and sat down on a chair, probably inventing invisible friends and/or talking to myself. I walked back to my car with a heavy heart.

Boy, I missed Colorado—I thought about my friends there often. I also wanted to see if things would work out with a girl I cared about in Denver. The seeds were quickly being sown that would yield my move back West, even though the prospect of moving up the corporate ladder at the record label was there in front of me. A few months later, the big decision had been made and I began preparing for my trek back to the West. And, yes, part of this process involved looking for work in Colorado.

Weeks prior to my resignation from KMG Records, I started sending out faxes to prospective employers. In 1999, e-mailing resumes wasn't common practice. There was a major concern over viruses from attachments, and it was still expected that materials would either be sent by mail or faxed. I had purchased a fax machine for around a hundred bucks for the occasion, as I didn't want anyone from work to get word of what I was doing. Dave Flomberg at *Boulder Weekly* received one of my faxes—the rest is, as the trite wording goes, history, and one of the reasons this book even came into being.

I rolled into the Denver area with high hopes of a full-time journalism career or a music business job, but neither happened. The desire I had for something possibly happening with the girl I cared about never came to fruition (about a year after I moved back, she proclaimed her lesbianism). I started writing for the *Weekly*, tested breathalyzers to pay the bills, lived with my parents, then went into cell phone activation for Nextel and moved in with some friends. I also joined a band that my college friend Chad was in called Breathing Eve. Life wasn't bad.

As a freelance writer, I was always looking for article ideas for the *Boulder Weekly*. During my research, I discovered that Bruce Cockburn was coming to town. He was one of those artists who had always intrigued me, partly because I did not know much about him. While growing up, I heard about Cockburn, but, as I've mentioned before, I was a metal guy. Dan Russell, who's worked with U2, Black Rebel Motorcycle Club, the Call, Vigilantes of Love, Sam Phillips—the list goes on—would promote him in his fantastic magazine, *NewSound*. I would read Dan's publication and devour every word during my pre-teen and teenage years, so I was well-versed with Bruce's album releases. However, I never went as far as listening to his music or buying any cassettes. The most I had heard of his songwriting was when a commercial for a live Cockburn record ran on broadcast television one day, probably while I was in the midst of watching one of my favorite shows of all time, *Unsolved Mysteries*. Strangely enough, there was a pastor of a church in the southern suburbs of Denver who looked exactly like *Unsolved Mysteries* host Robert Stack. It was sometimes hard to listen to his sermons because of this. Maybe I thought he'd break out a picture of a missing person, tell his or her story, and ask if we had seen that individual.

I pitched the Bruce Cockburn article to my editor, Dave. He was open to the idea, and I was excited to delve into the work of an artist I was unfamiliar with but interested in discovering. Cockburn's publicist quickly sent me his last two records, *The Charity of Night* and the recently released *Breakfast in New Orleans, Dinner in Timbuktu*. The latter disc contained the single "Last Night of the World," which was receiving a considerable amount of airplay on Boulder's KBCO-FM. I fell in love with both discs. The excellent guitar playing; the spiritually, socially, politically and environmentally conscious lyrics; and the musical compositions themselves, coupled with Bruce's warm, occasionally sarcastic voice, made me a fan.

During my first couple days with *The Charity of Night* and *Breakfast in New Orleans, Dinner in Timbuktu*, Chad, the guitarist in Breathing Eve, paid me a visit at my apartment on Dayton Street, right outside the Denver Tech Center. He had dropped in so we could solidify our parts for a song we were recording the next day. It was going to be a mammoth recording session for Breathing Eve—nine or ten songs, live, in a day at Lakewood's FTM Studios, without much time to fix errors. I grabbed my 1979 Rickenbacker 2001 bass, Chad pulled out his Parker Fly electric, and we planted ourselves on my couch and played through "Hereafter." I had written a new part or two for the song, and the first time we played it through, it sounded wonderful—everything fit perfectly. Afterward, I recall having him take a listen to Cockburn. This was new territory for me as a music fan. It wasn't the sugary-sweet pop I devoured at the time, and there were dimensions to the sound that I knew Chad would enjoy. While he didn't become a fan, I think he appreciated the fact that I was discovering and listening to something that was a complete departure from power pop.

Not long after Chad's visit, I got on the phone with Bruce Cockburn. The interview went exceedingly well. His sense of humor and his well-spokenness and friendliness made it seem almost as if I were talking to a friend. He was intelligent, engaging and not afraid to laugh at himself, and he was not limited to a pat, North American view of world affairs.

As often happens when I do an interview, I received tickets to the upcoming show. I brought my roommate at the time, Tim, as I knew he had grown to really enjoy Bruce's music. He picked me up outside my best friend Chris' wedding reception. I got into the car, pulled off the tuxedo, threw on some street clothes and we were off.

The concert at Denver's Paramount Theatre was stunning. Our seats were well-situated in the orchestra section, row U (I was in seat nine). The three-piece band (drums, bass), including Cockburn on guitar and vocals, was well-suited for the task. Unfortunately, Cockburn covered up his guitar amplifier and guitar effects with a sheet or tarp, so it was never clear how he was achieving his sounds.

Another interview with Cockburn took place about a year and a half later after the Paramount show. I was living in a house in Highlands Ranch, a suburb of Denver, at the time with a couple of friends, including Tim.

I paced around the kitchen while speaking with Bruce. He had just won an award, but he was not someone who paid much attention to them. The microcassette recording of the interview, for some reason, had such low volume that I had to decipher Bruce's words with the dedication of a crime lab technician. It worked, but I could only unscramble enough for a limited number of quotes. The piece itself landed in a short-lived local magazine, and whoever edited the piece spelled "Berklee"—as in Berklee College of Music—as "Berkeley," like the college in California, even though the article had the name spelled correctly when I submitted it.

Regardless of sound difficulties and one misspelling by an editor, each of the three times I interviewed Bruce Cockburn, I encountered a kind and talented musician willing to share his heart, mind and sense of humor unreservedly—along with information on his vast international travels outside his native Canada. His unflinching honesty has always been welcome, and I've appreciated our conversations.

****

I know you're well-traveled, and I know you have done a lot of work with Amnesty International and organizations like that. With your travels and the types of things that you've done, what has been your most memorable experience?

Oh man, there have been so many. It'd be hard to pick one, you know?

Is there one maybe recent ...

Well, yeah, the most recent thing—I haven't actually worked very much with Amnesty per se. I am a supporter of that organization, but my travels have been more connected to different ones, although they have been involved sometimes, but more sort of development agencies, aid agencies and that kind of thing, as far as what I have been working with, but in the last few years I have been involved with the land mines issue. I went to Southeast Asia in connection with that; to Vietnam and Cambodia in the spring, which was a really amazing trip. A little too short in duration for my taste, but a couple weeks long, and it was really very moving and [a] rich experience. Vietnam is so beautiful. They have had some bad typhoons and that sort of thing, and flooding in recent months, but it was so beautiful when we were there, and everybody's sort of getting on with life and in such a way that you would hardly know that there ever had been a war except for what's in museums and downed jets and so on that have been preserved as those monuments, but really there's not a sense that it's a war-torn country. It's a very poor country but incredibly beautiful. People are really easy to get along with.

It was interesting to me that they sort of seemed to view what they call the American War—of course we call it the Vietnam War—they view the American War in much the same way they view having fought off the Mongols in the 1200s. You know, it's just history now, and they talk about it the same way. Cambodia, on the other hand, is a country in a state of permanent disaster, and it's really on its knees and also beautiful in a different way. It's a pretty flat country, very moist and sort of classic muddy tropical, and it also has fantastic ruins at Angkor Wat, and temples and palaces that have been abandoned for many hundreds of years. And they're sort of the archetypal temple overgrown by jungle and really, really stunning.

So as far as the land mine issue, what has been your involvement been so far? I am not that familiar with it. I have heard a few things, but if you could give me a little bit of background on it and what your involvement has been with that so far.

I got involved in '95. The international campaign to ban land mines started up a few years before that, maybe two or three years before that, and I wasn't aware of it. I was ignorant about land mines. I knew they existed but didn't know what they represented in the world until I was asked by a group of Canadian aid agencies that were working in Mozambique to go to that country on their behalf and look at the situation regarding land mines. What's happened is that all these third-world countries—particularly, although we are all aware that there are land mines in Bosnia and Kosovo and so on—but primarily third-world countries who have had civil wars in the last twenty years have a major land mine problem. What happens is once the war's over, the soldiers give up their guns and they go back to their farms or whatever it is they do. But the land is saturated with land mines, so it makes farming difficult and—difficult is obviously an understatement—and yet they have to do it because it's their only way of getting through. So what you end up with is populations that have a significant number of amputees among them, and death and so on, and in addition to the tragedies that these things cause to individuals and families, they are a huge public health problem because these are countries that can't afford to supply prosthetic limbs and ongoing medical treatment for victims. As we talk now, there are about one hundred million land mines in the ground in the world. In Cambodia, which has a population of about ten million, there are eight million land mines. And that is down from a few years ago, when it was basically one land mine for every person.

Yeah, that is significant. Wow.
Land mines are weapons that are not primarily designed to kill, although some of it depends on which type of mine you are talking about. The most commonly encountered land mines are designed to maim rather than kill, thereby making you a burden. In a military sense, if you kill one soldier you just killed one soldier, but if you badly injure one soldier you've taken three out of the fight, because two of them have to carry. So the mines are designed to shatter your lower leg or more of your body depending on the type of mine, but not to kill you. Which means that a lot of people who encounter mines, civilians, end up dying a horrible, agonizing death over a period of time in the bush because nobody can find them or people are afraid to go get them because there are more mines or whatever, and the life expectancy of the mine in the ground is about fifty years on average.

So they are intergenerational.
That's right, and no matter what peace agreements are made and how binding they are, the mines keep on fighting. They don't care who they fight against. In the world, it's a plague and it's a plague that we visited ourselves in the latter half of the twentieth century. It was never an issue before that, obviously. So there are a lot of people working on trying to ban land mines. One of the very encouraging steps that has been taken is that there was a treaty signed a couple of years ago, spearheaded by the Canadian government actually, signed by now I think we are up to one hundred and thirty-six countries banning the manufacturing and use and sale of land mines. Unfortunately, that one hundred and thirty-six does not include the United States or Russia or China or India or Pakistan or a couple others. So there is work to be done still in terms of bringing the holdouts on side.

Now, obviously, "The Mines of Mozambique" was written about that. It seems like most of your songs are written

from experiences you've had or things you've seen. How does that go through a filter and become a song—what's the creative process you use?

Well, the initial thing is my emotional reaction to the situation, and that's the trigger. "The Mines of Mozambique" is a kind of a landscape piece in a way, but it's an attempt to get the sense across of what it feels like to be in a landscape that is mined, because the rest of the landscape of course still is whatever is normal for that part of the world. It's really an emotional response to something that I've encountered and then writing down lyrics. In the case of "The Mines of Mozambique," I wrote that in one night looking out the window of a hotel room I was in in the city in central Mozambique.

When you are in a place like that, what kinds of feelings go through your mind?

All kinds of feelings, man. From horror to the incredible poignancy of how hopeful people can be in the presence of the worst difficulties. Really, that's taught me more about hope than anything else I've experienced in my life—not necessarily Mozambique, but that kind of travel, generally, because people survive. People survive just about anything. And there's this incredible grit in the human spirit that allows us to do that. It's easy for people like us to sit around and get hopeless because we look at it from a distance, and it looks overwhelming. When you're right up close to it, you have no choice but to survive. And in order to survive, you are likely to have some hope too. It kind of puts the—what's the word?—the discouragement that we might feel in North America about these kinds of issues in perspective as a kind of a luxury, really. We can afford to feel despair because we don't have to deal with the shit.

Is that part of what you go through when you are writing a song then is dealing with all those emotions?

Yeah. It depends on the song, of course, but it can be, and the actual process of writing the song is—I was writing the words and then finding music to carry the words. The writing of words, to me, is the most enjoyable aspect of what I do. It's kind of like being a bloodhound on a trail. You are chasing this idea or these images and other elements down and trying to make them into something that works, and at the same time it might be harrowing because you are re-living stuff or looking clearly at stuff that you'd rather not be looking at. It's also fun.

In your song "Lovers in a Dangerous Time," there is a line, "Got to kick at the darkness 'til it bleeds daylight." Do you feel that kind of typifies your career?
I suppose. I don't think about that very much, but I think that's probably true, yeah. I think the job is to tell the truth as I understand it and try to share my understanding of truth with people. And the challenge is, of course, to make the songs, in the writing and presentation, effective vehicles for whatever that truth is.

"Last Night of the World"—they have been playing it a lot here in Colorado—can you give me some background on the song? I read what was in your bio, but is there anything special that goes along with that? I know there was a little blurb from you. Maybe if you could expand on that a little, what it was like being there and writing that song?
Yeah, I don't remember what I said in the bio, so I may repeat myself or I may make up something completely different. Catch me if you can. I was in between residences at that point for a period of time and staying in a room at a friend's place in Toronto, and one night sitting up listening to the radio, drinking rum, I started writing the song. A couple of the ideas had been in my notebook for a while, and the idea of champagne as an accompaniment to the end of the world was—this is probably in the bio—it was really something that I'd had in my head for years, for I guess four or five years anyway, from when Sam Phillips was touring with us in '91 or '92.

Sam Phillips is great.

Sam Phillips is incredible, and she's an incredible individual as well as being a great songwriter and performer.

I don't know if I like the Leslie Phillips's solo stuff, but …
No, she would agree with you on that. But Sam is one of a kind. She was opening shows for us on the *Nothing But a Burning Light* tour, and we were walking around someplace, Seattle or somewhere with big hills, and I'm lugging this backpack that I always carry around which has everything in it that you might need on the road, from PowerBars to flashlight, whatever, notebook …

Duct tape.
Yup. Yeah, usually. She saw me lugging this thing up this hill and said, "What do you keep in that thing, anyway?" And I said, "Oh it's everything I need for the apocalypse." And she looked at me and said, "What do you need for the apocalypse besides champagne and a couple of glasses?" I thought that was the most perfect observation about that that anybody could make, and it had to be a song. It took me some years to figure out how to make use of it. And in the meantime, she had forgotten she ever said it, of course. It was just an off-the-cuff remark. Be careful what you say around me, because it could end up getting used. That is not the first time that kind of thing has happened.

As far as the whole album—the new album—what was it like recording that? It seems like it's a more intimate record than *The Charity of Night* was before it. *The Charity of Night* seemed like it had a lot more of a harsher balance to it than this one, just with the sounds and everything. This one seems more personal. What was it like recording it?
They were actually recorded in almost exactly the same manner, but of course with different people playing and different material. So the actual recording process is we assemble a band and go in the studio and play the song and record it, and then we do overdubs and whatever else needs to be done and then mix it. They always tend to be pretty live,

these things. At least on the last couple of albums, the stuff that Colin Linden and I have produced together has been treated this way. It's colored by, as I said, the material itself and which particular musicians are brought in to play on it. I think the songs on this album are less dark than on *The Charity of the Night,* with one or two exceptions, perhaps, so it suited the different kind of feel, and I think that the feel was captured by the people we got to play.

Are there any memorable moments that stand out from the record, maybe one in particular?
Really the stuff that's the most fun for me is when I'm not working. So when we are doing the overdubs, then I can sit back and I can listen to what other people are doing.

Like what Ringo Starr used to do after he was done [recording drums]?
I guess. I don't know. But hearing Margo [Timmins] sing "Blueberry Hill," that was a complete knockout. Everything else was live off the floor on that song, but she came in and overdubbed her vocal part and we couldn't believe—Colin and I were looking at each other and laughing our heads off because we couldn't believe how great it was. Not that we expected it not to be, but it was sort of beyond our expectations. And Lucinda [Williams] too, doing the wonderful parts, especially in "When You Give It Away" and "Isn't That What Friends Are For."

Yeah, she has a really distinctive voice and it definitely added a lot of flavor to those songs.
Yeah, yeah. Like I said, it's fun for me because I am not responsible. I am sort of steering the ship, but I don't have to actually perform anything. It's harder to be objective about things when you're sort of in the action yourself.

What are your plans for the future? What comes next? Is there anything that you haven't accomplished yet in your career that you would like to?

The word "career" is OK because it's a convenient way to talk about whatever that thing is, but it's not a word I use, and I don't make plans. I go where I feel called to go, and that's something that you have to do moment by moment. I have no intentions other than to get this tour done. That is what we are embarked on right now, and that's kind of occupying most of this year. That's the big project at hand, and of course I've got a couple other songs on the go now. We've got a new instrumental piece that we are doing in the shows and things like that. So it does continue. And I suppose, too, I am probably due for some time off once we finish all this. It's been a few years since I've actually had much of a break.

Well, it will give you more time to drink some rum too. ["Last Night of the World" mentions a specific liquor—this is what I was referencing. -Ed.]
Well, yeah, although I am trying not to be too involved in that at the moment, but yeah. One of the things—I have joked about this sometimes—one of the things you encounter in exotic travels is exotic booze from everywhere. Every culture has its intoxicants, and some of them are pretty unusual, at least from my experiences.

Well thanks for doing this, Bruce. I certainly appreciate it. Was there anything else that you want to mention that you didn't get to mention?
Just looking forward to playing in Denver again, in the Denver area, and my only regret is we are not going to be there long enough to hang out like we usually do.

What can people expect when you come to Denver? What can they expect from the show?
Well, it's a trio format. It's the same band that toured with *The Charity of Night*—Steve Lucas on bass and Ben Riley on drums. The show leans obviously fairly heavily on newer material, stuff from the new album and the last couple, and the rest of the show is made up of a selection of older things that's slightly different from the selection of older things that we did on the last tour.

Will you be switching out between electric and acoustic?
Yeah.

Thanks a lot, Bruce. I wanted to say I appreciate the way you have been able to articulate your faith and not be preachy, because it always comes through and I think it's really cool that you are able to do that.
Oh, thanks for saying that.

I am sure it's hard and it's tricky sometimes to do that, and I am sure a lot of people miss it, but I think if they really look at it, they see the hope that is in there.
I think so, and I think it sort of comes down to the issue of telling your truth as you understand it. If that's what you're doing, then it's not a rhetorical exercise, you know. My particular faith is, at least ideally anyway, in everything I do, and it doesn't have to be spelled out all the time. In the beginning, when you discover something new and important you want to share with everybody and then that's when you run the risk of really belaboring it, perhaps, but at this point it's part of everything.

Well, I worked in the Christian music industry, so I know all about that. Christ is going to come through in whatever you do because He's God, obviously. Well I appreciate it Bruce. I hope the tour goes well and I look forward to seeing it when you come to Denver.
All right, Chris. Thanks a lot.

THE SAMPLES (SEAN KELLY)

Tuesday, March 21, 2000
Article: *Boulder Weekly* **(March 30, 2000)**

Sean Kelly should be sitting on piles of money. Well, hopefully not sitting, but at least enjoying its benefits and the sort of recognition that arises from a job well done. Kelly, known to many '80s and '90s college graduates from across the U.S. as the voice, guitarist and main songwriter of jammy pop band the Samples, has the oft-too-rare gift of crafting lush pop songs that can sparkle like a warm, sunny afternoon or cast a shadow like a heavy storm cloud. The Dave Matthews Band used to open for the Samples back in the day, and while Matthews and his band went on to radio chart success and enduring jam-band-fan love, Kelly and company were successful on the college and club circuit but never received the accolades and financial rewards that should have been given them. Through 1989's self-titled debut (originally released on Arista Records) to the self-released *Rehearsing for Life* in 2005, Kelly and company hit the road, touring as much as possible and taking the time to record albums, with various lineup changes occurring every so often since '97.

I discovered the Samples while cruising around the mountains outside Boulder in August of 1993. I was going to start my freshman year of college a week later. It was one of those easily impressionable times in my life—a major life change was about to take place. And here I was with my brother and a family friend, cruising around the foothills.

The family friend, who had just moved to town and was going to start his freshman year at CU-Boulder, asked, "Have you heard of the Samples?" I think I may have heard the name around town and seen posters, but I really didn't know much about the band. At that time, I was mostly listening to Christian metal and alternative music and sometimes other stuff, but nothing local and certainly nothing college oriented (the closest I got to college-oriented rock was the Alarm). Anyway, I liked what I heard coming through the speakers as we made our way along the curvy mountain roads. It must have been the Samples' sophomore studio album, *No Room*, we were listening to, as their third, *The Last Drag*, had not been released yet. It would come out a month later.

I liked what I heard. It was pop songwriting with instrumentation that reminded me of the Police. It was crisp, clear and undeniably good. I remembered that night, but it wouldn't be until my sophomore year of college that I would actually start listening to the band. I happened to be in a used CD store in Littleton with my roommate, Brian, who played the local Christian rock circuit in the band Twelve Tears. We were scouring the racks, and my fingers happened to come across a copy of *Autopilot*. Since Brian had cash (he had a job in college—I tried but failed miserably), he purchased the disc after I described how good it would most likely be. And Brian and I truly enjoyed the album. Soon after, Brian found a VHS copy of the Samples video documentary, *10 Wheels*, and we watched and liked it. We had both discovered a new band we truly appreciated.

Once my sophomore year of college ended, I would forget about the Samples for another year or so, but my love for the band resurfaced during my senior year of college. The band, by that time, had a deal with MCA Records, and I had to hear their new album. Walking down Boulder's Pearl Street Mall that summer, I exited the main path, headed to the record store right off the mall and saw that *Outpost* was in the listening section. I listened and liked it, but I didn't have the cash in hand (at that time, I had yet to get a debit card—I was strictly a cash and check man).

It was on my way to start my senior year that I stopped at a record store off Wadsworth Boulevard in Arvada, close to the Sam's Club, and purchased *Outpost*. The year was 1996, and that was when I truly fell in love with the Samples. I started off that year blasting *Outpost* through my Fisher three-and-a-half-foot-tall stereo speakers. I would make regular trips to area stores, purchasing all the back catalog

Samples titles in the original W.A.R.? paper cases. I think the unrequited love affair I had with a beautiful blonde female soccer-playing neighbor led to several purchases (I did get to eventually kiss her—I don't think I had to make any Samples purchases for a whole month to six weeks!). Music fans are always able to lie on the cushioning pillow of a new CD to help them through hard emotional times.

Toward the end of my senior year, the Samples announced two shows at Boulder's Fox Theatre (THE place to go see a live show in the Denver/Boulder area). This was the first time I had ever seen the band play, and I actually went alone to this show on Tuesday, May 13, 1997 (I rarely go to shows alone—I am too much of a people whore in constant need of companionship). My anticipation level was high, and I kept hearing talk of these being the band's "final" shows. I didn't want to think about the scenario of no more Samples. Here I was among people who had seen them numerous times and I hadn't seen them once!

The show started and I was blown away—it was everything as it should have been and more. Jeep MacNichol kicked the doors down on his drums, playing all his intricate parts and wonderful drum rolls. Kelly held center stage, as much a front man as I thought he would be, allowing his signature guitar parts to ring with clarity and beauty and his vocal intensity to shine through. Andy Sheldon added his thick, melodic and syncopated bass lines to the mix, along with his warm backing vocals. Al Laughlin brought in his keyboard parts with finesse, coloring and contouring the sound as required.

While in the process of getting back to my car, I heard a trio of concert attendees mention that the Samples were no longer on MCA. I was shocked. This new bit of unnerving information—combined with the rumors floating around the Fox and Sean's comments from the stage that some major changes would be taking place with the Samples—had my mind spinning.

Well, the band didn't break up, but Jeep MacNichol and Al Laughlin left the fold and other members joined the ranks. The Samples also went back to What Are Records?, the

Boulder-based label that had been their home throughout most of their existence, except for a couple instances.

I discovered this label reunion after I relocated to Nashville, a week or so after the Samples show. I walked into a Tower Records after living there for a couple months and saw that the guys had just released *Transmissions from the Sea of Tranquility*, a mostly-live double disc containing twenty-seven songs. I was relieved. "Yes, yes, yes," I said to myself, or maybe out loud, but in a whisper in the aisle of the store, "They didn't break up!" This may have been followed by a little jig. I'm not a dancer, but sometimes you've got to dance.

During my two years in Nashville, I saw the Samples perform a couple different times—once at the club 3rd and Lindsley [I think] and another time playing a frat show at Vanderbilt University. The Vanderbilt show was the first time I ever spoke with Sean Kelly. I saw him walking off after the show and simply said, "Thank you for keeping on keeping on." I walked away and realized that was a pretty stupid thing to say. Why couldn't I have thought of something better? Perhaps something like, "Wow, I loved the way 'Still Water' went over tonight. Great job!" or even, "Fantastic show, Sean!"

Once I relocated back to Denver and was writing for the *Boulder Weekly*, I knew I wanted to write about the Samples. I finally got the chance when the band played at the Fillmore, a large live music venue on Colfax and Clarkson. When I got Sean on the phone for the interview, I found him to be an extremely kind, likable guy. We discussed things like the recent placement of the band's music in a Disney television advertisement, Sean's unique guitar sounds, cheap places to eat in Boulder, butterflies, prairie dogs and Dr. Seuss.

Sean and I kept in touch from that point on—the Samples would play either in Denver or Boulder and he would put me on the guest list, once even hanging out with a couple of friends and me on the Samples tour bus outside the Gothic Theatre in 2001.

The tour-bus visits continued, oftentimes with my buddy Eric, a former college radio DJ. We would help out where we could and would do shots of tequila with Sean prior to shows. The unspoken arrangement at that time was that I would show up with a friend or two and a bottle of Souza Hornitas and we would all be on the guest list. Once, during a visit on the bus, I somehow managed to lock myself inside the bathroom. I heard Eric and Sean chatting and drinking tequila and then all of a sudden I heard Sean ask, "Chris, are you okay in there?" I finally managed to get out with their help. Eric used to chuckle as he'd remind me of that experience.

During another of these visits, when I wasn't trapped in the restroom, I casually mentioned that I played in a local band. A couple of years later I received an e-mail from Sean asking if our band wanted to play a handful of Colorado dates supporting the Samples on their upcoming tour. Of course we said yes, and the band (Crash Orchid) and I had a blast playing Fort Collins, Colorado Springs, Denver and Vail. We had never played in front of that many people before (and didn't after), and we were paid each time for doing so. It was the dream of every local musician—having an artist you truly admire and respect, and whose career you have followed for years, contact you and ask if you would like to open a handful of shows on their upcoming tour. It was a true gift and a magnificent, otherworldly experience.

I didn't see the Samples play again until a special New Year's Eve show in 2010 at Denver's Herman's Hideaway. The lineup for that concert, surprisingly enough, happened to be all the guys who played in the band during the mini-tour Crash Orchid had played on several years prior. It was great to see them again, and they sounded good. That same year, I would see the Samples play at the Denver Day of Rock, a large outdoor event held every Memorial Day weekend by Denver-based charity Concerts for Kids. This was followed some time later by a performance at the 40th anniversary party for the Bull & Bush, one of the premier brewpubs in Denver (also a great restaurant, but definitely try the Man Beer). By this time it was Sean and some guys I didn't recognize, but the songs were still there, and Eric, my pal who had been on the tour bus with me years before, joined me for the show along with my friend Peter. Again, it was a great memory.

Sean has been playing and recording with a new Samples lineup for some time. The professionalism and execution of the live shows makes it sound like a rejuvenated band.

The last time I interviewed Sean was in mid-2009 for a piece in *Westword*. He remarked how he didn't miss the road. I hope that has changed, because fans around the country should be able to hear what Coloradans have been enjoying recently.

****

Are you guys on tour right now?
It starts in Colorado, so we are not on tour right now.

What better place to start the tour?
Exactly.

I know you guys had the song in the Disney ad—how did that happen?
Well, basically just—I think that somebody over there was interested in having our music in it. So they contacted us and asked and that's how it happened.

What did that feel like, to have your song on an ad campaign like that?
I haven't seen it yet, so I don't know what it feels like as far as actually seeing it myself, but, you know, in the beginning I guess there were a lot of people that were like, "Oh, we heard your song on there," but I really haven't seen it.

Which song did they use? "When It's Raining" or...
No, it's a song called "Taking Us Home."

OK, OK. Yeah, it's the last song off of *No Room*.
Yes, exactly. And I don't even know if my lyrics are in it or not. It probably tells you how much TV I watch.

Well, you know they did make a Muzak version of, what was it, "Weight of the World."
They did?

Yeah, I was in the grocery store and I heard it.
No way? Are you being serious? I'd be flattered …

I was in Nashville too.
Really? Where would you ever find that? I would love to get a copy of that.

I know that it was a Kroger store—which is the same company that owns King Soopers. There is a Muzak version of "Weight of the World."
That, to me, that would be most flattering thing to hear that. That is just hilarious.

You guys have a good sense of humor. I saw the *10 Wheels* [documentary] video several years ago. What has been the funniest thing that has happened to you so far in your career with the Samples?
Yes, there are a ton of things. But I was actually just telling a story to someone recently and it's a total *Spinal Tap* [*This is Spinal Tap* –Ed.] story. One of many, you know, but it goes back to the time we were on Arista [Records]. It goes way back and it was with the original guys and we all flew into New York to—we flew in and we were on a tour, but it was our—I guess—signing party? Is that what they call it when you are signed and everyone gets together? We had the album made before we were with them, so they actually took on the record from us, and so it was delivered to them. We showed up about fifteen to twenty minutes early and we met at the Arista building in New York, and we were in this room full of very silent people, really silent, and we were like, "Mmm, maybe we are not in the right room." So we were all looking at each other, and it was loaded with food and pictures of us on the walls. So we were like, "Well, we are definitely in the right vicinity." No one is saying a word, and we start eating all the food and it was great—just like chips

and strawberries and stuff. And then, all of a sudden, I think that word got out that we were in the room because I think at first they thought we were the janitors or something—I don't know who they thought [we were] because we don't really dress in a way that [would] show that we were part of the meeting, but maybe they thought we were some field staff or something. All of a sudden there was this explosion of music and talk and conversation, and it was the most kind of staged thing I had ever witnessed. All of us looked at each other and we were like, "This is right out of *Spinal Tap*," because they didn't know we were in there. We got a kick out of seeing how that stuff is done almost in a fashion where it's set up to maybe make the band feel a bit more—in their defense, I don't know how else you could do it. It's not like people are going to be in a room, fifty people all excited for an hour, but it was so the opposite of what I ever thought it was going to be. We got a kick out of that for a long time. It's like we walked into dead silence and then this party broke out and then everyone is shaking your hand and "We are so excited you got here" and all this stuff, and it was like, "Man, we know exactly what was happening in here five minutes ago, and it was like a show."

So they pretended they didn't know who you were five minutes before?
Well, it wasn't that they pretended. They didn't know. We came early. We were supposed to walk in right on cue. And it would have been like this huge party going on, but there was no party beforehand, and everyone was still in there. It was just that—it's an act that people put on. But it certainly was neat to see the "behind the scenes" and it was hilarious because we were like, "Geez," you know? It's kind of hard to describe. That was always a funny *Spinal Tap* for us. That is one among many.

You have always had a strong fan base backing you. Always a grassroots thing. What does it feel like to have that kind of dedicated fan base?

Oh, it feels terrific! It's the thing they can't take away from you, which is number one as far as the industry goes. With the fans, it's basically—I hate anything to be black and white, but I can't think of an industry that is more black and white than the music business as far as it really tailors itself to proactive and reactive audiences. And I think the corporate aspect of music and rock 'n' roll, or whatever you want to call it, tends to really know how to cash in on the reactive and doesn't know how to nurture the proactive. And our fans are totally proactive. They buy all of our CDs. They go to tons of shows. They spread it to their friends. You couldn't have a better support team, and we do really well. When we tour we still sell out a lot of good-sized places, and even though we have been through some changes and stuff, we have people sticking right by us and new people that don't even know what changes went on. So that is the part that I think is awesome. I can't think of any other way to describe it. It's just a very proactive audience. Bands like Phish have learned to capitalize solely on the proactive aspect of their audience, and then there are bands that are solely at the helm of MTV and the radio play that they get, which doesn't always raise— well it often doesn't translate into people and attendance at shows. So we kind of walk a fine line because we are a total ready-to-hit-the-radio pop band, but with a garage twist to it and with an enormous amount of integrity that has sometimes gotten us into trouble, but I can live with myself at the end of the day.

Has the whole radio aspect—I mean, that has to bother you somewhat. You write these great pop songs, and then it seems like mainstream radio doesn't know what to do with them or doesn't do anything with them.
Well it's payola, and it still happens. We are huge fans of Neil Young and stuff like that. And to me, here is a guy that all of his songs are hits as far as I am concerned, but that certainly doesn't prevent them from playing and touring and having a wonderful audience and a great career. I think that realizing what it takes for it to happen is not so much a letdown. I don't take the whole brunt of it and be like, "Ooh, maybe our

songs should have more choruses or it should go into the middle eight part" or some catchy thing. That would reduce it from a cool song to a radio song. Radio is notorious for being a very sketchy aspect of music. I think radio is frustrated with us, too, because they tend to believe that it's radio first and then the band is known, and that's never been our case. When people have played us, we have had plenty of support from radio when it does happen here and there. We're just grateful, but we don't tailor our music—cater to that medium. It's just not our thing.

I know with your songwriting you wear your heart on your sleeve—is it hard for you to be that person, or is it something that comes naturally?
I think music, at least for me, the need to express yourself came far within the forefront for me as far as what I was into it for, so I think each person is different for what foundation they built their musicianship on. That comes right from me personally. I can't think of doing it any other way. It's not so much that our experiences and our songs are totally true also. We take some songs that are just about concepts that we have, thoughts that we are thinking, and we put chords to them and they relate to something and tie into some part of their life, but that may not have anything to do with our lives whatsoever.

You and Andy [Sheldon, bassist] have weathered the storms—what is at the core of that relationship that keeps it going?
Well, he and I go back to Little League or baseball. We used to be on the same baseball team at a high school we went [to] just a year before I quit. Rob Somers, who also joined the band, was in a band with the three of us back in 1982. So we just have a thing where we go so far back. We were talking recently about how we never rehearse, we never practice. We haven't in years, and I hope somebody doesn't read that and go, "Oh yes. It figures. No wonder they sound so crappy." But we have gotten so tight as a band that we really don't need that, and we do it live mostly when we do our new

songs—we just try them out live and three shows later we have got it down. But he and I, we go way back. And we are both from Vermont, so we have Vermont roots.

Are you working on a new record?
We are working on several different records. I am doing a solo record. We are going to do a live record and we are going to do the new Samples CD. And we are also doing a video thing—kind of a documentary that is going to be kind of like *10 Wheels*, but up-to-date. That is almost finished.

That should be interesting. I am sure you guys have a lot of footage.
Yeah, we really do. We are waiting for this next tour to really finalize getting the final footage done for that.

Now, the current tour you are talking about—that's the one that is starting at the Fillmore?
Yes, exactly.

What can people expect from the Fillmore show? That's a big place.
Our core audience definitely knows what to expect, which is that you don't know what to expect. And we don't know what to expect. We are psyched to play there. It's definitely a good sign for us that we pretty much [have] gotten our careers right back on track. It took about two years to really be out there working hard, and with these new guys in the band, it really feels solid. We put a couple new albums under our belt, and I think we are just doing our thing. If people show up, they can expect that they will get their money's worth.

The career that you have had so far—do you have any regrets or anything you would have done over again if you had the chance?
I really hate to be the kind of person that has any regrets, because that plays a role in growth and growing. But my little hidden list at the back of my mind would definitely be that I would have had a better attorney. [If] this band would have

been under the rein of a really great attorney, I think that things would have been a little different.

Sure. I mean they always say the record business is run by accountants and attorneys.
That's all it is.

It's great that you guys have survived. A lot of bands would have packed up and quit.
Oh sure.

What has kept you going? Is it just the desire to make music?
The music has kept us going. We have cool music, and we have got a lot of it, and we're not held to just one album, and we never had to be in a position where we'd become competition with ourselves, like we have to beat the last album. Our albums are like—one's a flop, one's great, one's marginal, one's great. The music, and challenging ourselves to do better and write better songs and to express ourselves and to get better as musicians, always keeps us going, because none of us have any formal training in music whatsoever, so the fact that we get up there and manage to get through a night of banging these instruments, making people happy on some level—we get so off on that. And we are not classically trained. It all comes from our gut. We are out there expressing ourselves, and it feels really good.

I know your guitar playing style is unique and the different sounds you use. How do you get the sounds? What equipment do you use to get it? I know you use the Roland Jazz Chorus [amplifier].
Yes, the Roland Jazz Choruses are pretty cool. I think the main thing is the type of distortion. I have been using a compressor, which really squashes the sound a lot, and I always have a little delay on it so it sort of rings it out a little bit. I started with the Jazz Chorus amps, which are typically not—they are really like keyboard amps, but I have this synth guitar that I actually still play.

Is that the one that was covered with electrical tape?
Yeah, exactly. I had one many years ago and it got stolen and I got my hands on another one. It was bright white and I didn't like it. It looked too strange to be playing this bright white guitar and the other one I had, the previous one, was black and so I just took black electrical tape and put it on there and it's been on ever since.

Is that the black electrical-taped guitar that you are usually playing?
Exactly. Yes, I play it all the time.

And that's the ...
I may have two that are covered with black electrical tape because I do have two and they were both white and I just didn't like it.

Are those both Rolands?
No, they are actually made by Guild and they have Casio insides or something.

Okay, that would explain it, because the sound, especially on *The Last Drag*—on some of the guitar parts on, like, the beginning of "Still Water" and ...
Yeah, that's interesting. Yes, it's really cool stuff. I don't know why they stopped making that guitar. But I am constantly desperately reaching out to see if anyone knows where I could get another. [I'm] checking all kinds of different websites all the time of where I could find it. It's a very rare guitar.

That's interesting.
Yeah, they make them now—they have these Roland set-ups that you have to attach to a guitar, but they don't come near how cool this guitar is that I have. Because the stuff is all internal and it's all built right in, and we've got an incredible guitar tech who can take such good care of them, Dan [Korpal]. Dan is the greatest. Without Dan I would not have those guitars.

Have you played around with the VG-8—the new Roland?
Yeah, I think I have one of those. I think that is what I put on my acoustic, and I have one here when I am doing studio stuff. But you can't control it the way I can on the electric. You could have either—you can blend them and you can do certain things, but this like—I can hit octaves on it and that's how the beginning of "When It's Raining"—I just hit a patch on it and put it on a low octave and it creates this sort of sound that I couldn't find anywhere else, not even with the pedals. I tried it. And so that's what is really cool about it. You can just do these things.

I have always enjoyed the guitar sounds. They are always unique. No one else really has them.
Cool. Most of them are by accident for sure. "Still Water" is the next one—find a sound, you know, in four minutes.

As far as the Samples, what are your future plans as far as the band is concerned? I know you mentioned the new record and you have the upcoming tour—what are your plans after that?
I think, and I don't want to jinx it, but I think somebody's come to us from the Blues Traveler camp and wants us to play with them at Red Rocks for the Fourth of July. I really don't want to jinx it, but that sounds like a great thing. So we'll probably maybe see if we can do a couple more dates. If not, you know, it would be nice to be back at Red Rocks. We set our careers in stone over the last two years and really proved to people that it's still there. It's going over really well as far as the changeover of people. Because we thought that was it. I thought for sure that was it. And it just worked. It worked really well, actually. We got a chance to refine the parts of how it didn't work before, and any parts that were dysfunctional, we got a second chance at refining ourselves as better people and better musicians. And we have pretty much everything in order.

Sean, I definitely appreciate it. Is there anything else you want to add?

Tell everyone we are very excited to be back in Colorado.

Is there anything anyone can expect that's special since you will be back here?
I do know that we are going to be doing a semi-private show at Tulagi's on the twenty-ninth. That's going to be for anyone who just wants to come down. It's going to be semi-acoustic. That will be on the twenty-ninth and that will be cool. That is sort of our way of just being back, and I think it's like five bucks to get in and, you know, come in and drink some beer or tequila and have a good time.

You guys, in your beginning stages, played at lot at Tulagi's before it went out of business for a while.
We played at Tulagi's so much. It was like our definite club in Boulder. Then we started playing J.J. McCabe's. Is the Walrus still there? I think that's changed over.

Yeah, I haven't heard of it.
The Walrus. It's up the street from the old McCabe's—it's full of pool tables. It used to be—that was a place we played all the time, also. That was a cool place. Some of the places we played, the buildings aren't even there anymore. There was a place next door to that that we played a lot at and—yeah—played many parties. We had the best times of our life playing in Boulder.

I mean "13ᵗʰ and Euclid" is based on a party you played isn't it? [Oops, I goofed. I had heard the song a million times, but gave the incorrect title! I did that once during a Lisa Loeb interview a few years later. You _never_ want to do that. -Ed.]
14th and Euclid. Not just a party, but we were the house band there because—this is another funny story that came up recently. It's a coincidence because somebody I know is trying to start a band, and they want to know how we did it, because the cops keep breaking up these guys. I said, "Well, we were really lucky because we played every party there was." We were the band that was like, "You want us, we are

there," for free, of course, always. Just the chance to play, but the environmental police kept coming with their sound equipment and finding out that we were too loud and shutting us down. Then we accidentally played a party at 14th and Euclid—that huge brick house.

That's on CU's [University of Colorado] campus, isn't it?
It's pretty close. It's right up there on the corner. I don't know how to describe it, but it's the big brick house on the corner, and that place was soundproof because of the bricks. It turned out that there wasn't a party we played that ever got busted. So we ended up playing until three, four, five in the morning, these incredible parties with, you know—who knows what drugs people were on, but it was a really fantastic time for us and a way to get in front of people long before we were good enough to even play in front of people. So it was how we [found] our sound and our environment and got to learn about people. The actual goal was to play in front of people. And most bands get practice studios and practice and practice and practice, but never really learn the art of interacting with your audience. We picked up on that immediately. That is why we always include them. But back to 14th and Euclid, it wasn't just any one party. We played there all the time. It's like every weekend. Samples. And we never got busted. I don't know who lives in there now, but I would like to go back there and play. I wish someone would throw a party in that place. That is something that I would like to ask. If you can ask whoever lives in that brick house on 14th and Euclid, if they set something up, we would be there.

That would be a cool promotional thing for—if this thing works out with this new label. Fly out to see the Samples play at 14th and Euclid.
That is a great idea!

You should do a tour of just frat houses.
Well, it wasn't a frat house, which was cool. I don't know if it is now, but it was just students. There were students living in

there and then they let us practice in their basement. So it was soundproof and it was the coolest thing for, like, three years. And then I think it got taken over, because it became such a nuthouse. It became a real nuthouse. I think the cops were up there a lot, and it was just crazy. It was like glow-in-the-dark parties long before raves and stuff. It was basically raves that were going on in that house.

You guys have always had an environmental conscience—have you kept up with the developments in Colorado as far as all the land that is being gobbled up?
Well, I always get really depressed every time I come through there and I see how much has gotten gobbled up on 36 [U.S. Route 36] coming into Boulder. Our keyboardist lives in Boulder, Alex Matson. That is where we found him. He's always been very active with the prairie dogs and he is always doing something in Colorado. He went to Estes Park recently to protest against some zoo that was being put up, which actually worked. They wound up putting an end to it, which is great. I get a lot of information from him, and the sadness from the prairie dog situation can speak for itself as far as I am concerned in Colorado because that has been going on—I remember making a speech about that in 1987 or '88 or '89, when we were at Red Rocks, because the big thing [that] was going down was they were having the prairie dog shoots in Colorado where people were claiming that they had like tuberculosis or some disease that they were proclaiming that they had.

I think it was rabies or something?
It wasn't rabies. It was something. Some other thing. It was so stupid because they would show pictures of these people holding their tails as rewards. And you were like, "Why the hell would you be touching this animal?"

If it had a disease?
Yes, and so this bullshit. It was stupid, and somehow Colorado didn't clamp down on it and that to me—did you ever see the movie *The Lorax,* by Dr. Seuss?

Yeah, I read the book a million times.

Same here. And that sums it up for me. It's like, you know, businesses and all—the song "When It's Raining" was written about some of the situations in Colorado. I just didn't really want to point it out to bum anyone out. But it was really along the lines of developers and blueprints and architects. There used to be that greenbelt law, I thought, that protected, but the mighty dollar always has its magical way of coming in and taking precedence over ...

[Somehow with tape transfer to digital means, my own technical lackings, or pure carelessness on my part, some of the conversation was deleted at this point. It begins again here. I believe that Sean was discussing some of the negativity that was surrounding the Front Range of Colorado at the time that this conversation starts again. -Ed.]

... don't know where to go, but unfortunately it's always negative. The Ramseys and the Columbine [high school tragedy] and a few years ago there was a girl who was murdered in Boulder. It was really negative stuff, and I don't think that should reflect any of the things that I was there during, that I liked about it. So all of a sudden I am watching some news thing and it's this special and they are zipping through Boulder chasing down people, but I wish that there was a little bit more of an awareness. It's just sad. I mean it's what you have happen in exponential growth and you are going to have a million people. I moved there because it was beautiful. And I had to move out because people thought it was beautiful, too. And that is basically what happened, because it loses that magic, as do most places. I remember the last time I was there, I think I got a fine in my car for going around one of those little rotaries. I must have been going two miles an hour, but he claims he clocked me at like twenty-five. It's like it's such a business there. You can make so much money off of students and the cops became very conservative and almost nasty. It was right around the time of the riots when I left.

Now that was when you played—that was when the original lineup played the final two shows?
I don't know. I ...

I know in August of '97, or no, it was like May—you guys did a show at the Fox—Charles [Hambleton] flew in for it. [The two final Samples shows featuring the longstanding lineup were in May of '97—I went to one of the two and it was held on Tuesday the thirteenth. -Ed.]
Yes, you are right. Oh wow, you're a fan of the band?

Oh yeah. I was glad I got the chance to do this. I think Alan Scully got to do it last time ... [Alan Scully was another contributor to the *Boulder Weekly*. -Ed.]
Oh, cool. Where are you from?

I live here. Boulder. Well, I grew up in Broomfield but I lived in Boston for nine years.
Oh, did you? Boston's great.

Yeah, it's a great town.
Now, have you gone down to the Butterfly Pavilion down there, [in] what is it, Broomfield?

Oh, over in Westminster?
Yes.

I have seen it, but I haven't been there yet.
You've got to go check that out. That place is really awesome. I mean, what a great educational tool for little kids, and it's completely done up right. All these butterflies are flying around and they are hatching and it's this really cool thing. It's so developed there now.

It is depressing. You've got Highlands Ranch. It's is a town that they basically created.
Really? That is amazing. I remember Boulder when you went up to the Hill and you—what is the name of that pizza place? Is it still there?

Abo's?
Yeah. That was like the big thing on the Hill. Abo's. There was a movie theater. There was …

Or there is The Sink.
There was always The Sink. And there was always the food court, trying to do something in there that wouldn't work. And Jones Drug. And it was just really mellow up there. And I haven't been up there recently. It's crazy. That place has changed so much. I have [an] old eight-millimeter film of filming the Hill with us running around and it was like—it was like a hot dog place that was across from the Dairy Queen. All crazy.

Was that Mustard's Last Stand?
Was that what it was? Maybe that was what it was called? No, no, because that's lower down the Hill, isn't it?

Actually, yeah, you're right. It's right near one of the original Starbucks.
I remember all the food places because they were cheap. And then there was Thank God It's Friday's or whatever—that place with the phones. You went in and ordered by a phone.

Oh yeah, Round the Corner.
Yeah.

Yeah, that place is gone. You're living in California now, right?
No, right now I am on the East Coast. Connecticut.

Do you like it up there?
Yeah, it's cool. It's good because we still tour and travel so much that I don't know if I really feel like these are roots by any means. But my grandmother lives in an old folks' home about six exits away, so I get to see her a lot. And I've never really been able to make that connection with her, and she can hardly speak English and understand me, but there are a lot of family roots.

That is cool that you are in a job where you can do that. What part of Connecticut is it?
Danbury. And I was born in Norwalk, so I go down there. It's an old stomping ground for me.

Wow. I used to go up to Stratford a lot.
Oh, really?

Well, Sean, I certainly appreciate it. And, I was going to ask you—I don't know who I'd need to talk to about this, but is it possible to get a few tickets for the show?
Oh, absolutely.

I'd love to come back and meet you.
Now, which show is this?

The Fillmore.
The Fillmore. What you've got to do is e-mail—let me give you an address to e-mail—I don't know if I have it here. I was going to try and give you our tour manager's e-mail—e-mail me at the address you sent to and hopefully I will have checked it by then. If for some reason you get to the show a little earlier, come bang on the bus. We will get you in no problem. It's just a matter of being reminded, and I have so many little things that I could put your name on and wind up losing by then, but it's no problem getting you in.

I appreciate it.
Yeah, no problem.

All right, thanks a lot, Sean.
OK, man.

And I hope the tour goes well.
Thanks a lot. We will see you soon.

Vigilantes of Love (Bill Mallonee)

Sometime in April 2000
Article: *Boulder Weekly* (April 27, 2000)

It's hard to describe what the songs of Bill Mallonee have meant to me. And it's even more difficult to approach Bill's work with an open mind as I'm both a huge fan and a friend of Bill's. These are easily two roadblocks to journalistic integrity.

Mr. Mallonee is the type of talented individual who makes me ask the same question I have regarding Sean Kelly of the Samples: "Why isn't he on the iPods of millions and on the wide-reaching radio waves of stations worldwide?" Plenty of others share this frustration.

I discovered Bill's music shortly after my sophomore-year college roommate Brian bought *Blister Soul*, Vigilantes of Love's powerful 1995 full-length. He was excited as we walked out of his fiancée's parents' house in Arvada and went out to his car to retrieve the CD. Brian was reluctant to let me borrow the disc and wanted to make sure I gave it back soon.

I remember putting *Blister Soul* in a CD player for the first time—it didn't do anything for me. I hadn't embraced the alt-country thing yet, but I gave it more time, partly because Brian had said, "Yeah, this thing rocks. It's soooo good." He had a way of making words stretch out their letters and syllables so everything sounded exciting. He could have been describing a Subway sandwich, our history professor's elf-like boots or a new CD. He was full of information, sometimes too much.

Brian got me to listen to *Blister Soul* more than once, but I still could not fully embrace the disc. I had some respect for Vigilantes of Love because Dan Russell was managing the band. Dan was a New England guy and I had grown up reading his music magazine, *NewSound*, which was focused on bands that appealed to Christians. I discovered the Alarm because of Dan. He had done a lot of cool things—he started record labels and put out albums by guys like Andy Pratt; he promoted concerts in the area featuring top Christian artists; and he did a huge amount for Christian metal bands like Barren Cross. He even created a yearly music festival.

Dan was a guy I deeply respected. He had an understanding of the Christian industry and of a lot of cutting-edge, creative Christian artists, but he also had his ear to the ground in the mainstream world and would also cover those thought-provoking artists (the Call, the Alarm, Bob Dylan, World Party, etc.) in the pages of his magazine. And, as I mentioned, he was managing Bill and the V.O.L. guys. I honestly asked myself regarding Vigilantes of Love, "What's *wrong* with me? What am I not getting here?"

I would soon understand Bill Mallonee and his music, and it would be a musical freight train hitting me in the aural spectrum. During the summer of '96, I had an opportunity to do an internship in Austin, Texas, with *HM* magazine. I had met founder and former editor Doug Van Pelt during a trip to Nashville for the annual GMA Week (a Christian music event put on by the Gospel Music Association) in the spring of 1994 and had been writing for the publication since, covering various Christian rock and metal artists for his magazine. I was a communications major, and this seemed like the perfect internship. I simply asked and Doug said, without any reservation, "Yeah, that sounds great. Come on out." My mom had a college friend who lived in Austin, and she and her husband invited me to come stay for the summer.

I had a great time in Austin. The associate editor, Brian McGovern, was also single and about my age, so I had an instant friend to do things with. We quickly hit it off and would often hang out on weekends and after work. Austin had a great road (Sixth Street) that was littered with bars, clubs and restaurants and would be closed off to traffic at certain times on the weekend—I think it may just have been late Fridays and late Saturdays. I gained fifteen or twenty pounds that summer due to Brian introducing me to Guinness in large quantities.

The great thing about magazines like *HM* is they received countless promo CDs and often these discs wouldn't be anything the publication would cover. It was sometimes as if a publicist didn't do the proper research and went with a mass mailing to *all* music-centered publications of a certain size. So in came a retrospective by Vigilantes of Love, called *V.O.L.*, and Doug asked if I wanted it. I said "yes," but I wasn't anticipating that I'd enjoy the music any more than I did back when Brian let me borrow *Blister Soul*. Boy, was I wrong about *V.O.L.* I have been wrong before, but this time I was really wrong.

I got back to my mom's friend's house, put the disc into my Sony Discman and cranked it up through the headphones. The first song that came on was "Welcome to Struggleville." The great instrumentation drew me in, but the lyrics sold me. They were earnest and painfully honest. They weren't religious, they made no apologies, yet the songs were rooted in a real, dynamic relationship with the Creator that wasn't always easy. There were no pat answers, but there was hope, there was faith, there was love and a lot to say. The music was often gritty Americana rock with plenty of sometimes lush, sometimes dirty guitars, great bass playing and solid drumming, but always the right amount of energy. And the songs didn't just float into the wind—they stuck with you. You would find yourself singing them and realize you were often living them in one sense or another.

When I arrived back at college that fall, I got my roommate Tim into the band. We really, really grew to love those guys. I was able to interview Bill for a college project and got to know him a bit through the kindness of Dan Russell.

I also knew a couple of guys who worked with Dan—Harold (Harv) and Dan Hallas (Danny Horrid)—from years before. Dan sang for a great local Christian band in New England called Clinic, and Harv was the manager. Clinic would open for touring Christian acts. Once when they were opening for Mylon and Broken Heart, a well-known Christian rock band, they received more applause than Mylon and his band. Christian artists like Mylon sometimes would preach more than they would play—this could get frustrating. I always understood the reason for the preaching and appreciated it, but I came to see a concert. Sometimes Christian artists who would preach at their shows would have really cheesy keyboard parts going along with the speaking portion, especially as it neared the altar call, a time for people to decide if they wanted to accept Christ's forgiveness for themselves. Again, this wasn't a bad thing, but it would often take a long time.

I had met Dan and Harv eight years prior to my Bill Mallonee interview. Dave Stewart, my incredibly kind, patient and thoughtful youth pastor, knew how much André Salles and I liked rock 'n' roll, and he fronted three hundred dollars from the church budget for Dan's band Clinic to come play a high school retreat. The show was fantastic and something I have never forgotten. There were something like forty high school kids in a large dining room of a retreat center in the middle-of-nowhere New Hampshire, and the Clinic guys played their hearts out.

Harv, Dan and I stayed in touch from that point on, and I featured them in a horrible music newsletter I sent out to five people or so on an infrequent basis. Later on, André and I played in a high school band together and got to play a talent show because someone passed off a song from a Clinic album as our own. The guys who put on the talent show quickly realized that the band on the tape was not us, even though we warbled through Clinic's "Children of the Rock." Maybe it had to do with the off-pitch backing vocals, the bass drum pedal falling off, the timing issues or our overall horrible rendition.

Anyway, eight years later, the time to phone Bill Mallonee for the college project interview arrived. I called him at his home in Athens, Georgia, in the fall of 1996 and he answered the phone. I introduced myself and politely asked if this was a good time to do an interview. He said, "Oh, hi Chris. Yeah this is a good time." I heard some whispering in the back and Bill quickly said, "Hey Chris, just a moment." Then he came back a minute or so later and said, "Yeah, that was my wife. She was wondering how you got my number." This was Bill and this still is Bill—always transparent, always honest. He lets you know exactly what's going on—this has been true since then to present day.

It got even better when V.O.L. was booked by our college to play our winter retreat at the YMCA of the Rockies in Estes Park, Colorado, four or five months later. I was excited. My roommate Tim was excited. I don't think we could concentrate on school or really anything for several weeks.

As soon as we had settled in at the Y, Tim and I walked over to the auditorium. Bill and V.O.L. hadn't shown up yet, but within a few minutes of Tim and I planting ourselves in a couple of old-style auditorium chairs, a short thin guy walks in, shakes a few hands and walks to the mixing board and starts conversing. I realized right away it must have been Bill. But he wasn't how I thought he would look. I was expecting someone taller who looked more like the voice and the emotions I had heard on disc. Still, Tim and I spoke with Bill a bit and told him we were glad he was there. We found out the next morning that Bill and the guys had beer, specific tasty types, on their tour rider but struck those off due to our Christian school being an alcohol-free zone.

The following night, when Bill, Tom Crea (drums) and the very kind Chris Bland (bass) took the stage, Tim and I were beyond mesmerized. We sat off by ourselves to take it all in. Bill was driving his emotions into a beautiful Les Paul Goldtop guitar, and his vocals poured out in ocean-sized waves of honest feeling. Chris' bass playing was fantastic, as were his backing vocals, and Tom's in-the-pocket drumming topped it all off. The guys played "Love Cocoon," a newer song that was to be on their upcoming record, *Slow Dark Train*. It was a very open song that Bill wrote about enjoying the act of sex with his spouse, and it was told with very Solomon-like specific detail in modern terms. I looked over at Jim, our dean of students, and he had an incredulous look on his face as the song progressed, but I think he realized what Bill was unabashedly communicating.

The next day, I saw Bill in line in the dining hall and simply asked him, "What happened to your long hair?" It had been on my mind since he arrived in Estes Park with short hair. All his promo pictures showed him with shoulder-length hair dyed blonde. Bill didn't bat an eye and simply answered, "It started falling out so I had to cut it."

I saw Bill and V.O.L. play several times after that, and I continued communicating with Mr. Mallonee as much as possible. I was working at a label in Nashville a year after the Estes Park show, and Terry Taylor, our head of A&R, and I wanted to sign Vigilantes of Love. Bill sent me an unmastered version of *To the Roof of the Sky*, a recently completed disc, but a label deal with us just never happened. Bill's material seemed too risqué for a Christian-market label that had to contend with Christian bookstore chain music buyers. I was extremely happy that Terry thought we should sign Bill and it only furthered my respect for the very kind, talented and revered Christian music legend.

When I got back to Denver and was writing for the *Boulder Weekly*, I wanted to cover two bands badly: V.O.L. and the Samples. I was able to write a piece on the Samples, but Bill Mallonee and company didn't have any upcoming shows in the area, and their forthcoming album, *Audible Sigh*, wasn't due to release until summer. Usually I had to have a show to base my article pitch upon, but due to the kindness of my editor, Dave Flomberg, I was able to author an article. Bill and I had a great time catching up over the phone. During a stop a year or so later, the band I was in at the time, Breathing Eve, secured the opening slot for V.O.L. at Denver's Soiled Dove (located at 20th and Market at the time). The best part of the evening was when Bill told me he liked our set—what more could I ask for other than praise from a songwriter I truly respected?

Bill long ago hung up the Vigilantes of Love hat and embarked on a solo career, still doing a ton of recording and touring. I've kept up my friendship with him over the years and he continues to amaze me as an artist. I hope that, over time, many others will discover Bill and his art. His solo studio efforts directly correlate to the quality work he did with Vigilantes of Love and prove him to be a relevant, formidable and enduring songwriter.

****

Do you ever question being so honest lyrically?
Well, that would probably imply a little bit more of a strategy behind what I do, and I really don't have any strategy. I pretty much let it happen. I consider myself to be a confessional writer. There have been a number of people who that tag would fit—there was a whole group of fellows in England, I don't know the exact time period, but I guess John Donne was one of them—actually a minister and a poet and he considered himself a confessional writer just because it implied a lot of things. It implied a system of belief that he held because he was actually a minister of the Gospel in the Church of England, and he was also a poet. And his work tended to be pretty—the work would be like penitential, which would mean penitent, exposing of oneself and at least the dark side of oneself. One's failure and inability to come up to standards, whether they were personal standards or the standards of God. That is why he called himself a confessional writer. There have been a number of people who have done that. I think basically I am a religious writer, I guess, on some level. I don't think I'm a pop writer; I don't think I'm an alt-country writer to the degree that the genre of music that we have is kind of bold rock, and so it implies being able to kind of draw from everything from gospel to country to rock 'n' roll and all points in between. I think thematically I tend to kind of be a confessional writer. I don't really think about what it is I'm doing. It's just something that initially started for me being a way to kind of just get it off my chest. It was more therapeutic than anything else, I suppose, than like sitting in front of a shrink.

Kind of a cathartic thing?
It was very cathartic. That's a good word for it. Rather than having to pay somebody ninety bucks an hour to tell your woes to, it's a little cheaper to write a song.

Let the record company pay for it.
Let the record company pay for my therapy.

What does it feel like to have the listening world know your thoughts? Is that ever an uncomfortable thing for you?

It's not an uncomfortable thing ever, because I think the world more than ever has—in spite of all our channels and abilities and ways of communicating with one another— probably never before in the history of the entire humankind that's ever been recorded have people felt more alone and alienated from themselves and from one another, which is kind of interesting to me. It's kind of strange that as technology makes it possible for more communication to take place quicker, we still don't seem to be able to scrape off the warts and pimples and the scabs that allow us to be honest with who we are and how we feel about things. So I look on songwriting as a way of kind of putting words in everybody's mouth, and I think if people can relate to that or interface with it or whatever it is they do—if they can react to it in a way that allows them to say, basically, "That's how I feel when he speaks. He is speaking my words," or "I understand what he is saying, even if I don't understand completely everything about the song." I think in some ways that is the highest praise for a songwriter. Let me qualify all of that by saying that I think the two ingredients to do such a thing for a songwriter—and it can backfire on him or her— are risk and vulnerability. [They] sort of reinforce each other, but I think you pretty much have got to be that kind of songwriter, and I'm really not interested in hearing any kind of songs or songwriting that don't at least make me think the songwriter is at least taking that risk.

Yeah, to kind of be true to themselves.

Yeah, I mean it's like I just want to hear something from somebody that's got something to say.

You have been through two different record deals—the thing with Pioneer and then Capricorn. What did you carry away from that? [Actually, Capricorn was before Pioneer and there were other deals/arrangements before and after both labels. –Ed.]

Let me go to the positive side first. The positive side is that we learned that the record business is just that. It's mostly about business, and there's nothing wrong with that. It kind of forks at the bottom line. The negative side of it for us is we didn't realize until it was too late that people will lead you to believe that it's really about other things. They'll listen to you or they'll make you feel listened to, but really it's about moving lots of units. That's not accusing record companies or industry types of duplicity—I think they are in an uncomfortable position of wearing two hats. First, they have to be able to appreciate and recognize some semblance of artistic credibility or genius or something like that. But the other thing is they have to be able to figure out is can they sell it in mass, and I think when we went into it we just figured that ingredients of passion and vulnerability and sincerity and just that sort of punk, Athens, Georgia, do it yourself, that sort of indie kind of passion, would carry the day. And we were really excited about aligning with record labels, because we heard countless bands out there that were doing the same thing that weren't getting a break to be on a minor-major label like Capricorn. It really was a minor label with sort of a major push behind it. And Pioneer, definitely— that was the label that never got off the ground. We definitely made a good-sounding record [*Audible Sigh*], and I think they had a vision for the thing. And with Capricorn, we made three records, didn't sell enough of 'em. We got great reviews for them, five-star reviews all over the country, and just didn't sell enough albums. The band has always maintained—as do I—that there are reasons for that that have nothing to do with the band per se, but everything to do about the industry and the superstructure because it has to run itself. I think being a record person, it's an unhappy marriage of art and commerce and trying to figure out where they meet or if they can meet, and if they can meet in such a way that allows the band to grow and develop and mature. And I think the problem with Vigilantes is, to sort of footnote that, I think it's just a little bit more visceral, organic and a little harder to package. We went in and re-recorded songs for singles and all that kind of stuff. That's frequently what you do and what you're taught to do. It's like, "The record company doesn't care about my record, they just want a single." They want a song they can play on the radio, and we gave them that and we did it not because we were trying to be contrived about it, we did it because we thought, "Well, this song is a good pop song. It's got something to say, and we are not violating our sense of integrity by putting it out." We felt like we did good things with it. But there's so much more than radio singles. There's money to drive the single. There's press. There's tours. There's playing in front of a thousand people as opposed to one hundred and fifty people like we were used to playing. There's all kinds of variables that kind of have to drop in the pocket—distribution all of that stuff—and it just never did it for us. It hasn't to this point. The new news is that we've signed to Compass Records out of Nashville.

Is that something that can be published?
It probably would not be—yeah, I mean, we've put it in our list. I think we haven't actually had an official national kind of press release on it.

I can leave it out if you want.
Well, you can say that we have recently signed to what they call a boutique label. You know, the kind that deals with specialty niche market kind of things, but has an extremely strong distribution [channel], and they seem to want to spend the dollars on the marketing end of it.

How many dates do you play a year?
Generally, for the last three years, except up through this past year, we play about one hundred and eighty dates a year. We're gone one hundred and eighty dates a year. More like one hundred and sixty dates scattered over one hundred and eighty days, and that would include the UK. So we have been going to the UK a lot the last couple of years.

How has the touring been going? Has it been pretty successful?

Some weeks are better than others. The strange thing about touring is you get into a mindset where you're not sleeping very much. When you are under those sort of sleep-deprived conditions, a lot of stimuli-response sort of things [start] going on, and it becomes a somewhat surreal kind of experience after a week or two on the road. And we tend to tour for three to five weeks at a time. So it leaves you some nights feeling extremely supercharged or elated because of the performance, and sometimes you just feel like you're beating your head against a stone wall and it's just not ever going to give or nothing's gonna break. I liken the experience—and I have actually written a song with that same sort of thematic crossover—my twelve-year-old, he's playing Little League baseball and his whole life rides on the next pitch, and if he swings and misses, his whole life, his whole world crumbles, and if he gets a hit he is on top of the world again. Likewise, the band goes into a town, plays in a small club in front of three hundred people, plays a killer seventy-five-minute set and gets an encore ending, and you think, "Tomorrow the world," or if it was a just a dismal night and there's hardly enough money to get a hotel to sleep in, you feel like, "Why am I doing this?" The pendulum is swinging between extremes, and the real trick, I think, for the touring musician, is to figure out how to get inside one's music and say, "This is my little piece of what I have to say to the world." Whether there's two people there or twenty, play like there's two thousand. Play as if your life depended on it, because in some ways it does. Get inside of that and really not worry so much about all the other stuff, whether it's people showing up or the club owner being happy or the industry thinking you're the greatest thing since the Beatles— whatever it is, you can fill in the blank. There's a hundred things. It's just being extremely satisfied with the music that you're making and to the degree that that represents what you have to give. I think that we kind of dealt with that right after the Capricorn deal. And it's been, on the whole, extremely satisfying ever since.

With *To the Roof of the Sky* and ...

Yes, *To the Roof of the Sky* definitely—the live record and the *40 Watt* live record [*Live at the 40 Watt* –Ed.], the record we cut over in the UK, *'Cross the Big Pond*. It's available over here through different distributors. We made it in four days. It was done in a little out-of-the-way rural studio in England and we loved it.

What was it like recording *Audible Sigh*? I know you worked with Buddy and Julie [Miller] on that one.
Stylistically and music-wise, it's just sort of focused. I think it's probably the best record. I think *Roof of the Sky* was really good, but it was an indie record. There are some quieter, fragile things on *Roof of the Sky,* like "Farther Up the Road" and "This Time Isn't One of Them" and "On the Verge"— they're not there on *Audible Sigh*. Now, in having reworked three more songs—like "Solar System" and "Resplendent"— those songs are there. It's a very, very good-sounding, radio-friendly kind of record. It's got a number of great names on it to help take it up another level. We were between drummers, so we used Steve Earle's drummer in the studio, taught him the songs and just went with it. A good friend of mine who's just a great session player, Phil Madeira, plays keyboards on the record.

Phil's great.
Phil is great. Emmy [Emmylou Harris] guested on a track. Julie, Buddy's wife, sings on it. We really had a great chance to take the songs that we have been playing in clubs for about the last year and kick them up a notch, and I think it's beautiful. I think the whole record really, really feels good. It has a sort of desperate, going for it, kind of swinging for the fences kind of thing, sort of a Hail Mary kind of approach and well I shouldn't say that [Really faint, can't clearly hear what Bill said. –Ed.] ... that sort of desperate kind of an approach, and I think that is what a lot of what this band's been about. But it's there, and it sounds good, and so far the initial response from radio and press has just been really, really good. But like you said, the record's not necessarily young anymore—I mean, we made it over a year ago; it just hadn't

found a home. Compass will be releasing it in the mainstream on June 13 and it will be out in England like two weeks before that, so we're real excited about that. It will be easy to find. I can guarantee it'll be pretty easy to find.

Who distributes Compass?
Koch. They do like Ani DiFranco—they're huge. One of the mac daddy kind of distributors.

Ani DiFranco—she's been selling tons and tons of units.
She's huge. You know Ani is one of those people who's basically got her vision; she knew what she was going to do. She does it with her band. She does it solo. She is like the complete package as an artist, but she doesn't think about that. She's just who she is. She's an urban folk musician with a lot of punk sort of influence and enough business sense to know that if she were to trade away that precious thing that's her music to somebody else, they would just screw it up. She's said that, and I think she's exactly right. In our situation, I think it's more of an age thing at some point. I've got musicians in my band that I want to take care of, and I'm married with two kids, and I want to make sure there's some stability there. We've been very picky about the labels that we've negotiated with in the past. Not to a fault, but at the same time we've said, "Okay, well we want you to understand, we will do this, but we won't go and do that." But at this point, the label we're talking about, Compass, is so behind it—they don't want us to change a thing. It's more of like entering into a partnership with the band. It's already established its own kind of superstructure and way of doing things. They're sort of trying to reinforce what is that we do and use the tools and resources to do them better. [Discussion of possible label deals prior to Compass along with past Vigilantes of Love band lineups—not included here. –Ed.]

When I talked to you before, you mentioned you were changing the musical style a little bit with acoustic guitar pumped through a small amp.

Yeah, it's kind of more of a grindy, sort of semi-psychedelic folk rock kind of thing. I mean, it still has a lot of the nuances and sort of the lighter side of [Unclear in the recording. –Ed.], but there's also more trippier kind of stuff coming through, and I am just not sure how we are going [to] augment that in terms of a fourth player. Obviously in the studio I can overdub those parts. We've been working with everything from piano and a string quartet to Mellotron and keyboard and things like that, and just [a] straight-out sort of psychedelic guitar kind of thing. I mean more along the lines of just ... [Unclear. Ah, the wonders of analog tape transferred to MP3 format! By the way, the sound that Bill is describing just before the recording became indecipherable was captured perfectly on the final Vigilantes of Love record, *Summershine*, a pop masterpiece that truly took the band in new directions but never received its due. -Ed.]

Kind of like "Black Cloud O'er Me"? [A song that had what sounded like an acoustic guitar with a ton of distortion on it and was on *Audible Sigh*. -Ed.]
Yeah, to a certain extent. There's some newer stuff that is even a little more developed than that, but yeah, probably that might be kind of a close sort of thing. It's definitely got that sort of folk-rock thing, but there's a bit of a sort of underground garagy kind of trashy thing involved in it, but I think melody-wise, vocal ability, it's a little trippier, maybe a little bit more Beatlesque in some ...

I was impressed when I heard *Audible Sigh*. It was a different-sounding record, but I really enjoyed it. It was definitely a step in a different direction going from *To the Roof of the Sky* and then *Slow Dark Train* before that. Those are much more live-sounding records.
Oh, definitely. I mean that's definitely one of the styles as far as the mixing. To use the close mics instead of what they call ambient mic-ing, where you let the room be part of the track and use the big, wide-open mics. I think it has an increased intimacy factor for me. You feel like the instruments are sort of right there in front of you. But I like some of the energy on

the *Roof of the Sky* thing. We rerecorded two songs from *Roof of the Sky*. One was "Paralyzed" and one was "But Not for Long." In some ways, I almost prefer the *To the Roof of the Sky* versions because they have some sort of organic energy that's maybe just a bit too harnessed. Bands that do what we do are always splitting the difference between, you know, how does it sound live, you know ... [The first side of the microcassette ended—I had to flip it over to continue recording the interview. –Ed.]
... sort of ride the fence between the two of those extremes.

They have always sounded good, though.
I love what we got. I think Buddy [Miller, producer of *Audible Sigh*] did a great thing in sort of coming up with the sound and an approach that worked for what we were doing and still allowed people to hear the record and love it and then hear the band live and say, "Wow, that was a great band."

What do you hope people take away from your songs?
I hope that they see their lives as something very significant and very precious, and that we have the ability to do a great deal of good and harm to ourselves and to other people about what we say and what we do. Without putting that statement necessarily into a religious context, I really think that for me I sort of settled that question—time to time—but hopefully they will realize that for us, anyway, this song—it's a testimony to a certain extent about what life looks like living behind the wheel of a van and on the stage of small clubs in America and doing the kind of music we do—which I think is basically folk-rock music. But I think it has a broader application, and for us—I mean, the interesting thing about this record to me and the way I write is that—some people said "Oh, it's another country-alt band," and it's like well, yeah, but most of the country-alt bands that I read about in magazines like *No Depression*, the guy's writing songs that sound like songs that were written about getting drunk in some bar, losing a job or going home with somebody's wife. You are not going to find those types of songs on our records, because to me that's just another form of posing. With all due

respect to bands that cover that genre, it's just posing. Most of the kids that I know that are playing that kind of stuff are suburban white kids that grew up with all the advantages of being white middle-class kids, and they may have been listening to the Ramones at the same time as they discovered Hank Williams. There are definitely bands that break the mold on that. I think Ryan Adams and Whiskeytown have been able to grab that genre of music and be comfortable with it and wear his heart on his sleeve about what he feels without writing songs that are sounding like they were some sort of paint-by-number. You know what I am saying? I don't think that just because it came from a college graduate and wound up on a stage and in an indie [form] that that legitimizes anything. It might just be as much posing as anything else. But I think with Vigilantes, if I haven't made this completely convoluted at this point, I'm trying to write about themes that I think have a little bit more eternal aspect to them. Automatically that might weed us out of people who want to stay a million miles away from that sort of thing. But I do think, like I said at the beginning of this long harangue, I think life is pretty precious, and I think the older you get the more you realize that sort of thing. A little bit of good you can do for yourself and others will mean a whole lot.

I appreciate it Bill. I know this was kind of last minute.
No, thanks for getting inside our records so much. This is so easy to do because you have been such a dear friend. You have just gone out of your way to immerse yourself in it and get it and understand it. I remember when you were living in Nashville and doing KMG [Records], you were always sending me postings and made me think, "Hey, Chris is looking out for me. He's got a lead here and we're going to change this." But I totally appreciate you getting in touch.

If people want to buy *Audible Sigh* now, are you halting the sales over the net?
No, they can buy it now. They can buy it from True Tunes. I mean it's only a Christian market that you can get it through there. You can find it at Christian bookstores, but I think we

are trying to minimize that thing right now. I mean, we are glad for True Tunes, and we love them, and I think the same number of folks would buy it in that market whether we came out and said it's a [Christian] record as not. I think the thing is, a lot of times we have sort of been hung by the proverbial throat by people visiting our website and thinking that it's a band with an agenda.

TIM FINN

Tuesday, June 6, 2000
Article: *Boulder Weekly* (June 15, 2000)

Sometime in 2006, after Tim Finn's *Imaginary Kingdom* album had been released or was about to be released in the U.S., work was on the brain in the Mile High City. I happened to glance at my cell phone and saw a text message pop up from a friend offering a well-needed break for my computer monitor-weary eyes: "Hey, Chris, it's Beki. Tim Finn is going to be at the Walnut Room tonight. It's only five bucks! You want to go? I'll get you a ticket if you want to come." Unfortunately, Beki's husband and my buddy, Randy, had to work.

It turns out the show in question was a promo gig, acoustic, and the radio station had only announced it a few minutes prior. Of course, I said, "Sure!" to Beki's text. I've always been a fan of the brothers Finn. And then there was the price—only five dollars. Who has shows that are only five bucks? Most local concerts are at least that amount.

So I grabbed another buddy and we met Beki at the Walnut Room, famous for their delicious thin crust pizza (with an amazing sauce, I might add). The small place was absolutely packed to capacity. Apparently the tickets sold out in an hour. We were treated to a wonderful happy-hour-time set by Tim (playing guitar and singing) and an accompanying guitarist. It was raw, earthy and earnest. The performance itself couldn't have been more than forty-five minutes long, but the length was perfect to whet the appetite and give fans a reason to check out the new record.

I first heard of the genius of Tim Finn, and younger brother Neil, while living in Nashville. Kent Songer, my boss at KMG Records, loved the Finns, and that, coupled with Neil Finn's fantastic new radio single released around that time, "She Will Have Her Way," I was compelled to purchase his just-released *Try Whistling This* disc. It took another couple of years before I actually listened to Tim, however. About a year after I was back in Colorado and writing for the *Boulder Weekly*, Tim's new solo record, *Say It Is So*, was about to be released. Better yet, Boulder-based W.A.R? (What Are Records?) was putting the disc out stateside. I had a good relationship there and, heck, the newspaper was Boulder-based, not to mention he was going to perform in that very same city. I pitched the idea, and my editor was more than happy to let me author a preview piece. Soon, I was on the phone with Finn, discussing the new record, his career and life in general. His insight into parenthood was something I appreciated. He had waited a long time to have kids and discussed what that was like.

I had been listening to *Say It Is So* a lot and enjoyed it, especially the songs "Underwater Mountain" and "Death of a Popular Song." I remember often hitting the repeat button for "Death of a Popular Song." The combination of the strong hook, the pleasant melody and the combination of Tim's rustic, weathered voice and background/harmony vocalist Julie Miller (wife of Americana giant Buddy Miller and a respected artist in her own right), along with the guitar notes, made for a fantastic composition.

Unfortunately, I didn't make it to Tim's acoustic show for *Say It Is So*. But several years later, on February 16, 2005, I took a girl I was dating to see the Finn Brothers play at the Boulder Theater. I have seen few shows so stripped down that managed to be so intense and full of sound. Tim and Neil were touring behind their new Finn Brothers disc, *Everyone is Here*—an album that was receiving a nice amount of airplay on Boulder's KBCO-FM.

Neil was under the weather, and apparently the show was almost canceled. The flu had been taking its toll, and he made the comment that some good whisky was giving him strength.

One would not have known that Neil was sick. He was that good. Each song soared with Tim playing acoustic guitar and sometimes snare drum, Neil on electric guitar, and Tim Smith (of Jellyfish and Sheryl Crow fame) on bass. Neil sang the majority of the lead vocals, Tim did some, and all three men sang backup and harmonies. It was simply staggering. The most memorable visual is Tim playing snare with his foot, while playing guitar and singing. Who else can do that?

The only downer to the whole show was that it was standing-room only and the girl I was dating and I are both short. I'm not sure why this is, but people with elevated height seem to be magnetically drawn to the spaces directly in front of my field of vision.

****

I was reading through your bio, and you made a comment about the album [*Say It Is So*] being largely positive. Are you trying to write positive songs, or is that just what seems to come out?
I am not trying to do anything. I just do what I do. I don't consciously try and write anything particular. I just— whatever I'm feeling at the time. I don't think it's necessarily positive or negative music. It's just music, you know what I mean? It can be uplifting. Somebody said it better than me— they said it's all about beauty, and you're either celebrating beauty or you're bemoaning the lack of it, but it's still about beauty, so in the end, that's what I believe.

Definitely. How do you usually come up with new material? What is the process like for you?
I like to get in the car and drive and listen to tapes in the car or just compile tapes of songs, good songs, and just drive out into the landscape of Eden. [Yes, this was in 2000 and people still used cassettes. –Ed.] I don't write while I am doing that, but it kind of frees me up a bit. I've got a music room in my house, and that's my sacred space, if you like. I go down there and I work, and that's a pretty exciting place to be. So it's just gathering impressions and experiences and feelings, and then just having a place where you can go where no one can get at you.

One of the songs stood out to me lyrically. I think it had to do with pride. It was talking about, "There's always something wrong when there's always a need to be right." ["Need to be Right" is the tune in question. -Ed.]
Oh, yeah.

Is that from a personal experience with pride, or is that just something that you wanted to speak about?
There's usually some intense experience that leads to a song. It may not [be] straight away. It might be weeks, months later, but I very rarely write from the abstract. That was from a very specific fight that I had. I actually wrote it only a few hours after the fight when there was still a very strong feeling in the air. And yeah, it's a terrible sort of trap to fall into to think that you have to be right. It can cause a lot of problems. So I am not trying to make a statement or a message. It was just a very personal experience that happened.

Now, as far as what Neil is doing now, has there ever been any jealousy between you guys as brothers and both doing music?
I'd say more like a friendly rivalry. Even then it has subsided a lot. I guess we're growing up more. It's never been bitter. It's never been what I would call jealousy, but there's been rivalry. I mean, he's six years younger than me, so I taught him everything he knows. He acknowledges that, and I'm the older brother, but he's very, very talented and carved his own path.

I noticed on the new record [*Say It is So*], you recorded in Nashville in Buddy and Judy Miller's studio. Why did you decide to come to Nashville to record?
Actually that's not correct. [I should have read the liner notes and remembered them, but at least Tim was nice about it. -Ed.] I recorded it in Nashville at Woodland Studios. Julie Miller sang on the record, but I decided to go to Nashville because it was the last—I didn't decide to go because it was the last place on earth that I thought I would go, but in fact it

was the last place on earth, and the perversity of that idea really appealed to me. That is literally true. This friend said to me, "I've had an epiphany. You must go to Nashville." It was such a stupid idea that I went immediately without knowing anybody there or knowing anything about it. I had tried more logical approaches for the preceding year of demo-ing and thinking about cool places to record, and I'd gone up a lot of blind alleyways and I'd scraped [up] a whole lot of material, so I guess in a sense I was desperate for an illogical idea.

Now I noticed, too, and I know it talks about this in your bio, why did you decide on so live a record rather than the more polished approach that people usually take?
Well, I just again really decided to do that. I was paying for myself, so I had no options. Somebody once said, "Freedom is absence of choice," and that was the case for me. Within that complete lack of choice, I had a tremendous freedom because I had to do it then, it had to be right, and I didn't have any opportunities to second-guess myself. I think what it reminded me of was that I am a live performer. I'm my best live, so to try and be live in a studio is now my constant aim.

How has being a dad affected your music? I know you have a son, Harper—what has that done for you as an artist?
Well, it's done a lot for me, as a man, to be a father after all these years. Any parent can tell you—it's very hard to talk about it, and it's a day-to-day ordeal which has great amounts of joy and also great confrontation with self, and it's not always a pretty sight. But as a songwriter, it's very difficult to say how it has affected me. It's not a theme. I don't write about it, but it's there, I guess, between the lines. You do get an immediate, almost biological sense of ongoing-ness from having a child, and that is quite a strengthening sort of feeling. So there is strength in this record. There is less vulnerability, perhaps, or less fear. There's certainly some dark spots in it, but I think I'm more confident as a human being on the planet. I feel more connected. I mean, I was

amazingly—I had no idea what everybody was up to all these years. My brother, my two sisters, even my parents—I mean, they've all done it and I hadn't done it. So now I feel stronger connections with family and just friends in general.

I've noticed that *Say It Is So* seems to have been received well so far, with *Rolling Stone* doing reviews and all these other newspapers—what's that like for you to be so well received after all these years?

It's a good feeling. In the end it's really nice to be judged positively and all the rest of it. I don't read my reviews, so I am lousily ignorant. It's just that obviously when I get a good one, somebody usually mentions it, but I just get told, "Oh you got a good review in so and so," and I don't go and dissect it and read it, because I've learned that in the end I learn nothing from them, either if they're positive or negative. They don't actually aid me as a human being or as an artist. But it's part of the process of getting people's attention, and they're tremendously valuable for that, and I'm very grateful for that if it's positive, because it gets the word out. I think over the years I've been treated fairly well in that respect. With Split Enz, we certainly had our share of amazing, glowing press, and I'm no stranger to that process, but I've also had, you know—there's a balance, and you get the odd real bad one and that's—I guess you don't take any of it too seriously. But I think this is my strongest record. I've been doing this for over twenty years, and I really believe that I've made my best record, so it's very exciting from that respect, and I just want to keep going. I don't want to spend another five years waiting to do another one. I've already written the newest one, so I am hopefully going to record that next year. And I would like to work with Jay Joyce again. So there is a great sense of ongoing-ness and a passion for what I do and those are the things that nourish me.

I wanted to say how in your lyrics, they're never heavy-handed but you always put a Biblical perspective in there. Is that a hard thing for you to do?

I'm not sure how to give a perspective—there is a kind of balance, you mean. It doesn't get too bogged down with how hard things can be. I think there's an upliftingness—I'm generalizing, but there is a pastoral kind of quality. A hopeful quality to a lot [Unclear. –Ed.] music I think, and part of just being in a far-flung place where you don't have the same intense urban concentration which can lead to despair and defeat. I think the landscape can just enrich you and all of that. The music and the water—the ocean. There's a lot of water imagery. I've done a lot of trips down the coast. It all seeps in there, and it's very uplifting when you have those experiences with oneness out there in the world. So when you have that, then you can talk about dark stuff, but you always know that there's a bit of a larger picture, I suppose. So when you said is it hard for me to do that—it probably isn't, because it's just a part of how I live my life.

I was going to say some of the songs seem pretty personal as far as your relationship between yourself and God. Almost songs of thanks.
Well, I don't actually believe in a personal God, so when you say "God," I don't know what you mean, but what I mean by it is the patriarchal feel that I was taught about as a child. I no longer believe in that, but there's a sense of spirituality in the work that's fantastic. To me, to be spiritual is to feel a oneness with other people, with everything in the world, and that's what music can do. I've seen it do that and a room full of people become one. And that, to me, is a religious experience. I do believe that despite its ephemeral and somewhat superficial nature, pop music can be a healing force in the world. I really do believe that.

Well I appreciate this, Tim. Thanks so much for doing this on such short notice.
Oh, no problem.

I hope the tour goes well for you.
Thanks so much.

KING'S X
(DOUG (dUg) PINNICK)

A week or two prior to August 24, 2000
Article: *Boulder Weekly* (August 24, 2000)

As a preteen and early teenager, I thought heaviness equated to musical talent. My friend Brian showed me how to play a power chord one day. I think a trickle of urine cascaded down my leg the first time I reared back and ripped out an "A" power chord with amp cranked and my parents racing for the aspirin bottle. I had a small white Gorilla amplifier, and I would take my jet-black Memphis electric guitar and create all kinds of noise. I was a fan of bands that did the same, albeit with much more ability and songwriting skills.

Later on, I would move away from my power-chord-dominated listening diet. I began to listen to musically advanced bands like Rush and King's X, and I quickly realized that any twelve-year-old could take a guitar pick, drive it against six thin metal strings, risk a wrist/fingers injury and play power chords at a volume level that, years later, could result in Pete Townshend-like hearing repercussions.

There is certainly a lot of Townshend and the Who in King's X. Singer and bass player Doug Pinnick followed bassist John Entwistle's amplification setup (you get the highs of a guitar and the thundering lows of a bass)—Pinnick courteously described how he achieved this sound in a postcard he sent me around the time of the *Dogman* album tour in 1994.

Part of the initial draw to King's X came because my friend Roger told me about them and I respected his opinion. He was really into thrash and I tried to love it because it was the most extreme metal music at the time—head-banging, fast drumming, screaming vocals. Roger and I met one summer in New Hampshire at a Christian camp called Camp Berea. The mostly-volunteer staff members were loving and really cared about the kids that came.

When I first met Roger, he was sitting in front of me at a chapel service. We were thirteen or fourteen. He was proudly carrying his yellow drumsticks striped with black electrical tape. Needless to say, he loved Stryper. We quickly bonded and, in fact, both wore our Barren Cross *Atomic Arena* 1988 tour shirts the exact same day with every ounce of teenage metal fan pride we could muster. We kept in touch after camp, and once, I sent Roger some Christian metal albums. One of the cassettes was by Swedish Christian hard rock band Jerusalem. Roger said his older brother thought the band sounded, strangely enough, like the Who. I thought that was more than cool as Jerusalem was my favorite band. To this day, they remain one of the most passionate, emotive bands I've heard.

Anyway, Roger told me about this band, King's X— apparently all the members were Christians, but they were a mainstream band. That was paydirt. Back in the day, we loved the bands that refused to be limited by the Christian music industry. Even better, King's X's debut, *Out of the Silent Planet,* was distributed by a major mainstream label, Atlantic. Roger drove his recommendation even further by comparing their musical skills to Rush, a band I revered and appreciated for their musical skill. I quickly went out and bought the cassette.

King's X was sensational. They had the Christian fans—the title of the *Out of the Silent Planet* album was borrowed from a C.S. Lewis novel, the first of his science fiction trilogy.

The band, it turned out, also had the respect of a slew of mainstream metal acts. I would read about them often in *Heaven's Metal* (later *HM*) *the* place to get your Christian loud music news.

I was a huge fan, initially due to the musical aptitude of the members. Later, I would realize that the band's decidedly Beatlesque vocal harmonies and pop hooks were just as much of a draw, if not more so. My dad, as I've mentioned before, schooled me on the Beatles' "White Album" courtesy of his reel-to-reel tape machine and metal-grilled Kenwood stereo speakers, so appreciation of catchy tunes and harmonies was unavoidable (my mom told me my dad used to play his music at high volume levels on the same stereo system when they lived in Germany, much to the chagrin of their neighbors).

I came to a place in my King's X appreciation where I realized I judge melody and harmony based on that very same monumentous double disc released by the Fab Four in 1968. How could you go wrong with the Beatles? How could you go wrong with a metal trio who combined the Beatles, Rush and Christian-themed lyrics?

It was a three-way combination that worked oh so well, and I wasn't the only one in my social circle who was affected. My buddy André (who appears often within these pages) and I stayed up all night once, discussing the band's lyrics and trying to figure out their hidden meanings. Were there any? Regardless, I'm sure we were a mess the next day with very little sleep and probably trying to make it through our Sunday school class.

Years later, after several other discs and tours, I was able to interview bassist/vocalist Doug Pinnick, courtesy of the *Boulder Weekly*, during the tour for the band's then-new disc, *Please Come Home... Mr. Bulbous.*

Doug was cordial during the interview and agreed to talk to me at the last minute. We discussed mutual acquaintances and more.

The concert itself was at the Aztlan Theatre on Santa Fe Drive in Denver. The area has been rebirthed in more recent times as a vibrant arts district. Unfortunately, the sound was horrible—I'd seen King's X a couple times prior and this was never an issue and hasn't been since. I hate to say it, but I only stayed for a song or two. My friend Chris and I had a hard time with the definitionless wall of sound coming at us. Part of the joy of the King's X sound is the vocal harmonies, and those were impossible to distinguish from the auditory mush.

I will, however, always fondly remember seeing the three-piece at the Ogden Theatre in 1994, when they played a rock-solid, crystal-clear-sounding show. My buddy Chris was present for that concert as well. During the performance, I remember my future college roommate, Brian, looking up at me and taunting me with grins, jeers, and gestures as I was twenty and was relegated to the balcony, while he was twenty-one and could be down on the floor close to the stage.

King's X is, and remains, a testament to great musicianship, solid songs, odd time signatures and awe-inspiring harmonies live and on recordings. My friend Doug Van Pelt, founder and former editor/owner of *HM,* has stuck by these guys since their first disc and I can see why. I've done the same.

****

[A mutual friend] says "Hi."
Tell [him] I say, "Hey." I was supposed to sing at his wedding, but he never got back to me. I don't know what happened.

Yeah, I wasn't sure either. I don't know what happened. He was a friend of mine when I lived out in Nashville, but yeah. First question: The three of you have known each other for like twenty, twenty-five years. What was your first impression of those guys? [There was a problem with part of the question being cut off. –Ed.]
First impression of Jerry? I don't know. When I met Jerry I never thought anything but that he was a drummer and he was flawless. I didn't even think about it. When I saw Ty—I saw him play at a spring fling, it's called, with a little band. He was in the background with his Les Paul, playing. He was like eighteen years old, and he moved up front and did this little eight-measure lead, and I was really impressed. And me and Jerry actually tracked him down—but we had met him earlier—and then Jerry played with Ty in a little group for about a month, and then I played with Jerry for a little bit and then we finally got together.

Was it Jerry and Ty that did the thing with Phil Keaggy for a while?
No, me and Jerry did that.

What has been the most vivid or memorable experience?
The most vivid and memorable experience is driving down the highway in an RV on our first tour, and the drain for the toilet was broke. And we couldn't open it. So we kept taking a shit in it anyway. And it filled up to the point where when the bus went up a hill, stuff would roll out the side. We were riding down the highway, and all of a sudden we look out the window and there's a guy honking at us, yelling and screaming at us, and what happened was it broke – the toilet thing busted and shit flew all over the street, the road, the highway, whatever you call [it], on this guy's car. He had the top down. He had a Camaro. That's the most memorable experience to me. And then we pulled over and tried to take care of it, and it smelled so bad. I think Jerry and Ty started throwing up. I'm not sure. That's the most memorable experience besides playing Woodstock [1994].

I have actually found a bootleg video of that. And that was huge.
That's one bootleg that has been going around. Everybody has seen it, and now we just need to put it out.

That was a good concert. Was that pretty freaky, playing that thing?
Yeah, I thought we sucked. I hated it. I was all nervous. I thought I was an idiot and I wanted to quit, and then afterwards they said we were the highlight of the day. Go figure.

What was the transition like for you from Atlantic to Metal Blade?
One day we were on Atlantic and the next day we were on Metal Blade and we went out and toured. I don't remember any transition really. We were just happy to be on a label and be able to put another record out and go tour.

I know you have your own studio and you did the Poundhound project and Ty has his Alien Beans thing going—what's that like for you guys?

It's really the coolest thing in the world to have your own studio because I can go in at any time I want to and do what I want to, and Ty too—we can make records when we feel like it without the pressure of everything—of money, of a producer, an engineer, or whatever. It's all ours. It's like being at home, and I love it.

When you guys were writing the new material, did you get together to write it or did you write it on your own?
No, we wrote everything from the ground up on the music on *Mr. Bulbous.*

Oh, wow.
I think ten songs in ten days.

Was most of it recorded live, or did you do a lot of overdubs?
The basic tracks were live, and then [we'd] overdub vocals and stuff like that later, but the basic tracks were done live.

Wow! What was it like recording that record?
Quick. We set Jerry up in my studio and made up a song in about ten minutes and put it down. "Let's go home, come back tomorrow and try another," you know. It was pretty simple. We have been together for twenty years, so it's like—what we do nowadays I don't even think about it. I don't think about a formula or approach or anything. It's like breathing, being in this band. We don't think about anything. I don't, anyway.

Is there any chance you'll record any of the stuff on the— I don't know the name of the song, but it was "Johnny cut his hair, now he looks like a punk?"
Who knows? We might pull out that stuff and put it on some from the early days, "King's X in the '80s" or something. But I don't know. Those are cool songs, but life goes on. It's sort of like opening up a yearbook and you look at yourself ten years or twenty years ago, and it's like, "It might have been cool then, but it ain't now." [King's X did eventually put out a

studio album, *Black Like Sunday*, that featured many of these early songs that were newly recorded, including the song "Johnny," mentioned above. –Ed.]

I hear you. Has there ever been a point where you guys were going to just go your separate ways?
We thought about it every now and then. Just because we felt that financially or successfully we couldn't survive, but then we just decided to stay together anyway and keep going. This is my family, you know. My brothers. We ain't going nowhere. If we sold a couple million records we'd probably break up and spend our money and go travel.

I noticed on this record, in particular, that you guys all have Yamaha endorsements. What led up to that? Because I know originally you were using Hamer and Ampeg.
One day Yamaha signed up with Ty and Ty said, "Hey, do you guys want to endorse Yamaha?" and we go, "What's the deal?" So he told us, and we said "Sure." And the next thing you knew, a couple days later, we are all on Yamaha. It was pretty simple. No big cosmic story happened there.

Do you miss the twelve-string [bass]?
Nope. I mean, I still have them, but I haven't played them in like five years.

Is that thing hard to play?
It is sort of difficult to play, but it's pretty cool. I don't know. I just lost interest in them after a while. I will pull them out again. Probably in the future.

Well the tune up—I think that would be a bastard.
Not really. Once you get into tune, it stays in tune. That was the good thing about it. But you had to get it in tune.

Where did the album title come from?

Mr. Bulbous? It was sort of a joke. Ty made that up. We had been running that title around for a couple years, and this time we just decided to do it.

Cool. What do you hope people take away from the record? Do you have anything in mind you want them to take from it?
No, I really don't. It's just us expressing ourselves and just another record by King's X. Hopefully our audience will like it, you know, or whatever. It's just another child in our life.

Do you have any favorite cuts on the record?
"Julia" is my favorite.

Wow.
Just because it's such a bizarre song. It's so simple but yet so complex.

It is a great song.
It took us a [long] time to try to make up a melody to it because it's a really bizarre chord change.

Yeah that song was interesting. Because it sounded like—guitar wise—it sounded like something that Ty would usually do, but it sounded like it just lowered a key or two.
Yeah, sort of. Some of the weird changes I made up on my bass, and then he brought the guitar in to make sense of it.

Any regrets so far?
Any regrets?

As far as King's X is concerned?
Oh no! We're legends. What can I ask for? You know, what more can I ask for? My name is in history. We will go down as one of those bands. I love it.

What is your opinion of the newer, younger bands that are coming out now?

Every new band that comes out, I think it's great because everybody just wears their heart on their sleeves and then the next generation is going to have something to say and they come out with their attitude and they do it. And I love the new rap metal and all that stuff —whatever you call it.

Like Limp Bizkit and Korn?
Yeah. And I just tuned into Taproot. I really dig them a lot. I love all that stuff, just because it's low tuning and groove, and that's just me. I love that shit. So anytime you turn down and groove, I'm there.

Was there anything else you wanted to add?
No, I never have anything to add. I always just answer questions because I have said so much in my life in the last twenty years being in this band, I ain't got much left to tell you. So I just answer questions now.

Any chance you will revive the old fan club newsletter?
That could be a possibility, but I have no idea. We do things when we feel like it. One day we will just wake up and say, "Hey let's start the newsletter again." "Cool. OK." We're pretty happy as a bunch of guys these days.

What can people expect from this tour as far as the show? Can you tell me anything that you're playing that you haven't played in a while?
Well, basically we handpicked these songs for our enjoyment. And so people had a hard time with it at first, but now they like the set. We are not doing everybody's favorites anymore on this tour. We did it last tour—we did everybody's favorites. We just did them all. This time we said, "Let's do it ourselves and have fun." So we are doing stuff that you probably won't normally hear. I can't tell you, though.

Can you tell me one song?
"Everybody Knows a Little Bit of Something."

Oh cool. That was a great album. It sounded like on *Faith, Hope, Love*, you guys had a blast making that.
Those three albums were really rough. I can't even listen to those records, but I'm glad people like them. We had more fun later with *Dogman* and, especially *Tape Head* and *Ear Candy*, we had a great time. [A brief discussion ensued here regarding the music business. -Ed.]

Well again, I appreciate it, Doug. Thanks again for being so honest. I know when Doug Van Pelt [then-editor of *HM*] interviews you, you always put your heart on your sleeve, and I appreciate that.
Yeah, I put my heart on my sleeve way too many times. It's like, "There it is. Now there's nothing else to Doug—know it all."

Keep it up, man. God bless you.
Well, thank you.

Just keep doing it, because that is what people need to hear, is people being real. I hope to meet you in Denver.
Yeah, come out and say "Hey."

I should be talking to [our mutual friend] tonight.
Tell him I said, "Hey" too.

You were supposed to be in his wedding?
Well, he wanted me to sing, I think, "I'll Never Get Tired of You," but I guess it never worked out.

I know in the past—like ten years ago you sent me postcards and stuff, and that was really cool. Picture from the Marquee club.
Yeah, I used to do that stuff. I wish I had time to do it now.

Well, have a great tour and have a great show tonight.
We will see you in Denver.

RUSH
(ALEX LIFESON)

Thursday, August 1, 2002
Article: *Boulder Weekly* (August 22, 2002)

Rush was one of those bands that I fell in auditory love with the first time I heard them. I owe much of this attraction to the genius of television. Growing up in New England, I didn't have many friends during my early elementary school years, aside from a guy, James, who lived around the corner and was as passionate about cars as I was.

"Chris, what do you think of the new Chrysler LeBaron? I love it. My dad says it drives really well. The seats are nice. Nice vinyl seats. I really like riding in it. And you should see the engine. I bet it could beat Mr. Hunsaker's Buick station wagon if we were to race them." Yes, that is how our conversations went.

Then there was my neighbor, Jeff, who is discussed in detail in the Stryper chapter of this book. And, sure, there were some others. But I was the odd guy. I loved guns, cars and reading but hated sports and for some reason people liked to point out those differences. It could get kind of tough at the school bus stop—once I had to take a piss really bad. The bladder walls were knocking the liquid contents back and forth like a heavy, wet towel in a clothes dryer. We had these huge rocks, boulders actually, all over the place in our neighborhood. I think there were two or three just in our yard.

So I'm walking home from school and my bladder starts demanding immediate attention. I walked up a small dirt- and rock-covered hill on the side of Chicatabut Avenue, stood behind one of the boulders, ripped open my zipper and began making a river. It was cold outside, so I wasn't thrilled about river-making. I really wanted to be done with it.

My brother knew what was going on, as he and his friends had been right behind me on the walk home. He saw me climb up the hill and go behind the gigantic rock, so he decided to investigate by peering behind the boulder when I was in midstream. He yelled, "Hey, come look. Chris is peeing! Chris is peeing!," while laughing. I didn't bat an eye, lifted my biological cannon and covered his jacket with the remaining contents. Horrified, he ran off toward home with the oft-said, "I'm gonna tell Mom and you're gonna be in trooouuble!" The best part is that, yes, even though he beat me home and informed my mom about where my urine had landed and what it had drenched, my mom chuckled while I told her my side of the story. Strangely enough, I did not get into trouble.

Most days when I got home from school—whether stopping to take a leak or not—I watched a lot of television. My mom worked, and my brother Andy and I generally had cool babysitters, and while he was out playing with friends or at a sports practice, I was home watching TV. It generally wasn't cartoons. I was more into '70s crime dramas like *Charlie's Angels* and *Wonder Woman*. We didn't have cable, so my choices were pretty limited.

When I was in the third grade, this all changed—not the cable portion, but the scope of what I'd watch on the tube. That was the year V66, a non-cable music video station, launched. I was in heaven. I watched video after video, falling in love with Tears for Fears' "Everybody Wants to Rule the World" and many more. In fact, I first became interested in playing bass due to seeing a bass at the local music store that looked identical to the one Tears for Fears member Curt Smith played in the video. If I remember correctly, the guitar in the store was a headless bass—not a Steinberger or other high-priced brand, but a knock-off that had a much smaller price tag.

It was through V66 that I discovered Rush. One evening, my parents were either out at a dinner party or had to work late. My brother and I were dressed in our pajamas, ready for chocolate milk and a night of television viewing. I was turning channels and settled on V66. A high-pitched voice was singing, "Red alert, red alert!" I was instantly drawn to the sound and the video. Our babysitter, L.J., was standing next to me, watching the video, and my brother was curious and asked who the band was. L.J. responded instantly, "That's Rush."

From that point forward, I liked the band, and as I became a musician, I revered them. I would listen to Rush with my friend Jeff, who lived in back of me—and later on, my friend Mike, who lived about twenty minutes away and played drums in a band with me. We would discuss them with lots of respect and admiration. While in college, I delved full-on into the band, and my listening habits included heavy, heavy doses of the Canadian trio's music. Eventually I got into music journalism, started writing for the *Boulder Weekly* and dreamed of an interview with a member of Rush.

I never thought it would happen, but Atlantic Records was very gracious in all our communications regarding an interview for a *Boulder Weekly* piece—it was the start of a relationship that has continued to this day. Their publicity department is full of great people.

So once the fine folks at Atlantic instilled a microcosm of hope for a possible Rush interview, I could think of few other things and probably even forgot to brush my teeth, apply deodorant or put on pants once or twice. I was pining away for an interview with Geddy Lee, as he had been instrumental to my playing as a bassist; or Neil Peart, Rush's monstrously talented drummer, as he authored all the band's lyrics. I was dubious as to whether an interview would even take place. Usually I was able to secure interviews fairly quickly, but scheduling seemed to take an eternity.

But then it happened. I was at work, sitting in my cubicle at an office building in the Inverness business park in Englewood, Colorado, and a personal e-mail message came up on my computer screen—from so-and so at Atlantic Records. The subject was probably "Rush interview." My innards started tumbling like the numbered balls in the state lottery machine. The content of the message simply said, "Alex Lifeson is available for a phone interview at one p.m. your time. Do you want it?"

I launched out of my chair and made a beeline for my manager, Mario's, larger, executive-style cubicle. He looked up after popping a handful of almonds into his mouth and asked, "Hey, Chris, what can I do for you?" I quickly explained that I had an opportunity to interview Alex Lifeson from Rush, but I had to leave right then and there to make it happen. His mouth opened, his eyes bulged, and I thought he was going to lose the almonds he had just consumed, along with anything else he had eaten during the last twenty-four hours.

"Chris, yes, go now. You're doing what? Rush?? Go now!" Mario, after all, had been a professional drummer and had a major label offer on the table several years earlier. Neil Peart was one of his favorite drummers.

I made it home with plenty of time to spare. Alex was a bit delayed in calling, and I started to worry. I picked up when the phone rang, and he immediately apologized for calling late. Something had happened to the record company cell phone he used for interviews and he had to call on his personal phone. He was professional, funny and incredibly personable throughout the interview. It's an experience I will never forget.

The Rush show itself rolled into the Denver area on Saturday, August 24, 2002, and inhabited Fiddler's Green Amphitheater for an evening. It was a very special occasion, as I had waited years to see the band live. The show was simply electrifying. It was even more special as I got to share that occasion with my dad, a true music fan.

****

Thanks for doing this. I know you are busy with interviews and whatnot.
Oh, that's okay.

I have some questions. Take them where you want to go. I'm trying to avoid the questions you have been asked the last twenty-eight years.
Thank you, I appreciate that.

No problem. What has been your overall feeling about the tour so far?
It's just been amazing. We have been having a great time. It's so nice to get out and play, but the thing I've noticed more than anything else is the audience reaction. Everybody seems so happy to see us, and it's just a wonderful feeling. I know that we have great fans, probably the best that anybody could hope for. They're very loyal. They're into what the band does, or they have been with us for a long time; it's pretty evident looking out at the audience every night. But there's a sense of joy that everybody seems to have at the shows, and it's a wonderful thing for us because we really feed off that and we have a really good time every night. I think we are playing really well, which is also a very key thing. Nothing worse than not getting off on what you're doing. But we prepared ourselves really well. We had six weeks of rehearsals and pre-production, and we have been on the road for one leg so far, and I think we're playing probably the best we have ever played. That seems to be the response that we're getting.

Any particular songs that are challenging to play currently?
Well, definitely there are a few that are always challenging to play. "Natural Science"— you've got to stay on top of that all the time. And some of the new songs, but they're already settling in and feeling really, really great. We wrote the songs, and even though we haven't played some of these songs in a long time, they don't feel particularly difficult to do. It's a question of stamina, I think, to play for three hours, but I'm really glad we are. Everybody prepared for it. We all started working out in the gym back in November, and then the rehearsals—the amount of rehearsing that we did got our fingers into shape and our chops together. So everybody is in really, really good shape and healthy and pretty happy, actually.

I saw some of the footage on your webpage from the Hartford [Connecticut] show—it looked like you were having fun.
Oh yeah, that was—I'll never forget that gig. That was amazing. That was a real magical night. I don't think we looked at each other for about the first six songs. We were so—I wouldn't say we were nervous, but we were just so pumped and excited. The audience response that night, I guess because it was the first show, was really special. I really had a lump in my throat [at] a couple points through the night. I was amazed by it.

That's always a good feeling, I'm sure.
Oh, yeah. Yeah, is it ever. You do something for twenty-eight years and you can still get so excited about it. That's pretty lucky.

I wish most people could say that about their jobs. Are you going to be alternating set lists and switching out songs from show to show, or will it stay the same?
Well, we do that with "Ghost Rider" and "Ceiling Unlimited." We alternate those two. The problem was that we wanted to do lots of new material, but our fans have been around for so long, you really have to play a lot of older material, or just balance the set. So we decided we'd have four new songs in the evening show and just alternate a couple of them. So far we've only done that with "Ceiling" and "Ghost Rider," but we worked up a couple of others and we will see as the tour goes on whether we will start including them.

Are there any songs you are extending out and doing extended jams on?
Well, there is "By-Tor and the Snow Dog" and "Working Man," those things. We like to stretch out a little bit at the end of "Bravado," and so far everything has stayed pretty fresh from night to night. We're not really repeating ourselves too much. You get into a groove after a while, and what was spontaneous for a couple of nights suddenly

becomes the norm. We are trying to keep it as fresh as we can, and we are being pretty successful at it, I think.

That sounds awesome. I can't wait until you guys come to Denver. The *Vapor Trails* album seems like it's probably the heaviest record you have ever done. Was that done intentionally, or was it something that just kind of happened?

Yeah, it's just the way we went. Geddy finished *My Favorite Headache,* and then he did some promotional stuff for a couple of months, and I produced a band called Lifer, from Pennsylvania, and they were kind of very hard rock, almost metal-ish. I don't know what you would call them, but they were pretty hard. The stuff that I do on my own tends to be a little bit on the harder side, and Geddy's a little more melodic, but once we started playing we really just got into the whole vibe of playing hard and playing loud and listening to it loud, and it was really inspiring. Then the fact that we made a decision not to have any keyboards on the record, I think, forced us to play a little more and we played a little harder because of that.

Was that the decision you both made, as far as the keyboards, where Geddy just didn't want to do them?

I really hoped that we could stay away from it as much as possible. I said right from the beginning that I really would rather develop guitar parts or do vocal things or do anything than have sample keyboards on the record. I just thought it would be so much better if it was really an organic record and it was all about us playing. Ged certainly had no problem with it—the only thing he said was, "Listen, I am fine, but if we find that we are missing something and we can find it in keyboards, then I'd like to reserve the right." I said, "OK, fine. No problem." But I never let him feel that way. Then once we got into it and I had time on my own to mess around and explore, he would come in and go, "Wow, I see what you mean. That's great." And then he started doing the same thing with vocals—vocal ideas, using vocal lines as curtains or coloring or whatever instead of going to that string sound or an organ sound or whatever.

Well, vocally it's a very dynamic record. It sounds like he really put a ton into it.
I think they're the best vocals that he's done in a very, very long time.

Now live, how is that going to translate? Are there going to be DATs [digital audio tapes] for some of the background vocals?
We've always triggered some samples between the two of us, and I'm singing a lot on this tour. I didn't expect that to happen, but I'm singing a little better than I have before. I work at it, and we supplement it with some vocal sampled stuff and then we just don't have it in some areas where we might have done it on the record and we don't seem to miss it. And I'm not so sure the audience really misses it. There's something about the live performance that makes up for what you don't hear from the record. But there's a lot of power in the new material, and it doesn't seem to be affected by little things that we may leave out.

I had a little bit of a different question for you. I read about the nineteen thousand dollars worth of cheese on the website [Rush's website, at the time of the interview, stated that Alex ate a gargantuan pile of cheese valued at this amount—a joke of course. -Ed.]. Is there any truth to this or maybe a decimal that's off?
It was seventeen thousand, and it was all soft cheeses. The dry, hard stuff, boy that's tough, but all those Bries and Camemberts, Saint André, they were okay.

I take it that it wasn't before a performance, or else you would have to depart for a while.
I don't think I would go to the bathroom for about a week if I ate that much cheese. On our website, there are some really funny, creative people there, and they thought they'd do these factoids and just make them all silly little things. And

it's incredible the response to questions like that: "What was it like to eat all that cheese?" No, I never ate that much —I think I might have actually eaten that much cheese on some occasions.

That's a lot of cheese.
That's a lot of cheese.

That's heart attack material.
Yes, exactly. Exactly.

You have been doing this for so long—do you have one humorous experience that stands out above the other things that have happened to you?
You know, those are really difficult questions to answer. Lots of funny little things happen, but there isn't any one overriding thing that happened in so many years as well, but no, I don't know.

If you were any cartoon character, who would you be?
Stimpy.

What about Geddy and Neil?
Geddy would be Ren, and Neil—would Neil be—I don't know. I don't know. You got me there. But you got Ren and Stimpy, anyways.

I heard when you did the three-disc live album a couple years ago that there was going to be a live DVD that might be released because apparently you have all kinds of footage from the *Test for Echo* tour?
Yeah we had—we shot the Toronto show. We did two nights in Toronto and we shot one of those nights and we intended to do a DVD from that footage, but of course everything stopped and it's there. Although we haven't spoken about it, perhaps we'll do the same thing on a show during this tour and combine the two. I don't know. We haven't really discussed what we want to do with that. But it's something

that we should probably pursue because it would be worth having.

Will you be recording on this tour as well?
No. No. No. We are finished with recording live for a little while, anyway.

You guys have done a lot of that over the years. Is that more intimidating when you know the tape is rolling?
No, you know, now it's not so bad. In the past, it used to be difficult because you picked seven or eight nights that you were going to record, and you knew it was on, and those were the nights where you always made dumb mistakes, but on the last tour, recording was a nightly event, so after a while you just didn't even think about it.

It seems like most of the people that have been really creative musically have gone away over the years, but you guys still remain strong. There is a big pop element to your music—is that something that has been done on purpose over the years, or is it just from the writing—the way you write—is it just something that comes about?
I think it's just the way we work, the way we write. The things that we're influenced by seep into what we do as a band, and individually we're inspired by different things. You know, we're really quite different from each other in terms of the things that we like to hear when we're playing. Geddy is more melodic. I am a lot heavier. Fairly broad, and then when we work together it comes out the way it comes out. But it's really quite different for all of us. So we're influenced really by all sorts of things, as I think most people are.

You, yourself—are there any future production plans, as far as working with more bands? You have seemed to take that road in the last few years.
Yeah, I would love to do more production. I really enjoyed it a lot. I love being in that situation. I really realize that being a producer is not just about the music. It's about a lot of different things. It's about being a cheerleader and about

being a coach and about being a dad. And being a diplomat and being a cop. It's a lot of things, depending on who you are working with. But I love what happens when you inspire somebody to do something or you subtly direct another musician into looking into different possibilities. And when you see that spark ignite, it's really a very gratifying thing. I'd love to do more of that.

You don't have anything scheduled out, but that's something that you would like to do?
Yes. Exactly.

Now as far as Rush—have you guys been talking about the next record, or has that even entered your minds yet?
Oh, no. We take a day at a time. This tour is going to take us to maybe until Christmas. But we just want to get through this. By the end of this tour we will have worked steadily for two years. Really solidly, with very little time off, and I think we all need to have a little bit of a break. So we're going to finish this tour, and everybody's going to relax for a bit, and then we'll see what happens. And I am going to take advantage of it next year and try and get some other work and work with some other bands or some other projects, just because I love working. I love being busy. But in terms of what Rush is going to do, I think we'll just take a break for a little while and then see what happens.

Do you have time—the three of you—during a tour to fly home and see your families, or are you just consistently...
We're out for four weeks and then home for ten days. So it's not too bad.

Well, thanks a lot for doing this.
Okay, Chris.

I hope everything works out with your phone.
All right. Thanks.

Sixpence None the Richer (Matt Slocum)

Friday, January 24, 2003
Article: *Boulder Weekly* (January 30, 2003)

Sixpence None the Richer rose to prominence due to their massive hit, "Kiss Me," which appeared in the film *She's All That,* and their cover of the La's' pop gem, "There She Goes." However, prior to all the hype, the band released the monumental *This Beautiful Mess*, their sophomore record, and were celebrated among those who listened to Christian music and appreciated great art—honest, heartfelt poetry put into catchy, atmospheric pop and rock tunes.

The combination of Leigh Nash's (then Bingham) honest and innocent—sometimes pleading and bleeding—vocals and Matt Slocum's melodic, shimmery, college-rock guitars played on the ears like nothing else around at the time. Add to that the stellar bass playing of JJ Plasencio and the expressive, spectacular drumming of Dale Baker, along with the additional vocal harmonies and guitar playing of Tess Wiley, and you had a group that could easily hold its own.

I remember catching part of their set at the Cornerstone Festival in 1995 and being blown away. I had never put much stock into the band prior and had dismissed them like I dismissed most Christian pop bands, but this performance threw me for a loop. I think my hesitance was due to my friend Tony (who in later years would ride his motorcycle from Tennessee to Colorado to work an annual road bike race) showing me the band's first cassette, *The Fatherless and the Widow.* I was into metal at the time, and this cassette cover looked like your standard Christian pop photo—which simply meant "avoid at all costs."

Tony said to me, with his usual raised eyebrows when he meant business, "Man, these guys are good. They are from

Texas, and their music is really good. I don't know that you'd like it though. It's not heavy." The Cornerstone show destroyed my earlier reservations and made me think entirely differently about the band, but it would take me a while to delve into their recorded material.

A few months later, the band was scheduled to play at my college, and I borrowed a copy of *This Beautiful Mess* to prepare for the show. I wrote for the school newspaper at times and thought I might be able to come up with something. I was mesmerized and blown away by what I heard. The disc didn't come out of my stereo for months. The concert at my school was as great as the Cornerstone show had been. I think they even played an instrumental college-rock version of Michael Jackson's "Beat It." Maybe the years haven't been kind to my mind, but I am almost sure this happened, and that it took a minute or so for me to fully realize that they were actually playing a Michael Jackson tune.

Later on, I would appreciate Sixpence more and more. Guitarist Matt Slocum and I had a mutual acquaintance in Steve Taylor—another artist covered in this book—and this made me appreciate Sixpence even more. Matt was close with Steve, and I was the acquaintance.

Any artist who called Steve a friend was someone I respected—after all, he had set the Christian music industry on fire with his poignant songwriting, full of satire and truth. And it had worked. He was always culturally relevant, his records were well received, and he had a good-sized fan base here and in places like the UK. (Later on, Steve would "retire" more or less from making music and launch a record company. One of his acts was Sixpence, and he wound up producing the self-titled third Sixpence disc—the one with "Kiss Me" on it.) Later, Steve wound up launching a career creating films and eventually re-entered the music industry as a performer.

By the time I was finally able to interview Matt Slocum, Sixpence had just released—or was about to release—*Divine Discontent*, which would be their final album for several years as they parted ways (they have since regrouped and have released new recordings and toured). I was able to secure an article with the *Boulder Weekly* when I discovered that the band would be performing on Boulder-based national radio show *eTown*, which taped live at the Boulder Theater, a historic venue right off of the Pearl Street Mall.

Matt and I had a pleasant chat, sometimes discussing mutual acquaintances and familiar places. He was incredibly kind and answered a plethora of questions. However, during the interview, it sounded as if Matt was taking a bath. I heard splashing, but thankfully, no quacking of a rubber ducky. Please, Matt, tell me you were washing dishes!

The interview itself was never used—I wound up writing a short preview piece with no room for quotes. The interview sat in a box and has never been printed until now.

After my conversation with Matt, I'm sure I started thinking long and hard about the upcoming Sixpence performance at the Boulder Theater. I was generally able to get myself plus-one on guest lists for shows when I did an interview. This time I was more than typically pumped up about the possibilities. I had gone on one date with a beautiful girl who lived a mile away from me, and I asked her to go to the Sixpence show for our second outing. She was excited about the concert—I could ascertain this by the sound of her voice when I phoned her to make final plans.

On Sunday, February 2, the day of the show, it snowed like a sieve. The white stuff just wouldn't stop floating down. I was concerned about driving to Boulder, but I managed to white-knuckle it the whole time in my cherry-red Honda Civic coupe. We arrived, had a Guinness and some food at Conor O'Neill's, an Irish pub near the theater, then went into the show, where strangely enough, we wound up with seats very close to the front row. This didn't hurt when trying to impress a girl.

The band, of course, was fantastic even though they didn't play for quite as long as they normally would have—after all, it was a radio show taping. I drove the young lady home after the show and was hoping for another date; I saw her once more a couple weeks later when she invited me out for Mexican food and a margarita—then it was over. Nothing was said; she simply ceased communication. I found out shortly after that she had reconciled with her fiancé. That was after I spent a good wad of cash sending her flowers on Valentine's Day—no name attached to the card. It's amazing what I've learned (or haven't learned) about dating in the years following.

****

Thanks once again for doing this. And congratulations on the release of the record [*Divine Discontent* –Ed.] a few months ago. It sounds really great.
Thank you.

What can fans expect from your Boulder *e-Town* performance?
I understand the *eTown* thing is more of an acoustic, stripped-down performance. Am I correct on that?

Sometimes they do that. Sometimes they have a full band. Cowboy Junkies played last year and they brought the whole band.
The whole band is definitely coming, but I think they were requesting that we do kind of a more stripped-down, acoustic performance. I think we are playing six songs or something like that. So it'll definitely be a full-band thing, but probably just stripped-down, more acoustic versions of the songs. [We'll] probably just play a mix of stuff off the new record and a few off the previous one.

So nothing from *This Beautiful Mess* or anything like that?
Because we have such a short amount of time, we'll probably just stick to those two records.

Are you planning a tour right now or anything like that in support of the record?
Yeah, actually Boulder will be the first date on that tour. We play Boulder on the second and then we're out all the way

until February 28. Boulder is as far west as we're going. We work our way back east from Boulder.

Are you still based out of Nashville, or are you living in L.A.?
No, we all live in Nashville. We're still based out of there.

I used to live there. I actually used to run into you in the grocery store.
Oh, really?

Yeah. I worked for KMG Records for a while.
Oh, cool.

With [mutual acquaintance].
Oh, yeah. OK.

I used to see you play cello at church and stuff, which was cool.
Oh, very cool. What church did you go to?

Christ Church.
That's right. Yeah.

So it's definitely a cool thing. Have you talked to Steve Taylor recently, since the whole Squint thing?
Yeah, we talk fairly often, maybe like once every month and a half or so. I know he is kind of doing producing and still trying to get his film work off the ground and doing a lot of writing. So he is staying busy.

Well, that's cool. I know Word [Records] gave him a couple million dollars [It was actually under a million. -Ed.] to make a film, and last time I talked to him he was showing me these movies with Frank Stallone instead of Sylvester, and he was talking about maybe going that route, but I hadn't heard anything since.
Yeah, I think he's still pursuing that.

I know he went to film school out here in Boulder.
Oh yeah, he's from Boulder, isn't he?

Yeah, that is how I met him. He and I have a mutual friend—he was this guy's youth pastor for years.

What has the rise to commercial success been like for you? You started off independently with Gavin Morkel [R.E.X. Records] and those guys and then wound up with Steve [Taylor, Squint Entertainment], and you're fully a Warner Bros. band now.
It's definitely been slow. Sixpence has been plugging away at it for about ten years now. So it's definitely been kind of a slow rise, and [we had] a number of setbacks with Gavin's label, R.E.X. That thing folding, that set us back a little bit, and then with Squint and that whole thing kind of falling apart a couple years ago—that was definitely a setback. I think there are pros and cons to every situation. I think what was special about being on Squint and it being an indie label was it was a very family atmosphere. Everyone knew each other and was friends, and there was a certain level of camaraderie there and artistic freedom, I guess. That was really nice, but being a full Warner Bros. band now, I think you miss a little bit of that camaraderie, but the pros are having that big muscle behind you, that big power to kind of push your music out into the public. So it's good. Like everything, there are pros and cons, but I think we all feel really blessed to have been successful and to be able to do music for a living and make a good living at it and have people hear that music. A lot of people don't have that opportunity. I'm glad that we have risen this far, because you meet a lot of people that work just as hard as we have, if not harder, and have just as much talent as we do, if not more, that don't end up where we are at. So it's been a good ride for the most part.

I had heard that *Divine Discontent* was recorded quite a while ago. I'm sure by now you have a plethora of new songs. If you were to go in and record an album right now, what would it wind up sounding like?

Well, to be honest, there really aren't too many songs in the queue right now. The first version of *Divine Discontent* was done in the spring of 2000, and then from there over that two-year span before it came out, we were still writing and recording and getting more songs and recording and adding on to the record. So we were pretty much writing and recording all the way up to the release of that record. Since then we have been doing a lot of promotion and a lot of traveling to publicize it, and for me, personally, I don't write very well on the road. I kind of need those incubation periods at home to spark the creativity.

Was that a pretty taxing experience, having taken so long to record the record?
I think it was a little frustrating watching the momentum of the last record slip away because obviously we had worked so hard up until that self-titled record broke and then worked really, really hard promoting it after it broke and built up a lot of momentum for the band. I love being in the studio. That's one of my favorite parts of making music, so that part is not taxing for me. I think what was taxing was just sort of watching the years go by and watching the momentum slip away. I think we've definitely felt the impact of that with the release of this record—just sort of having to start over in a way. It just took a long time for us to get that record out.

With your songwriting, do you feel like you get too personal? Do you ever feel like you reveal too much?
Yeah—on this record it's probably to a fault. I've always written songs that way because songwriting for me has been a type of therapy or journaling or sort of just getting things out that are inside. But that's only one side of songwriting, and I think as far as the craft, you can't focus on that all the time. You have to kind of get outside yourself and write songs about things external and tell stories and whatnot. So yeah, there's probably some stuff on this record that is a little bit too revealing, but I think it also kind of goes along with what transpired in those few years. So it's a balance, I guess.

When I talked to Rick Gershon [publicist at Warner Bros. Records] yesterday, he mentioned you guys were taping a show—what show was that?
You mean the TV show we were doing yesterday? It was *Sabrina, the Teenage Witch.*

That's cool. What was that like?
It was really boring. It was a lot of hurrying up and waiting. I've never really seen the show, so I don't really know what it's like, but I guess it will air next month and we got to see what it's all about. But yeah, it was just a lot of hurrying up and waiting. Leigh [Nash, Sixpence's vocalist] had a few lines and she did great. So it was all right.

Was the rest of the band in the show, or was it only Leigh?
The whole band was performing in this club and Leigh has a few lines. She interacts with Sabrina a little bit, but the whole band is performing during some of the scenes.

When you originally did the Letterman [*Late Show with David Letterman*] show for the first time, what was that like for you? Was that a pretty stunning occurrence? I can't even imagine what that would be like, knowing that fifty million people are watching you.
Yeah, I mean most of us grew up watching that show, and I watched *Letterman* from a pretty young age, so it's really mind-blowing to be in the studio and playing on his show and seeing him sitting over there to your left. It was great. I think it's one of those moments that you cherish in your career and definitely one of the high points and definitely a sign that you've had some success. So it was a lot of fun.

Do you keep in touch with Chris Taylor [front person for defunct Christian rock band Love Coma, an amazing, passionate band that most have never heard of. Slocum was in the band at one time. Chris is a gifted songwriter, vocalist, guitarist and painter. -Ed.]?

I do. I haven't talked to him in a while, but I do try and keep in touch as much as I can.

I used to see him a lot when he'd come through Nashville. I know you did the Love Coma thing for a while. What are the future plans for the band? Do you have any in mind, or are you taking it day by day?
Well, I think I said before, we're just trying to regain some of the momentum that we had from the last record. That is just going to involve probably a lot of touring and working hard and just getting out there and playing for people and reconnecting with the fans and getting new fans. I think this year is going to be filled with a lot of touring and promoting this record and just trying to get ourselves back on the radar. That's kind of the short-term plan. I think the long-term plan [is that] we just want to keep putting out quality records and keep having a voice in the culture and keep making quality art, and hopefully at the end of the day we've got a good body of work to show for years.

Do you know if there are any plans in the works to tour with Sarah McLachlan?
I have no idea. It's something that would be great for us and would be really great if it worked out. We signed with Nettwerk Management last year, and they have been a great company to work with. They have got a really great roster of bands and it would be cool to open up for some of these groups, and she would be a prime candidate for us, but I don't know at this point. There are no plans in the works for that.

Maybe you guys can arrange a Neil Finn tour. That would be cool.
That would be amazing.

I just interviewed him last week. Amazing guy—just a very soft-spoken and genuine guy. Have you met him before?

No, I haven't. I've seen him play numerous times. I just think he is one of the best songwriters working today. He is just amazing.

Have you heard the version of *One*—it's the last record he did, but it's the European version—the one called *One Nil*?
Oh, yeah. I've heard both versions, but I had *One Nil* first and then they kind of remixed it and resequenced it and released it on Nettwerk as *One All* and, yeah, it's just an amazing, amazing CD.

Cool, Matt. I really appreciate it. Right now I am doing a "pick of the week" for the paper, which will spotlight you guys, but next time you are town, I would like to do a larger article, and I will make sure I mention that to Rick [Gershon]. I have that Neil Finn thing going on right now, so I am trying to fit everything in.
Yeah, good luck with that. That's amazing.

Yes, I mean awesome guy. But, again, I really appreciate it. If you happen to talk to Steve Taylor, tell him I said "Hi." I haven't seen him since we were at the same wedding a few years ago.
I got an e-mail from him the other day and I was going to try and hook up with him and Deb [Steve's wife and an amazing painter. –Ed.] for dinner before we left on the tour. I might see him next week and I will be sure to tell him "hello" for you.

OK, thanks a lot, Matt.
Thanks, Chris.

NEIL FINN

Monday, January 13, 2003
Article: *Boulder Weekly* **(February 6, 2003)**

Growing up in the suburbs forty-five minutes south of Boston was kind of lonely until I got involved in music and church. I met some great people around the time I was in the sixth grade. I was held back and had to repeat the first grade when we were living in Blacksburg, Virginia. Maybe I was developmentally challenged—perhaps I should have re-done my year of kindergarten. Listening to directions was not my strong point.

Somewhere in the recesses of my parents' basement, in a box unopened for twenty-plus years, there is probably a pumpkin cut out of construction paper with the eyes where the mouth should be and a tail for a nose. Creativity? Maybe. An example of living inside my own world? Certainly. But at six years old, the classroom was difficult for me. I never experienced those sorts of issues again, and with the exception of math and science, did really well in school.

Fast-forward seven or eight years, to when I was able to enter into the junior-high youth group at our church in Medway, Massachusetts. That's when I met Jason, an aspiring drummer. He and I formed a group (I use the term incredibly loosely, since neither one of us had much musical training). Jason would bang on my mom's cookie tins and use a big round metal-rimmed shipping container as his bass drum. We would discuss music and were both metalheads. I first listened to a Deep Purple album with Jason and felt guilty for days as they were on the list of "satanic" bands.

But most of the music we listed to was Christian metal. Jason first turned me on to Rez Band—at the time those guys sounded like AC/DC. He also introduced me to Whitecross, the Christian band that sounded very much like Ratt. In our band we wanted to emulate those guys, and we invited the oft-mentioned André Salles, another guy we knew from church, to join us. André was the only guy out of the three of us who could play, and the band never formulated. We'd go on youth-group hay rides and everyone would sing to people at retirement homes while drinking hot chocolate, and Jason, André and I would talk about the band, and that's about it. I did discover that André had a love for Crowded House, Squeeze and other pop acts. This wasn't my thing, but it didn't stand in the way of our friendship or our desire to play music together.

André and I kept spending more and more time together and actually did form a junior-high rock band called M.D. (It stood for Ministry Delivered—we delivered plenty, but great music certainly wasn't on the list.) We invited my friend Brian to play guitar. I don't know what I thought I'd do in the band—perhaps play rhythm guitar? I knew a few chords and how to make noise, but little more. I thought to myself, "Well, I'll sing. It can't be that hard." So we all got together and André and I quickly realized that Brian excelled at guitar. We couldn't think of anyone else in our age bracket who could do hammer-ons, solo and play "Stairway to Heaven." Also, Brian had equipment—a nice Peavey amp (only thirty watts or so, but who cared?) and an electric guitar with a whammy bar! We were excited and soon played a "gig" at a church gong show. My mom did her best to keep people from gonging us, but there's only so much you can do when your son's vocals are off-key at best and there's a Casio keyboard drum machine serving as the rhythm section. We were gonged.

We played twice more after adding a drummer, Dylan— once for the youth group André and I attended and once in a talent show. Of course, as most musical ensembles go, our band broke up, but between that and another musical project I did with André that was equally as bad (Obliterator—just the two of us and the aforementioned Casio keyboard drum machine), lots of material was recorded. Over the years, I've gone back and listened to the compositions. I've realized how good (for our time and age) some of the fledgling songwriting was and how structured the tunes were. André would sometimes criticize me as the metal guy and I would tell him I hated his cheesy pop, but in listening to the material, I've realized a lot of what I missed out on listening to during those early years of being a musician and music fan. Probably one of the keys to André being able to write tunes with hooks was the influence of bands like Squeeze and Crowded House.

As the years have gone by, I've also realized that what's always drawn me to a song is a good melody and/or a strong hook. Once I got over my prerequisite of music having to be heavy and equating heaviness with complexity, I discovered—years too late—bands like Tears for Fears, Squeeze and Crowded House. I also realized that what I thought was cheesy, disposable and lacking in complexity was anything but. Most of the artists I've grown to love aren't just skilled songwriters, but incredibly talented musicians with a heightened amount of musical aptitude.

After college, when I was living in Nashville, I got bit in the hindquarters by the power-pop bug and couldn't listen to much else. It started with Jellyfish and went on from there. A college rock station in Music City used to play a variety of different stuff, and when the single "She Will Have Her Way"—from Crowded House leader Neil Finn's debut solo album, *Try Whistling This*—came out, it received a steady amount of airplay. Who with any appreciation of pop wouldn't love that song? It was beautifully constructed. I went out and bought the disc, and while it was a bit more experimental than what I had expected, there were still a few songs that captured my senses.

While I was writing for the *Boulder Weekly*, another Finn solo disc, *One Nil*, was released as an import. Some time later, a live record, *7 Worlds Collide,* and the American version of *One Nil*, called *One All*, were put out by Nettwerk, and a U.S. tour was announced. The *Weekly* allowed me to write a piece to preview the New Zealander's upcoming show at Denver's Gothic Theatre. Finn was all I could have hoped for—insightful, engaging, and very friendly. He also had a great sense of humor and recalled a very funny instance from a stay in Denver during a previous tour.

****

I just have some questions for you—take them whatever direction you'd like.
OK.

What are your thoughts when you hear yourself on the radio now, such as the old Crowded House songs: "Don't Dream It's Over," "Something So Strong"—things like that?
Well, I generally don't realize it's me for a while. Actually, I suppose I do on the radio if it's on in the foreground. But, yeah, I have this great habit in places like the supermarket and shopping centers when my songs come on of not picking it up at all, and Sharon, my wife, is going, "Oh there we go. What is it?" And to me it sounds slightly like an annoying song that I used to know, until I realize what it is, of course. I actually enjoy it—having it in a variety of contexts that they crop up in. It feels a bit that it's become a part of the fabric of life or something.

And plus it's good for when people are buying groceries.
I think my music must be calming, because they put it on [in] the supermarket a lot. The one down the road, I almost always hear one of my songs in there. And some of the other stuff they play is fantastic and some of it's really appalling. So I don't know quite how I feel about it.

I guess that's what happens when you have been writing songs for a long time—you wind up with one of the songs being played in the supermarket.
Yeah, and lots of other places too, for that matter. Some people may get a little upset about their songs being in that context, but I figure if you treat the songs as children, you can't really choose who they sleep with or where they sleep.

I interviewed Tim [Finn, Neil's brother –Ed.] a couple years ago, and he was telling me how he waited a long time before he started a family.
Yeah.

He mentioned how you started off fairly young and started having kids—what was that like when you were having a music career and raising a family at the same time?

It was challenging. But you can only know what you do yourself as far as waiting to have—I don't think there's any recommended age to have children, really. I think we had them young because we had a solid marriage. It was a little bit of a surprise the first time, but not too much, and we thought, "It'll be a good sort of challenging thing that will keep us together." Ultimately, it was physically quite difficult, but we were young enough to be able to cope with lack of sleep and all that. When you are twenty-three or twenty-four, you survive that sort of stuff, and the rest of it is mentally challenging but not too difficult. I made a point early on of trying to have the family with me as much as possible on the road. It actually works a lot better than people might imagine. Kids are really great, and my ones were really great in that environment—they used to hang out with the crew, and it is a sense of community traveling around. I guess if I had been going for a whole Motley Crue kind of existence that may not have worked.

I heard that there's possibly another Finn Brothers record in the works?

That's more than a possibility at this point. We have got quite a number of songs written already, and we're just working toward the recording of that sometime probably by the middle of the year.

How do you and Tim write together? Do you ever fight? How do you work out any disagreements?

We write together in a variety of ways. Sometimes he'll bring a piece and I'll add something to it, or sometimes we'll be sitting there and something will just drop out of the ether between us. And if we're enthusiastic enough about the first idea, we usually finish it and it'll be really strong. Sometimes a phrase he'll bring along will spark an idea for me, or I will have a riff and Tim will start drumming because we write on

REEL TO REAL BY REEL

guitar and drums basically. He plays drums and I play guitar, so we get quite a big sound going straight away. And, yeah, we have taut, fraught moments—little things that are Achilles' heels between us. I don't know if that's the right expression, but there's things that will spark off intense arguments or whatever, but this is a brothers' relationship we're talking about, so most brothers could relate, but we pull each other back really quite quickly. There's never been any lasting feelings other than enjoying playing music together.

You released *One Nil*—I think it was a couple of years ago in Europe. What do you hope to accomplish with the *One All* album that just came out here?
It was just a quirk of timing at the stage that when *One Nil* came out everywhere else, I didn't have a current deal in America, so the album was nearly a year late being released in America, and I was able to tweak it a little bit to get it to a point where I think it's, to my ears, a better record than *One Nil*. So delayed but improved was the hope. In terms of what I'm hoping to achieve from it, I am not expecting *One All* to set the charts on fire. It seems that the area I am in now is— when I look at the charts, there are very, very few singer-songwriters that I would relate to in there. So I can only assume that whatever happens for this record happens in sort of an underneath sort of way—through really good record stores and through really good radio stations. I saw the evidence of that when I came through last time, and I will this time, I'm sure. There's a little bit of intensity in the shows that is indicative of an audience that's been there for a long time and really knows the songs. A sense of celebration and community almost.

That's great. The current tour that you are going to be starting in America—what is the lineup going to be? Who's going to be in the band?
Okay, well we've got Sebastian Steinberg on bass guitar.

Oh, he's great.

172 | P a g e

He's an amazing bass player, yeah, and I was lucky enough to have him last time as well. Lisa Germano on—well, bits of everything, and her beautiful voice. Scott McPherson is the drummer. And Shon Sullivan is the one who's playing guitar with me—aka Goldenboy.

So some of the same personnel from *7 Worlds Collide*?
Some of the same personnel. Not the extended bands, because they're all working on their respective bands at the moment.

You were mentioning with *One Nil* that you don't expect it to burn up the charts [Actually it was *One All*. –Ed.]. Is it hard to create the songs that you do? You seem to be very honest with your songwriting, and it seems a lot of the stuff at the top of charts right now is fluff. Is that frustrating for you?
Only occasionally. Most of the time I feel very blessed to have the situation I've got. I've had a long career with a few peaks and a few troughs, but I've luckily never gone downward to a place where I struggle to go and do tours or whatever. At the moment I am in a really great position. I have been able to come to America and play three weeks of shows where I know they'll all be full and audiences will be completely up for it and I count myself a very lucky man. I think the songs deserve better, but in terms of commercial success, it's great to hear them coming out of a radio, and I don't mean to sound too humble about this, but I am also very conscious of being very blessed, and I think with massive success comes a whole raft of issues I don't have to deal with, which I am quite pleased [about] as well.

During the Crowded House era, you probably had to deal with more of that.
Yeah, I've had at various times, and with Split Enz before that a couple of times, and I've enjoyed them all, but I think the long run of twenty-five years now of writing songs and being able to travel the world with them and having a really strong, solid audience is a really exciting thing.

Oh, definitely. I know your son Liam has a band and appears on the *7 Worlds Collide* DVD. Are you working with your son's band, or are you involved with them at all?

Not directly, other than providing a few meals here and there and a bit of space downstairs for them to rehearse in. And I give them the honored piece of advice, some of which is initially kind of ignored, but then stored away and comes back a few months later. I have to accept that now, that it's not generally right to immediately respond to what Dad says. You have to kind of work it in slowly.

What advice have you given Liam about the music business?

Well, various things come up, I suppose—situations with managers and record companies. We advise him generally not to sign anything until—he's nineteen now. I think he's old enough to make reasonable decisions with a lawyer to help him. I sort of advised him to stay away from it as much as possible until he was about this age, because they were a pretty good band even at the age of sixteen. There was potential there for some Svengali guy to go and say, "Oh, a young band. Perfect, let's launch them," but I didn't think that would be very good for him. And I suppose just kind of stick to your guns, you know, decide what your parameters are for engaging with the music industry and then stick to it, because consistency is the really important thing. I just advised them not to sort of go all out, do everything straight away—all the interviews, magazines, papers, newspapers and then after a couple of years go, "Oh, I hate all of that stuff. I'm not going to do anything any more." I think that is a natural reaction to getting publicity. But I think you've just got to kind of decide early on what you can bear and then stick to it.

You have probably heard and experienced all kinds of horror stories regarding the business and publicity and whatnot, so is it hard for you not to give him as much advice as you would like to?

Yeah, I have to stand by a little bit and just let him have his own experience of it. You've got to acknowledge when you are an adult that your advice is not necessarily right anyway for your children. There will be some wisdom in there, but everybody's experience is different. But he's turned out to have a pretty solid head on his shoulders, so I am not too concerned about him anyway. [At] the odd time, I will suggest he goes back and try some vocal again if I think he can do it better, but that's about the size of it now.

Vocally, your albums have always been exquisite. You have always had the vocal harmonies, and so that's probably part of those areas where you have a really good ear for that and can probably hear things that he can't.
Well, he's still developing as a singer and he's getting better and better all the time, so it's very pleasing to watch. And the thing that's good about his voice is that it's got its own sound. You know it's him when he is singing. That's hard—that's not necessarily an easy thing to find.

What's it like to be doing what you have been doing for so long and to still have such incredibly dedicated fans?
It's a joy. I can honestly say that. The last tour of America that I did—and this is the same in other countries too—maybe because I hadn't been to the U.S. for a while on the last tour, I walked on stage every night and there was a sense of—I can't describe it really, other than saying it was a celebratory sort of feeling and a communal feeling, and it just felt like something was gonna happen. There was a great energy in the room, and I think that as a performer or as a musician, you just can't ask for more than that. I think that the years that have passed have actually intensified that experience for the people that have come along. I can honestly say I am enjoying playing shows more than I ever have.

On the *7 Worlds Collide* video, there is an interview with Lisa Germano and she mentioned that she thought she could pick up all your songs by ear and had difficulty

doing that because of the song structures and the chords and the keys.

Because they were all black keys.

Is that something that you consciously—is that just how you write, or do you consciously try to be a little different in your selection of key and chord structure?

I am not conscious of much of it, really. All the keys on the piano and the guitar are open to me, and I often find myself in flats, and that's because they sound like more interesting chords not often heard. And then there's just the odd difficulty for the bands I have. It's great, I think, for a listening experience because it means the songs sound less predictable, but for a band trying to learn them, it's a real bastard.

Well, with the band Squeeze, a lot of their stuff seems to be pretty straight-ahead and you can pretty much predict where it's going to go [Squeeze is an fantastic band, and Chris Difford and Glenn Tilbrook are incredible songwriters, so I'm not sure where I was going with this comment. –Ed.], and then you put on one of your records and its like, "Whoa, this is still really melodic, and it may even be in a minor key, but it's still really catchy." So it's interesting that she made that comment.

Yeah, well the ultimate downside of that is that I am the one who has to teach—well, since Crowded House broke up, I have had to teach dozens of people my songs, and it's quite a trial. You've got to go, "No, I'm sorry; in the second verse it doesn't do the same thing." So really it all comes back on me.

You did some songwriting with Jim Moginie from Midnight Oil—are you going to be working with him again at all?

Well, I wouldn't be surprised at some point, but I'm not sure when exactly. So, yeah, that's certainly a vague answer, isn't it? I really enjoyed working with Jim, so yeah, I wouldn't be surprised.

He seems to write songs in new and different ways too.
Oh, yeah. He's an interesting musician and a great guitar player. I love the way he plays guitar.

Is there anything that stands out in your career that has been particularly humorous that might be a story that you tell people about what you've done touring, anything like that?
Oh, these are always really hard to think of at the time. There have been thousands of things that have been humorous. Where are we now? You are in Boulder.

Yes.
OK, a humorous story from Boulder.

Or Denver.
Or Denver. Yeah, something's coming to me now. Yes, well in Denver—the last time I was in Denver was on the *Try Whistling This* tour. We have a particular fondness for toast, coming from this part of the world, late at night; particularly after a show. We had the impression that every hotel we were staying at had twenty-four-hour room service, so it's generally not a problem. Well, I came back to the Denver hotel very shortly after the show and rang up for toast and tea, which was the norm, and the guy there said, "No, we don't do toast." And I said, "Well, it's really so easy. Have you got bread?" He said, "Yes, we've got bread." "You got a toaster?" "Yup, we got a toaster." And I said, "Well, why don't you do toast?" He said, "It's after midnight. We only do cold sandwiches." And I got involved in this ridiculously heated conversation about probably the most ridiculous subject on Earth, really—toast. As it turned out, he just refused to do it for me even though it would have been the easiest thing in the world. We had all the band ring up, and my sons were on the tour too—everyone rang the guy up in the next half hour just asking for toast. We pursued the man, and the poor guy really lost it big time and got screamingly angry and the next

morning—unfortunately, we didn't really intend this, but he got the sack.

The on-duty manager came and one of our party was talking to him about it, and as the story grew, the guy was given the sack. A cautionary tale for those who work in the hotels that we're about to visit.

You would think he'd be able to make toast.
Well, it seems like it's the most simple thing in the world, doesn't it? I, unfortunately, don't lose my temper in the right situations, which is probably where I am facing injustice—true injustice—or bigotry. I lose my temper when I can't get toast.

It's probably just aggression from other areas coming out ...
It's finding its way out. There's something that's disturbing about taking out all your repressed anger on some complete innocent stranger.

Well, you know, the more angry you are, the darker the toast.
The darker the toast, the better the music.

Exactly. That will look good in bold. You have probably been asked this a dozen times or probably more than that—probably thirty-six times or three thousand six hundred times—any chance for a Split Enz or Crowded House reunion?
No—I mean, there are certainly no plans at the moment. It depends on a lot of things, so I can't really fully answer that one. It's not an interest for me, and any of those kinds of things would be far greater if a Split Enz reunion, for instance, included the very early lineup of the band that was before my time, so I can come and see it. When you're in it, it's sort of different. There's always the motivation of money to do it, but it's never seemed to me to be a good enough one on its own.

Sure, I can understand that. Well, Neil, thank you so much for doing this. Is there anything special that people can expect from the Denver appearance besides the request for toast?

Now we'll have toast being thrown up on stage. I just know it. It will be a band that's completely one hundred percent committed to the show and a lot of good music and [some] intensity, I think. That's all I can really promise. The details of it will be worked out on that night with the audience.

Sure. Well, thanks again, Neil. I look forward to seeing the show. Hopefully, when this article comes out it will raise some interest and hopefully the show sells out.

STRYPER
(MICHAEL SWEET)

Friday, September 5, 2003
Article: *Boulder Weekly* (October 23, 2003)

Jeff, my neighbor who lived in back of me during my formative years in Norfolk, Massachusetts, called me one day. I was probably eleven at the time and was undoubtedly trying my hardest to avoid doing Saturday morning chores. (Am I the only one who can still smell Pledge furniture polish when I least expect it?) This was the same Jeff who listened to Rush's *Moving Pictures* album with me during summer afternoons following an exciting game of Wiffle ball or a game of guns (when toy guns actually looked real, instead of a glow-in-the-dark bright orange).

Jeff was a drummer and a Christian, so we shared a lot in common. He introduced me to a lot of cutting-edge Christian rock. Rock music itself was absent in many evangelical Christian churches at the time. It wasn't like it is today, with drum sets and electric guitars in most modern churches— rock back then was often suspect and even "of the devil" in certain circles. It was like a lot of things that people failed to examine and use wisdom in trying to understand—it was easier to pass judgment on something because of how it looked rather than try to understand what it truly was and get to the heart of what the artists were trying to say.

Anyway, Jeff called me and was all excited and wound up. "Hey guess what?" he asked. "I went to Logos today (Logos was one of the only Christian bookstores in the area) and got a cassette. It's this band, Stryper—a metal band but they're Christians." I was mystified. "But get this," he said, "their tape, *Soldiers Under Command*, has a military van on it, painted yellow and black, and they have guns—some look like the submachine guns on *The A-Team*, the ones you said were made by Ruger. And I think there may be an M16 or Uzi too. And they list the Bible verse Isaiah 53:5 on the cover—and they are really good."

I think even then I knew that this would go over about as well with my mom as when I was four and asked if I could add the f-word to my vocabulary. But the urge to hear this band was stronger than my fear. "Wow, Jeff, can I copy it or borrow it?"

"Well, yeah, but it'll be a while. I'm digging this, so much better than Petra."

I was a tad bit pissed. Jeff had a thin Sony double-cassette boom box and could have easily made me a copy. We would both buy bricks (ten in a package) of Maxell ninety-minute cassette tapes. It was ten dollars for the package, and you could easily fit two albums on one cassette, unless the album went beyond forty-five minutes in length. I'm sure I had a blank cassette lying around.

But the Petra comment—I understood. I just could not get into that band at the time. When kids talked about Christian hard rock in the mid-'80s, it usually ended in a discussion of the hugely successful Christian arena-rock band Petra. They were an excellent rock band, but they were a far cry from metal. Stryper was different. They were a legitimate metal band and even recorded on a "secular" record label.

It wasn't that Stryper was the first Christian metal band, but they were the first to gain national attention as a mainstream band on a mainstream label with huge respect from at least a sizeable contingent of the "secular" metal crowd and even mainstream rock fans. Bands like Jerusalem and Resurrection Band had been turning up the volume since the mid-'70s, and after Stryper started gaining ground, an influx of Christian metal bands sprouted up due to their popularity. The rest is history and has been recorded well—if this is of interest, I strongly recommend checking out *HM*, a magazine that is now strictly online. No one has done a better job of recording and cataloging the genre than founder and former owner/editor Doug Van Pelt.

I became a huge fan of the burgeoning Christian metal movement. I was able to see several of the prominent Christian metal bands perform in their prime, and I did get to see Stryper live a few times—the first time in 1988, after the release of their album *In God We Trust*. I found out they were coming to the Worcester Centrum and quickly purchased tickets, assuming that a girl I liked from my junior high class was going to come. However, her answer was "no," and so fellow Stryper fan André Salles came with me.

The show itself was awe-inspiring. Hurricane, a Poison-like band and Stryper's labelmates, opened. Stryper's stage setup was unbelievable. They had a drum set that spun around on a drum riser with water that shot out of the sides of the elevated platform. The lights, the sound—it was unlike anything I had experienced prior.

I anticipated that show like few others. In fact, I went to the bathroom nine times before Stryper went on just so I wouldn't miss a song. To this day, I have a small bladder due to that show. The psychology took over.

I first interviewed Michael Sweet, Stryper's lead vocalist, in 1996 during a college project and was able to interview him again for the *Boulder Weekly* in 2003 as Stryper was doing a reunion tour. Michael was very thorough in answering each question asked, and it was a pleasure speaking with him. The reunion show, while not as over-the-top as the first performance I had seen, was still an impressive display of skill and showmanship. My friend Dan and I walked away from Denver's Ogden Theatre on the night of Friday, Oct. 24, surprised we had had such a good time and that the guys could still pull off an excellent show. It's not surprising that the band did regroup a while later, with most of the same lineup, and has continued to this day.

Whenever I think of Stryper, I can't forget the poster I had of the band hanging up in my bedroom when I was fourteen. My grandmother happened to glance up at the poster one day and said, while pointing at drummer, Robert Sweet, "Why isn't she pretty!"

[A quick conversation about Doug Van Pelt, creator of *HM*, took place for a moment before the "official" interview questions. Doug is someone we both know and a person who gave me my real start in journalism—if it wasn't for his kindness, I may never have gone into writing. He also has been incredibly supportive of Stryper and of Michael's solo efforts. -Ed.]

****

I just have some questions. Take them wherever you want to. Obviously they are going to have to do with the [Stryper] reunion. I guess the first question is, why the reunion?
We went in and recorded a couple new songs, which hopefully everyone knows about. I just figured since we did those songs and there's this new record out, why don't we go do a few shows? We originally were talking about the possibility of doing eight to ten shows. That turned into eighteen to twenty shows, and then it turned into thirty-one, thirty-two shows, which is where we are at now. It's an opportunity to go out and encourage some people that have been wanting to see a Stryper show for a long time and to also go out and have fun together again as a band—reunite for this one-off thing, this one-time deal. Go out and have a good time. We're not definitely officially back together as a band. A lot of people seem to think that we are. We're not. This is just basically a one-time, celebration-type tour. Get together, go out and have fun and then go our separate ways again. What the future holds—I don't know. I'm not saying "no" to anything down the road, but you know what I mean. So that's where we're at. And we're going out and doing it. It's right around the corner. Rehearsals start on the twenty-fourth of this month for shows on the second of October.

How has the response been from the public so far?
It's been really good. I'm a little upset over the label side of things, and I'm a guy who speaks really free and open, so I probably offend and upset people often.

[Discussion of frustrations and concerns over *7: The Best of Stryper*, an album released earlier that year. -Ed.]

183 | P a g e

And it's just really sad, because I think it could be an incredibly successful time to go out and tour and to meet many, many people, but unfortunately it's not as it was originally planned. Now, hopefully this will be a success. We're playing clubs—larger clubs—and hopefully everything will go well. And it's not that it's about the money, it's just you want everyone to be happy, the promoters to be happy, so they want to bring you back, and there's just so much that goes into the soup, and if people aren't happy and they lose their shirt, then it's a bad thing. It takes everyone working together to make it happen and I just really feel like the ball was totally dropped, you know?

How has everyone changed since you were together before? Was it easier or harder to play together?
In some regards it was easier; in others it was harder. The fact that everyone's continued playing music made it easier because everyone's somewhat kept their chops up and that whole thing, but everyone has kind of gone a different direction musically. So it was a little more difficult to be on the same page. You know what I mean? Not that difficult, but just a little difficult at times. Really, to be honest with you, it was almost like we just kind of picked up the ball and continued right on where we left off. It was pretty cool.

Has the approach to some of the older songs changed? When the Police performed at their induction into The Rock and Roll Hall of Fame, it sounded different. Are you keeping it the same?
We are going to, for the most part, keep it the same. It's going to be like stepping right back into 1986, '85. We might throw in some different endings and different beginnings, you know, things like that. But for the most part it's going to be the same.

Will the spandex make a return?
No. The guitars will be yellow and black. The drums will be yellow and black—yellow and black scrims in front of the amps. Probably mainly black clothing. I'm going to wear a lot

of black clothing. I have some leather pants and some black pants and some black shirts—lots of black. It's just kind of been my thing. But you're not going to see a lot of yellow and black clothes.

I just thought I would ask. I wasn't sure how much back into it—if you guys were going to do the full ...
No, we are not doing the big hair, full make-up, full glitzy yellow and black clothes—nah. To be honest with you, even if we had the resources and the finances, I don't know that we would do that. But we don't have the resources and the finances to be able to do that. I remember we'd have four outfits made from Ray Brown—who did Whitesnake and Bon Jovi—[and] it would cost us sixteen grand. And that stuff's not cheap, and we can't fit into the stuff we had before.

Come on—you're not still twenty-five?
I am still slim and trim, but man, your body changes. It's funny how that happens, but it happens.

It's like the episode of *Seinfeld* where Kramer tries to go back to wearing jeans.
Exactly. And it would be silly anyways if we put on those old outfits. If we had new ones made, that would be cool, but we don't just have the resources or the finances or the time to do that.

Several years ago you told me a story about a glass eye—can you repeat it?
Basically, we were in Australia. We were playing to a large crowd in an arena. We were in the middle of a song—I think it was "Free." I noticed this guy right at my feet—right down in the pit, screaming and pointing and screaming and pointing and screaming and pointing. The guy was really, really upset and frantic, you know, worked up. And he looked kind of like a pirate-type character—red bandana, beard stubble, earrings, tattoos, missing teeth—that whole thing. And I didn't really think much of it, and after a few minutes of this, I started to wonder, "Gosh, what's going on?" So he was

pointing at my feet. I looked down and I saw what appeared—registered in my mind—what appeared to be a piece of gum that someone had rolled into a ball in their mouth or in their hands and spit out or whatever, and he was warning me about gum. "Oh you are going to step in gum." Don't ask me why. That is kind of stupid, but that is what I thought it was. So at the right opportunity, I hit a chord—a sustaining open chord, and I bent down and I flicked what I thought was gum off the stage way out into the crowd and the thing went flying. But when I flicked it with my middle finger, it hurt. It was like flicking a marble. And the thing was just gone, and at that time I went back up to continue playing the song, and I could hear the guy screaming like twice as loud. And veins bulged in his neck and he was just furious. After a few minutes of hearing this guy scream and stuff—it was hard to make out because he had a really thick Australian accent, he was spreading apart his eyelid and there was—I looked, and there was nothing in his eye. It was just this open hole. After we ended the song, I could hear him saying, "That was my eye. That was my glass eye," and he was trying to warn me that his glass eye was on the stage, it popped out and could he have it back. So I flicked it. It was gone. It was crushed, probably. The guy never got his glass eye back. It's a true story. It's a very odd story, but it really happened and it was very uncomfortable. I didn't know what to say to the guy. I couldn't look at the guy for the rest of the show.

That's the type of story that *Spin* needs to run because they always do those stories in the back.
It was bizarre. After the show I told everyone what had happened and no one believed me. It was weird.

You are still living in Massachusetts doing the cranberries and stuff?
I'm not doing the cranberries anymore. I was for a while. It was a family-owned business, campground. On the property—it's like eight hundred-plus acres, four hundred campsites on the property, [and] there are eleven bogs. Like

really big bogs. So that's their other half of the business. I worked at the campground. My wife kind of ran the office, which she did growing up. They have owned it since she was born. She ran the office, and I helped people to their site and went around and made sure all the campfires were put out at night, drove around in a big Jeep. Everyone called me Ranger Mike. And I worked in the cranberry bogs. Actually from this time—from like right now through to the end of October, [I] would harvest the cranberries and corral them and load them on trucks and put on hip waders and get out there with rakes. It's quite a job. It's serious physical labor. It was a lot of work, but it was fun. It was a whole other life, man. I did that for about five years, four-and-a-half years.

What are you doing now?
I've been producing. I've been blessed and fortunate enough to be able to produce. I've produced a number of bands over the last three years at Kenny Lewis' studio called Mixed Emotions. That's where I do a lot of my work. I did the first version of *Truth*, the *Him* record, the "O Holy Night" single. I'm going to be doing the new record. So I work out of that studio and I've produced just a whole list of bands.

Is Ken based in Nashville?
Kenny Lewis? No, he's based in Massachusetts. He's up in Middleton—it's about seventy-seven miles from my house. It's quite a commute, but it's a great studio. It's a basement studio. He converted his basement and it's a finished basement and he's got [a] Pro Tools rig, two-inch analog machine—nice gear, man. ProControl, he's got an analog console, tons of outboard gear, tons of mics. It's like the best studio in town. Bang for the buck, you are not going to find any other place that even comes close.

And Pro Tools, I mean, it's such a relief to be able to make a mistake and go back and ...
Absolutely. He charges—I think his rate is four hundred twenty-five a day. His block rate. If you took that studio and put it in Nashville or L.A., he could probably get a thousand a

day, maybe more. His rates are unbelievable. And he knows his stuff. He's a Berklee grad of engineering. He's a drummer. He reads music. He's solid. I mean, he's one of those guys that could fix anything and just very smart and bright and musically bright. He's a rare find. You don't find a place like that here.

Oz [Fox] and Tim [Gaines] and Robert [Sweet]—what are they doing?
Well, Robert, I guess, is playing in a band called Blissed and doing some other things on the side. I don't really know a whole lot of what he's doing on the side, to be honest with you. I will find out, because I'm going to see him in a couple weeks. Tim is managing a music store, and I guess he and his wife, Irene, are preparing to move from the L.A. area out to Nashville. And then Oz is heading up a facility of JBL. He's been there for a long time, actually, soon after the band broke up. I think he started there in '93 or '94 and he's been there ever since.

Good speakers.
Oh yeah. Great speakers, great components. He's still doing music. He's got a band called Sin Dizzy.

Wasn't Tim in that band for a while?
Tim was in the band. They parted ways. Tim's basically musically working with Irene, his wife. She is a singer/songwriter. He is producing her stuff and co-writing with her, and they are really going after that. Real different. It's more acoustic rock, folk-type stuff.

What do you hope people take away from this reunion?
I just hope that people leave happy and encouraged, uplifted, hopefully renewed. Anyone that has problems, who is struggling—hopefully they'll come to the show and they'll leave renewed with an extra boost to go out there and get through this life, because that's what's important to us, is the message and being able to one-on-one affect people's lives

and help people's lives. That is really what is important to me.

When you go on this tour, you're going to find a lot of people that became Christians early on in your career through your ministry, and it's probably going to be incredible for you guys to hear these stories.
Well, I hope so. My gosh. It is. It will be. If we do come across a lot of people like that, it will be incredible. And to see the fruit and see what came from the ministry of Stryper—from the music of Stryper—it's going to be amazing, you're right. That'll make it worth it right there—worth the price of admission.

It's like Mike Peters of the Alarm. He said he got all these letters from people saying they turned away from suicide because of a song he wrote.
Yeah.

And he said that is much more important to him than any gold records he has.
Absolutely. That's what matters in the end. The gold records don't have souls, you know. They don't go to heaven or hell, and we as people do. We have to make choices and meet our Maker someday, and that's what matters—eternity and life after death and where we're all going from here. That's really the only thing that matters, and the choices we make to get to that point. That's all that matters.

Well, Michael, I really appreciate it. Thanks a lot for doing this.
Hey man, no problem. Thank you for calling and for allowing me the time to speak. I look forward to seeing you out on the road if you can make it to a show.

STEVE TAYLOR

Probably in late March or early April 2006
Article: *HM* (Issue 120: July/August 2006)

Steve Taylor is one of those people who have commanded and been given my utmost respect.

My first "real" concert experience was seeing Steve play at Gordon College in Wenham, in the school's gymnasium, the usual Massachusetts stop for most Christian artists back in those days (sometimes Eastern Nazarene College's gym would be used instead). I believe Dan Russell—the guy who managed Vigilantes of Love, was a figurehead in the New England Christian music scene and started the magazine *NewSound*—was somehow involved with the show. Dan was always bringing in cutting-edge artists, along with the mainstays. And I can certainly thank Dan for pointing me in the direction of the Alarm, World Party and, eventually, Bruce Cockburn.

For this particular New England visit, Mr. Taylor was touring behind his latest record, *I Predict 1990*. My friend Brian and I were really into the cassette version I had purchased during a church retreat in New Hampshire (most people my age didn't have CD players yet). As I mentioned earlier in this book, he and I were in a band with André Salles, a frequent guest in these pages. Brian had his guitar teacher at Walpole Music instruct him on how to play "Babylon," from *I Predict 1990*, so I knew he had become a true fan. I also realized that Brian would probably be interested in coming with me to see Steve play. I'm not sure if I bought the tickets (ten dollars in advance) or if my dad or mom bought them. Regardless, on Thursday, April 14, 1988, my dad, our youth pastor Wes, Wes's young son, Luke, Brian and I took the church van up to Wenham.

The sound in the gym was horrible, but I still was excited to see the opener, Whitecross—maybe even more excited than I was to see Steve. I was a Christian metalhead at the time and had recently spent a lot of time listening to their debut album. They were the Christian sound-alike to Ratt and had a guitar player who could play miles around most other players in metal, Christian or mainstream. They didn't disappoint.

Steve took the stage soon after Whitecross ended and had a crack band with him. The performance more than made up for the horrific sound. It's difficult to make a live performance sound good in a gym. Wes's son, Luke, poor guy, had cotton stuffed in his ears as Whitecross had dealt him a good sound lashing, so I don't know how much he heard. I'm not sure if my dad enjoyed the show, but he certainly didn't hate it, and I have to hand it to him for supporting me by going. Wes, Brian and I had a great time—Steve is just one of those gifted entertainers.

I also have to hand it to Wes. He was one of the first people I met in the church who didn't club mainstream rock on the head and try and kick it to hell. He once said, "Chris, it's important to listen to both mainstream and Christian rock. Balance is good. Don't completely rid yourself of Christian music, but there's a lot of good stuff out there that doesn't necessarily have a Christian market label." Understandably, he was also a big U2 fan back before *The Joshua Tree* launched the band into superstardom.

Steve's show was as theatrical as it was musical. He catapulted onto the stage, dressed in an ice cream truck outfit and throwing water balloons, to start the first tune, "I Blew Up the Clinic Real Good," a satirical tune about an ice cream truck driver who decides to blow up abortion clinics because he's afraid he will no longer have any clients. While the song is tongue-in-cheek and certainly doesn't support violence of any kind, it definitely opens room for thought, as Taylor's songs always do.

Three years after that show, I moved to Colorado with my family. Steve Taylor had spent a good number of his formative years there, so when I moved to the Denver area, I hoped I would somehow run across him. I had just delved into his excellent album with the band Chagall Guevara—a disc that took Steve's talents to a whole other level. It was a mainstream rock record, released on major label MCA, and the songs and musicianship were staggering.

While he had his large fan base in the States and in Europe, this record could have displayed Steve's song craft in front of millions and largely outside of the Christian market. Unfortunately, the Chagall Guevara record didn't get its proper time in the spotlight, despite the single, "Violent Blue," and the fact that the band had a tune, "Tale O' the Twister," in the movie *Pump up the Volume*.

Anyway, my first year in Colorado had a lot of this record playing in the background. It was that good, and it still holds up. Later on, I would try and play the bass parts on the album and realize just how skilled Wade Jaynes was at handling the low end on his Gibson Thunderbird. And the drums—something about the drum sound of that album, especially the snare, still causes me to drool a little at times. Of course, Mike Mead was a fantastic drummer and I had been listening to him for years, starting with the work he did with Christian artist Rick Cua.

When I entered my freshman year of college a couple years after hearing Chagall Guevara, I was in a communications class with a guy named Bob. He was older than the rest of us by five or six years, I'd say. I was the youngest on the roster anyway, as it was a junior- and senior-level class, but that didn't seem to matter. I still remember it fondly. Jeff Johnson, our professor, was a kind, compassionate man full of godly wisdom. Bob and I quickly became friends and often discussed Steve Taylor. He actually had Steve as a youth pastor many years before at Steve's dad's church in Northglenn. Once, out of the blue, he told me Steve was going to come speak at his youth group. I went and listened. It was incredibly interesting.

After Bob was done with school, he and I kept in touch. When I moved to Nashville after graduation, I gave him a call and asked if he thought Steve might be able to give me some advice on my job search. Steve was running a record label called Squint Entertainment at the time, and I wanted to get into the music industry. Bob was quick to reply and said, "Sure, Chris, let me see if I can get in touch with him for you."

I soon forgot all about my conversation with Bob, thinking that Steve and I would never meet. I mean, why would he have time for me? He was busy running a record label with artists like Sixpence None the Richer and Chevelle. One day I was out with my friend Shawn, eating the chicken tenders basket at the Applebee's about a mile from my apartment off of Old Hickory Boulevard and 70 South. Applebee's was one of the few places Shawn would eat, so we were limited. It was chicken or chicken. No Chinese food, no Italian food, just chicken. He was a great guy, but we did have that harmless limitation. Let's just say that I no longer like the chicken tenders basket—or chain restaurants at all, for that matter, and, last I heard, Shawn was the food and beverage manager for a restaurant. I'm guessing his palate has expanded.

I bid Shawn good night and came back from my chicken basket to an answering machine message. I pressed the button, thinking that it might be Christian singer/songwriter Michael W. Smith calling for my roommate, as they'd go see movies together—but, no, it was Steve Taylor and the message was for me. "Hey, Chris, it's Steve Taylor. I'd love to help you as much as I can. Bob gave me a call and told me about your job search. Please give me a call on Monday and we'll set up a time for you to come by the office."

I showed up at Steve's office in the Word Records building in the West End area of Nashville at the designated time. He went out of his way to chat with me and offer advice. We then discussed his affinity for filmmaking. He mentioned how he had just been given a sizeable sum of money to make a film. It was under a million dollars—not a huge sum when it comes to making a movie, as Steve explained, but it was still something. He walked over to a bookshelf filled with VHS tapes and started pulling some out, explaining how one of the ways to get attention was to get actors who were related to other famous actors. Instead of Sylvester Stallone, you'd use Frank Stallone. It saves you money and gives you that name recognition. He showed me the covers of a bunch of videos

REEL TO REAL BY REEL

from his shelf where the filmmakers did just that. I could tell Steve was excited about the prospect of making a movie. He always had tons of energy and it was certainly evident that day in his office. I mean, if you're not touring, dressing up in an ice cream vendor uniform and throwing water balloons, you've got to channel it somewhere!

The best part of the meeting, however, was at the end, when Steve asked, "Hey Chris, do you mind if I pray for you regarding your job search before you leave?" I didn't decline and walked away with an increased appreciation for a true creative genius.

Steve and I would run into each other from time to time during my tenure in Nashville, once even sitting at the same table at an out-of-state wedding, and he was always friendly and willing to chat. When I left Nashville and moved back to Colorado, I still touched base with him once or twice a year.

In 2006, Steve made a film called *The Second Chance*. I heard about the movie and pitched an article idea to Doug Van Pelt at *HM*. Doug liked the idea, even though it wasn't a music-based piece. He realized the quality and importance of Steve's art. Mr. Taylor and I were soon in touch and had a phone interview where we discussed *The Second Chance* and his choice of Michael W. Smith (the legendary Christian pop singer and the same guy who hung out with my old Nashville roommate) as the film's lead. He was the same down-to-earth, humble guy I had met years earlier—when I called him, he had just finished having a dodgeball game with his young daughter that involved a wadded-up piece of tape

Steve has since gone on to release the film *Blue Like Jazz*, based on the best-selling book. The film hit theaters nationwide in the spring of 2012 and is available on DVD. About a year before the film's release, I sent him an e-mail asking how the movie was coming along and he replied by asking, in his comical manner, "Chris, do you happen to have a million dollars buried in your backyard?"

I wish Steve the best as he continues with his creative endeavors, including his return to the music world as a performer in the band, Steve Taylor & the Perfect Foil. He is truly gifted.

****

How are things going with you, by the way?
Everything's good! I don't know if you heard, [but] I am a new dad—my wife and I had kind of an unplanned adoption when we were in Africa and we ended up meeting a little girl over there and decided to adopt her. It was a long process, and we are finally able to bring her home. We have had her for a year now. And she is just a really great kid.

Congrats!
She spoke no English when we got her. She has picked it up quickly. She is very lively and just a really great kid. We've been married twenty years with no kids, so it's quite a change all of a sudden having a nine-year-old African around the house, but it's also good.

I'm sure you have plenty of energy. I have seen you live.
Yeah, right.

All the youth pastor stuff is probably coming back?
That's right. We just finished playing a game of dodgeball with a wadded-up piece of foil, and so that was kind of bringing it all back for me.

Old Crossroads Baptist. What caused you to be interested in making movies? I know that you went to CU (University of Colorado) for film school. That was prior to doing any youth pastor work, wasn't it?
It was actually around the same time, because I started going into the youth pastor [position] the summer before I started at CU. At first, the youth pastor job was just supposed to be temporary until they found somebody—you know, professional—and then I was doing it for five years. Yeah, so I was studying film in college. It was a fairly new department, and they were very avant-garde-leaning. Possibly America's most famous avant-garde filmmaker at that point, Stan Brakhage, was kind of the mentor of the department, and so that was a lot of the direction the classes leaned. Of course, I

was more interested in narrative filmmaking. I think the first short that I did was a comedy—it was mostly comedy. So that was what I was doing back then.

I remember seeing one of your shorts. It was about a car salesman, I think.
That's right. It was based on a true story of a man and a wife who tried to trade up their baby on a Corvette. And I [made] it mostly for laughs, but I did kind of like the premise. It seemed totally absurd. It was unbelievable that it actually happened, but I thought that it was kind of a funny take on consumer culture. [It] just felt like a good topic to try to do a short on, and it was fun. Overall, it was a good experience. I pretty much did everything from start to finish—writing it all the way through to editing it, and then ultimately taking it through the sound process and out to film print. So it was very instructive from that standpoint as well.

The whole process was probably a lot harder back then.
It was. Yeah. Well, I was editing on one of those flatbeds, and of course you are cutting film together as opposed to doing it all in a nonlinear environment on a computer screen. So I actually started doing this totally old-school because the way movies are made really didn't fundamentally change, technology-wise, until now. Outside of the invention [of] sound—basic technology was always the same and it really hasn't changed until just recently with the advent of nonlinear editing and then, of course, high definition and all that stuff. It's all experiencing the change now, but it's still very much a traditional method.

With *The Second Chance*—was that filmed on film or was it video?
That was filmed on thirty-five millimeter film.

Oh, wow.
Yeah, even when I was shooting music videos—luckily, I always shot on thirty-five millimeter. I just didn't think anything else could touch the look of it.

Sure.
And the stuff always looked better, and so I kind of became a snob, and, of course, [when] you're on a tight budget, shooting on thirty-five millimeter takes up a pretty big chunk of that tight budget. But I just really wanted to. I had done a little bit of experimenting with high def just to see what might happen. The more I checked it out, the more I was pretty sure I wasn't going to like it. So [I] shot on thirty-five.

What was it about high def that you didn't like?
When you're shooting something that has a lot of outdoor stuff, I think that's where it really shows its limitations, especially in any kind of bright daylight.

Didn't Steven Soderbergh do a movie where he shot everything on high-definition video?
He did. In fact, I'm not even sure it was high def. I thought it might've been DVCAM. He had done *Full Frontal* on DVCAM [A good portion of the movie was shot that way per a little bit of Internet research. –Ed.] I haven't seen it yet, but I thought that might have been on DVCAM too. There's movies that I've seen that I thought were well done. The last *Star Wars* movie was shot entirely on high def, but they pretty much never left the studio, so that the lighting was always controlled. There are movies like *28 Days Later* that were shot on DVCAM, that I thought was a perfect use for the medium and actually made it more interesting, but there [are] not that many projects like that.

What led to *The Second Chance*? I remember in '97, I was speaking with you and you were talking about doing a movie and that Word (Records) was going to finance one?
That's right. Yeah, I actually had the money to do it. It wasn't a lot. It was like an eight hundred and fifty thousand dollar budget, I think. I had a story premise. We worked a long time on the script—Ben Pearson, my longtime collaborator, and then another guy, Willie Williams, and, man, after all that work we did a table reading where you get actors around a

table. It started off pretty well, and the more we got further into act two, the more sort of overcooked and convoluted it all felt, and it just wasn't working. I put that one on the back burner and had this other idea for something that felt a little more appropriate for a first film and certainly something that wasn't quite so—how do I want to put it? This movie—it's a movie that a more experienced filmmaker would need to make.

Sure.

So *The Second Chance* was writing things that I felt I knew those worlds pretty well and would be able to hopefully bring something new to the party. I've said this before, when I would see movies that were set in a church, having grown up in the church and having a dad that is a pastor—invariably these kinds of Hollywood movies or TV shows all felt like they were done by people who don't go to church.

There are some notable exceptions, but overall that's stayed pretty true. So I wanted to do something that felt realistic to people that go to church and something they could actually relate to, and since the story had its deepest resonance, I think, with fellow Christians, I wasn't as concerned about a project that felt kind of like an insider's view.

How did you get hooked up with Sony?

The movie was finished, because it was funded independently. Actually my house funded a third of it, and then some investors came on—kind of pseudo-partners—and then we finished the movie, like a rough cut, right before Debbie (Steve's wife) and I left for Africa to get our daughter. I think someone from Nashville that worked on the record-label side saw the movie, and they sent it to New York. Then that person saw the movie and Sony Pictures decided, "Let's pick this up, and we'll distribute it." I think their expectations were that this could be a successful project, but its best life would be on DVD, but they were still up for doing a theatrical run, so they gave us a fairly limited budget for what's called PNA: money, prints and advertising, and so that was how the theatrical release came about on February 17.

How did it wind up doing at the box office?

It's getting close to half a million at the box office, which is not bad. Some cities it played great in. Probably the biggest disappointment is it tended to not play very well in the South. I was actually hoping it would do a little better in the South.

Sure.

It was funny. If I went back to my touring days, it followed pretty much the same pattern as when I was a touring artist, you know.

Because you and Bob Jones were really good friends.

Yes, that's right. Very tight. Wow, you know, [in the] Carolinas it didn't do very well. [In] Alabama it didn't do well. In Georgia it didn't do well. And, of course, in Nashville it did great. Cities in the North and the Midwest and the places we opened on either coast did pretty good business too. So I don't know why that is. I guess it's hard to shake a sensibility, maybe. I don't know.

As far as a movie in general, what's most important to you going into a movie project? Is it the script, or how it's going to be filmed?

Nobody was going to entrust me with their awesome script, and so I never even tried that. I just figured if I was ever going to be able to make a movie, I'd have to generate a project myself. So the script became and remains the most important aspect, and it just takes a long time to get it right, especially when you're still learning. So, this script went through a lot of stress and a lot of revisions and a few different readings. It started off in a lot better shape. We did one of those table readings on *The Second Chance* like we'd done with [Another movie, not sure of the title. -Ed.] and immediately you could tell the difference. This felt like a movie and moved well and felt pretty well-paced, and then from there you just keep revising it until you feel it's ready to shoot.

Sure.
I just finished a comedy with two other friends. We've got a reading coming up this weekend—actually an acting company in town is doing a reading, so I'm both kind of nervous and kind of thrilled, because you find out so much when you do these readings, as far as what you have and what still needs work.

Yeah, I always figured that you would do something in the lines of comedy that would have kind of a sharp edge to it.
Well, it was a tough thing because I would have actually preferred to do a comedy first, and this comedy doesn't really have any great socially redeeming value. My original idea was to actually do this movie first, but it kind of depends. There's so much money involved in just trying to raise money even for an independent movie, and you end up kind of going with whatever project you're working on and where you can find the money. *The Second Chance* came, and in retrospect, that is probably good. I think *The Second Chance* gave me a little more latitude. The mistakes I made wouldn't be quite as glaring in this kind of a movie as they would have been in a comedy. So having said that, I can't tell you how many times we were in the editing room and we'd come up on some scene and some sort of problem to solve and I'd say to the editor, "If this was a comedy, I'd know exactly what to do here."

Can you say anything more about the story line for the comedy, or are you keeping it under wraps?
It's not like [a] big top secret thing or anything like that, but it would probably be more interesting once [I've] secured financing for a better press release at that point.

Will you contribute any music to it?
That's possible, but that's not necessarily the plan at this point. It would probably be an easier movie for me to contribute music to than *The Second Chance*. I was really involved in the music, of course, but mostly just as a

producer and then selecting other tracks to license and of course some guidance [that] I provided to Michael W. Smith and then John Painter, who also did some music on it.

John Painter is incredible.
Yeah, he really is. In fact, there is that movie *Hoodwinked!* Are you familiar with that?

I've heard of it.
[It's an] animated movie that came out and did really well. He did all the music to that. It's a really good movie.

How did Michael W. Smith wind up acting in the *The Second Chance*?
When we first started out, I talked to Ben (Pearson), one of the two other writers on this, and Ben also was a DP (director of photography) on the movie. We talked it through and started plotting it, and Ben had the idea early on and said, "Michael W. has always wanted to act. We should talk to him." And my question was everyone else's question, "Well, do you think he can act?" So we met with him, and he was excited about the idea. I spent an afternoon with him running lines and running scenes and had another actor there and left feeling—you know, "I think he can pull this off. We just need to write something that feels within his range." So we really wrote the part with him in mind, and I really appreciated not only that he was up for it, but that he was a very willing participant. I think other people in that position would have been a lot more cautious, or maybe because there's aspects about the character that he plays that are very unattractive and that could be construed as, "Well, this is the dark side of fame, and when you mix fame and Christianity and those types of things ..." Of course, really all I was doing was writing from my experience from being an artist and being kind of the center of attention and the tension that comes from being a follower of Jesus and being in the spotlight. So I think having Michael in that role added a certain extra something, even a certain extra realism that I'm not sure I would have gotten with someone else. And I've got to say, I

thought he did a pretty good job. He worked really hard and wanted to get it right and I think he pulled it off.

Was there anything that you can think of that was particularly humorous that happened when you were filming?
Oh, man. The very last day of the shoot was Halloween, and all the cast, unbeknownst to me or the crew, they all arrived in Halloween costumes. It was a really fun set the whole time, but it was also really hard work, because we were working on a tight budget, and everyone was working really hard. I remember that last day we had weather problems and we have to get done that day, and all this stuff's on and I'm trying to have serious conversations with my assistant director, who's dressed like a butterfly and has antennas flopping around while I'm talking to him about the next set up and things like that. We had a lot of homeless people on the set because they were a lot of extras, and that always made for interesting scenarios and usually really positive scenarios. Every day was trying to control chaos because we had so many extras and typically a lot of non-actors on the set. One example is there's a scene where there is a little African girl when Ethan and Jay go to visit this African family. They're cooking goat on a little charcoal grill on the floor and it's smoking up and we had to hire that entire African family—a refugee family to do this. None of them were actors. They looked like a family, and spoke another language, and it seemed like a good idea at the time. And it was, but their little girl, when it came time to do her scene, she just did not want to do it. We had already shot her in some other scenes, so we couldn't replace her. So we spent three hours just trying to get her to pass a little paper plate to Michael W., and I'm guessing that little three hours cost us like, I don't know, twenty, twenty-five thousand bucks.

Oh, wow!
She just refused to do it. We are doing everything. We're trying to bribe her. Michael, at one point is—he was really good with kids, and we just started filming, and we kept

wasting film because she would refuse to do anything, and at one point we were just trying to get her to pass the plate, pass the plate. At one point Michael just sort of gradually takes the plate from her, and I just started laughing because it looks like this guy is stealing her artwork. So finally we took her on a walk and she agreed to do it. We barely got the shot, but stuff like that is kind of par for the course.

What does it feel like to you to finally have a movie done and out? I know you have been planning this for years.
I've been talking about it for a long time. Mr. Big Shot. It felt good to finally get it done, and there was a certain amount of relief, because when you're editing you honestly don't know if you have anything or not. And we did what is called an assembly cut and showed it to people who didn't know much about the movie who were pretty harsh critics. It was kind of a sigh of relief when I left that screening realizing there's work to be done, but we've got something here and it's not going to be a catastrophe. Then the more you work on it the closer it gets until finally you've got it color corrected and you've got the sound and you show it in a multiplex that's got good sound and a good projector and it's like, "Oh wow. This actually feels like the movie. This is all right."

What were your thoughts when you first saw the movie completed and in a theater?
I actually really enjoyed it. I figured I'd be just looking at all the mistakes and being bummed out, but when I finally saw it in a theater with an audience, I actually really enjoyed it and then I started—we did more and more screenings, and for a really long time, I was actually enjoying every screening. After about the one hundred and fiftieth time watching it, it started getting a little old. It held up pretty well for quite a while.

That would be like mixing a record where you hear the same song five hundred times.
I think so, yeah.

Do you have any plans to do any more music, or are you kind of past that?
I am sure I will do some more music eventually, but there's so much at stake when you are attempting a filmmaking career. The stakes are so high that it just didn't seem fair to try to get people to invest in a movie while I was still having this parallel career in music. So, I felt like I'd better give it everything, as opposed to being someone who was a musician who thought, "This looks like fun. Maybe I'll just dabble in this for a while."

Well, I know Mike Mills from R.E.M. has done that. I think he just did a movie called *Thumbsucker*. [I spoke in error—Mike Mills the film director is not the gifted bassist Mike Mills who played in R.E.M. -Ed.]
You know, that's right! I saw that! I haven't seen the movie, but I wondered if it was the same Mike Mills. Oh, that's really interesting.

And then Michael Stipe did the—and that was actually a really good movie. I am sure it offended a lot of people in the church ... [The movie was called *Saved!*, but I never mentioned the name of the movie. –Ed.]
I never saw that. I saw it—but he also produced—or was one of the producers on *Being John Malkovich*, which is one of my all time favorites. So—he has got a pretty good ...

Who's the director of *Being John Malkovich*?
That's Spike Jonze.

That's right. There is a really good movie as far as—it's a Korean movie that I just saw that had some of the most incredible scenery and film coloring.
No kidding. You don't remember what movie?

It was called *Oldboy*.
Oldboy. I've got that on my Netflix.

It's really good. It takes a while to sink in on how accurate they are with the costuming and everything, but the editing and everything is great. It reminds me of **Punch-Drunk Love.**
Oh man, I love that movie.

Have you seen *Seconds,* with Rock Hudson; the John Frankenheimer film?
No, that is on my Netflix list too.

That is one of the all-time—as far as camera angles and movies I have seen, that is one of the most incredible.
Well, I'm going to have to move that up on the list because— that's Frankenheimer, right?

Yes.
Oh wow. Yeah, I will move that up on my list then. It's like one hundred and fifty deep, so ...

How many movies do you watch in a month?
Well I, you know, the same old cliché. I used to watch a lot more before having a daughter, but sadly I end up having to watch *Mary Poppins* and whatever animated movie is coming out. I have a hard time staying awake in those things, but I still get out to see movies quite a bit. I just saw this amazing French movie called *Caché.*

Oh yes, that was great! With the guy who filmed the family and left the videotape on the ...
Oh man, that was fantastic.

Yeah, I was really impressed by that. I love the way it starts where you don't know that they are watching the film.
Yeah, right. You don't know you are watching somebody taping something.

That was a great movie! Well, anyway Steve, I really appreciate you doing this.

Oh, no. My pleasure.

What does the future look like for you now? Are you going to continue doing movie making? Do you have other things that you want to try?
Yeah. Assuming this script gets a pretty good response, I would love to do this comedy next, and so probably start the fundraising process in May and hopefully be able to shoot it sometime—ideally even this fall. So we'll see how that goes.

Are you going to try to generate interest in the Christian market for it, or is it more of a mainstream movie?
I don't think it's an offensive movie or anything like that, but it's not a movie—I couldn't tell churches, "Hey, you need to see this," or youth groups, "You've got to go see this." It's just played for laughs.

Steve, thank you again. I really appreciate it.
Oh, man, I really enjoyed it. It's fun talking to a guy who knows so much about movies. So that's good. If you've got any other tips, feel free to let me know.

There is another movie I have heard that is really good called *Waiting*.
Waiting?

It's a fictional movie about a group of waiters that work in a restaurant.
Oh yeah, it's out on DVD, right?

Yeah, it's supposed to be really funny.
Wow! Yeah, I will check it out because I think it's got Dane Cook in it and ...

And there's a movie with Bill Pullman too, called *Rick*.
Called *Rick*?

Yeah, it was a Sundance movie.
Yeah, I haven't seen that one or heard of that.

It's actually kind of a moral tale. It's about a guy who is climbing the corporate ladder and then makes some mistakes and lives to regret it. It's a really good movie, and it couldn't have cost a ton of money for them to make.
Yeah, right Wow. *Rick.* Just R-I-C-K?

Yep.
OK.

Well, I will let you go because I am sure you have got other things to do this evening.
My daughter—it's her bedtime, so I've got to put her to bed. She was supposed to be in bed before you called, and it didn't quite work that way.

Thanks again, Steve.
All right, Chris. Great talking to you.

Good talking to you too.

THE ALARM (MIKE PETERS)

Tuesday, April 4, 2006
Article: *HM* (Issue 120: July/August 2006)

By the time I interviewed Welsh artist Mike Peters seven years after my first conversation with him, a lot had changed. He had been touring and recording for a good while with a new version of the Alarm, and a new Alarm record, *Under Attack*, was about to be released.

Also, Mike had been battling cancer for the second time, and I could tell he was physically exhausted. He still remembered what city I lived in, even though I hadn't mentioned it since we had last met during his 2000 show at the Buffalo Rose in Golden, Colorado. The new version of the Alarm played that night. After the show, Mike told my roommate Chad and me all about touring with U2 during the *War* tour, the recording of *Under a Blood Red Sky*, and how the Alarm played in Boulder the same night U2 played Red Rocks. Not bad for an after-show chat.

By 2000, Mike's musical direction had been changing for quite some time. Largely missing was the slick, spacious-sounding alternative material, and in its place was modern rock with gritty guitars and a juggernaut of sound. He had been exploring this direction in various doses for a good portion of his solo career, and it became clear that he had carried the sound over into the new version of the Alarm. A quick listen to the new Alarm lineup's first official, widely-distributed studio album, 2004's *In the Poppyfields,* left no doubt. It was an interesting progression, but he still managed to stick bits of classic-sounding Alarm fare into this and future records. *Under Attack,* the follow up to *In the Poppyfields,* contained a song called "Raindown" that sounded eerily like something the Alarm might have recorded back in the '80s, only with a more modern feel. The backing vocals on that song would—as I wrote in *HM*—have made Freddy Mercury proud.

When Mike Peters and I got on the phone to chat about *Under Attack* and his health battles in 2006, I hadn't authored an article I was excited about for *HM* in years. Usually I was writing about a Christian metal band of some sort, though I hadn't listened to Christian metal as a regular part of my musical diet since early on in my college years, with a few exceptions. However, that changed when Doug Van Pelt, founder of *HM*, asked me to write a piece on the Alarm. He's a huge fan and knew that I was too, so for him to assign the article to me was a huge deal and involved a good amount of trust, not to mention kindness. I also pitched a piece on Steve Taylor. The hugely respected Christian singer/songwriter had gone into filmmaking and was about to release his first film, *The Second Chance*. I had deep respect for Steve, his lyrical wit, his creativity, and his integrity, especially after meeting him and getting to know him a bit while living in Nashville, so to interview him and Mike Peters for the same issue of an internationally distributed music magazine was a big deal. These two artists were far from the confines of Christian metal.

Back to Mike Peters—I did get the opportunity to see him live again seven years after the interview for *HM* was conducted. He had taken on an additional musical role as frontman for legendary Scottish rockers Big Country. The group had just released a new disc, *The Journey*, and made a stop in Denver. So, on Friday, June 14, 2013, Mike and the lads performed at the Marquis Theater and my buddy Greg Glasgow and I were able to attend. The band put on a spirited show full of loud, boisterous rock 'n' roll. The crowd of maybe one hundred and fifty sang along with the more established songs, and celebrated the new material with aplomb. Mike, as he is known to do, had the crowd singing along and celebrating the experience with dancing, raised fists and loud cheering. Early on in the set I could tell he was struggling a bit. I had a couple of friends who had spent some time with Mr. Peters that afternoon and had mentioned that he seemed tired.

I immediately became concerned and realized it may be tied to his cancer battle. My perceptions proved correct. As he was performing, I noticed that Mike would hold his head from time to time, wipe his brow and put his hand over his mouth. In between one of the early songs, he asked the crowd to carry some of the vocals for him as he had just had a round of chemo a couple weeks prior and was dealing with its physical repercussions. The supportive, spirited crowd did just that and another special evening took place. My prayers and thoughts go out to Mike and his family as he continues this ongoing battle.

****

A couple of years ago you played the Cornerstone Festival in Illinois. What was that like for you?
It was a great experience. It was nice to meet up with all the people at the event. There were some real great Alarm fans, and it was really quite an emotional night. It was a great concert, for a start. And we felt we made a good connection with all those people that had been interested in the Alarm for years but never seen us at an event like that before.

Had you played anything like that before—like Greenbelt?
We've done those, yeah. [I asked Mike about Greenbelt back in 1999 and he discussed it a bit. I should have revisited that interview prior to conducting this one. –Ed.]

Now this year you went to SXSW [South by Southwest]— what was that like?
It was really great. For me it was great because I wasn't sure if I could go right up to the last minute, because of health, so it was great. It is something I have done every couple of years for the last ten years. So it was a good event for us to go [to] because it keyed up our album for the U.S.A. to come out on the thirteenth of June. I think it's coming out [then]. So it was all partly to run the flag up on the album coming out in the U.S.A. and to play for all the fans that could get there. And

also for all the team that [were] involved in the record on that side of the planet and the American record label, they were all down at the two gigs. And it just makes it all a very real and personal thing, because *Under Attack* is the first domestic U.S. release we have had for the Alarm for a long, long time.

What label is that coming out on?
It's coming out on Eleven Thirty.

What was the response like at SXSW?
Amazing! Both gigs were great. The first one at Elysium was the one that was advertised and it was packed out, and a lot of emotional fans, again, because of the situation with my health. A lot of people, including myself, were thinking whether I'd ever get a chance to play in America again. So to beat those odds and get out there was an amazing thing. And the fans were amazing. The first seven songs of the nine-song set that we originally were playing were all from *Under Attack*. So it was pretty new for most people, but you would have never thought it from the response. Everyone picked up on it instantly. That was the great thing about this album; it breathed a whole lot of life back into the Alarm. The old songs are benefiting from having these songs to be played alongside them. It makes the concert really exciting, and it's almost like seeing the Alarm again in 1983 for the first time, if you are old enough to remember those times. But with the new album being as powerful as it is, especially to play live, from our point of view, it's converting people really fast to the band in a way that I can only liken [to] the early times, when people were seeing us for the first time and didn't know anything about the band. You know, young college students coming through to see us play and going with their friends, not knowing anything about the band, and hearing "Sixty Eight Guns," "Spirit of '76" or "The Stand" and then thinking, "Wow, I'm rushing out to go buy all the records." That's the sort of experience we're generating on this record. So it feels really fresh and exciting for us, and I think it does for the fans, and that part's coming across to us on stage. The

e-mails and the response that night after the gig were—one guy wrote in straight after and said, "Oh, I've seen you about twenty times in America—the original lineup, [the] 2006 lineup," and he said this is the best gig he's ever seen. So it was great from our point of view to get that sort of response back. Being SXSW, you're not supposed to do encores or anything like that because it's a tight schedule. It's fifteen hundred bands being accommodated across the whole thing, but no one would let us get off the stage, so encores were happening, and that was exciting. And then we played a second night on Sixth Street, an unannounced show just for the Eleven Thirty staff and the few people that we could tell about it that we sneaked it out to. And that was in a smaller place, more intimate, and that was a fantastic gig as well.

What was your final encore for the announced show?
"Blaze of Glory." We had a vote, because we only had a few minutes left, so we had a quick vote and that was the one that came up, so we went for that. We played "Sixty Eight Guns" the first night, but the second night we didn't play "Spirit." We did "Sixty Eight Guns" in the set. But we did it as an encore on the first night because we did a sort of medley of "Spirit of '76" and "45 RPM" in the Elysium set.

As far as "45 RPM" and "Superchannel," what does it feel like to be having hit songs right now? For a long time you did your solo records and *In the Poppyfields* came out and then *Under Attack,* and all of a sudden you are on the charts again.
It's great from our point of view. It makes it all exciting. I think it creates a buzz around the gigs for the fans. For the people that have been with us for a long time, it's nice for them to go into their workplace and workmates have heard the record on the radio or something like that. It sort of brings it all out into the open again. It's a vindication of some sort for all the blood, sweat and tears we've put into the band through the years. There are so many trends [that have] come along since the beginning of the '90s, when the Alarm sort of fell off the radar, that it's been a long way back for us

to create the environment where people have listened to the Alarm again without thinking of us as being from the '80s, or that all we had to offer was a greatest-hits package. So to overcome those obstacles, it does take time and an endeavor, so having these couple of hit records kind of helps to put some marks in the sand that we are actually winning on our objectives. We've got a long way to go, because we are only achieving that in the UK at the moment, but we're breaking barriers down internationally. We are always working from a small base, a small committed team of people that actually work within the structure of the band, and then there are fans that are all part of it as well, so it's a real community of people working toward the same aim, all putting a lot of love into the thing that they get a lot of joy out of. It's a good family network. I think it's sort of what punk rock is all about, really. It's kind of like there are all these fans, and everyone's involved in the band, and everyone's doing it for the right reasons. We haven't got a million-dollar marketing budget behind it, but we have got far more than that in terms of love and enthusiasm.

What does it feel like to have EMI behind you again?
It's good. It's been good for us in the UK, and it gave us resources. We're not the priority act. We're not Robbie Williams at EMI, or Coldplay, by any stretch of the imagination, but we have access to some of the resources that I think have helped us to make a better record. We also made a film for every track on the album, which is again something we might not have been able to do if we hadn't been with EMI. All those things are helping to take it all forward, I think. And I think they're learning quite a lot from us as well, because they're still a corporation at the end of the day, and the wheels turn very slowly and can be a little bit frustrating. Whereas we are much more of a guerilla unit on the ground and can move a lot quicker. I think in some ways we've got much more [Unclear. –Ed.] on the Internet and the underground than they have. So I think it's a learning process from their point of view, as well as for us. We know what majors are about because we have been there in the past in

some sort of shape or form. It's not helping us to sell a million records—not yet. But it's helping us to get across to other people and retouch base with our audience, some of the people that we have lost along the way. A lot of our audience who started with us in the '80s, they're bringing up their kids and their family, and they are fighting for their careers, and they don't buy music magazines or have time to switch on the music channels or surf the Internet to find out about their bands, but if we can get to them, they'll come to a gig and maybe that will relight the fire for them. Having EMI behind us has definitely helped us to get out to all those people.

As far as your health battle, how is that going right now?
It's going as well as I could have ever have hoped for, really. I have just had my fifth round of chemotherapy treatments for the leukemia, and I think they're getting all back down to a manageable level. So my blood levels and health levels have come back to normal, and hopefully I will be able to get myself into remission in a couple months' time, and then I've had some long-term tests done, which have predicted how it's going to move for me in the future, and they've come up really good for me. They've come up that I've got a slow-moving illness, and it was indicated that maybe when I was diagnosed ten years ago, it was the start of what I am having now, really. So it's possible it could go away for quite a few years before I have to consider more treatments, and then when it comes back—which it will do; the history of the illness says it will come back—then it's how I respond, whether my illness has learned to combat the treatments, and then we'll look at what the options are. I've got options of stem cell transplants or just more chemotherapy. There's all sorts of options for the future, and also there's the possibility that new cures, new treatments might come along that can stave off having something as heavy as it sounds for a long, long time. So I've got to be hopeful with the outlook. I believe a lot of it is about positive thinking, so my thoughts are all gonna be, as soon as I get into remission, it's going to be a ten-year remission. That's my thinking, but we will cross

that new bridge when we get to it. My outlook is very good at the moment, so I am very happy.

That's fantastic that things are going better. If any of these questions are too personal, please let me know. How did you find out it had come back?
I went to the doctor—just routine, every year I go for a road test to my doctor because I was diagnosed with lymphoma ten years ago. Whenever you've had cancer, there's always the feeling that it never really goes away. I think there's always that fear in the back of your mind. So I've always stayed in touch with my doctors and had check-ups, and this time I went to see him and he spotted some lumps in my neck through my glands, and he thought it was wise that I go for some blood tests, which I did at the hospital, and that's when it revealed that my blood count had gone up to half a million white blood count. The normal count is somewhere between six and seven thousand. So I was in danger of having a thrombosis at the time. They started treatment the next day, it was so high. It was quite a shock, because I felt great inside. I had just come off holiday. I felt great. I felt really confident. We had a great album in the bag, and I got a son, and he is the light of my life, and life couldn't have been better, and then boom, out of the blue, just through a routine blood test, I was diagnosed with leukemia, which is a horrible word to hear about yourself. You don't know that much about it when it comes along, and it's very frightening, but I dug deep with my wife, and we got a family behind us, and I made an announcement on the website, and the fans are great. We learned a lot from the culture of the fans. We've got a wide fan base across the world, and this illness has touched various members of our fan club community in one shape or another, and through them we were able to get a lot of information and some health tips and alternative therapies I've been able to add to my lifestyle. I believe all that has been helping me, and I've come down from the half-million white blood count to absolutely normal levels. I did that two months ago, and that was quite an amazing jump, according to all the doctors. I even went to the Baylor Institute in

Dallas, and UT Southwestern while I was there, with two of the leading guys in the world, and they both gave me a fantastic outlook and said I have an amazing recovery. They wanted to write to my doctor in Wales, which is an amazing testament to my man here, Dr. Edwards. They wanted to touch base with him because they said he has obviously worked out your illness absolutely brilliantly and got the right treatment for you and brought it down amazingly well. So I'm very lucky. I could have been in another part of the world where—I read a lot about CLL in other people. I am involved in a digest with other CLL sufferers and some of them—their treatment has been nowhere near what I have had, just because some of the doctors are slow on the uptake of future developments. I'm lucky that my guy here in Wales has obviously done his research and he is right on the front line.

Is this the same doctor who initially helped you ten years ago?
Yeah, he was part of the team really. The main doctor about ten years ago was a guy named Dr. Gozzard—he has moved up into management on the hospital administration board. Dr. Edwards was more of his sidekick then, and he was definitely part of the team for me ten years ago. That's what I like about him. He knows the history, and even ten years ago, although they weren't very happy about me going on tour, they understood that I had to be right mentally. They were able to monitor me all the way through and keep checking it out, and although they weren't sure what happened to me, I've always stayed in touch with them to be checked up here and there. Obviously, somewhere along the line these last few years, the brakes have come off my immune system and the count's gone up and here it is big time. So yeah, he's a good guy to have on board.

Has the cancer coming back changed any of your views on life, or has it made you view every day differently?
It does now, because I've got a son. I think everything changes when you have a child. That changed everything as

well, so I can't be as foolhardy as I was ten years ago when I refused all the treatment. I thought this time I was too far gone. I had to have treatment. I've got a boy. I've got to be around for him, so I couldn't be as devil-may-care about my health. It's made me reassess a lot of things, which I'm always doing anyway, but we have been lucky this time. Because I've got my boy, I didn't want to go on these gigantic tours and get lost in the world touring. And we decided to do shorter time-scale events—weekend events or a week of dates here and there. We would [Unclear. –Ed.] it all up so we could do it in manageable little chunks and make it more fun and eventful, and I think that's worked really well for us. Luckily, with my illness coming along when it did, we were so glad that we planned it that way, because if we had a full tour booked we would have had to cancel it all, and that would have been the death knell for the album and maybe even the band, but because we've got these one-off dates, we've been able to keep them in the calendar. I've been able to build my treatment around it so I can go and do it. It's given me some [Unclear. –Ed.] in my treatment. I would have been devastated if we would have had to cancel a tour and I was sitting at home having to have chemotherapy thinking, "Oh, I would've been playing in Denver, Colorado, tonight." That would have been awful, but luckily I didn't have to face any of those dilemmas. I think for the meantime, for the future, we will just keep it the way it is, and if something really good comes off that I can do within the guidelines of keeping my health and keeping my future intact as a human being, then we'll do everything we can, because I love playing rock 'n' roll, and this is a great album to play, and I don't want to drop the ball on the Alarm just because I've got leukemia. I think me picking up the ball and running with the band helps to combat the leukemia, rather than vice versa. So I want to keep playing, but we'll make it meaningful. I don't think my interests would be served just playing a hundred dates across America or something like that, which I've done in the past. I think it would be much better to keep them to a minimum but make them really carry a lot of weight when we do play them. I think it will make it more exciting and fresh. I still want to make more albums and write loads of songs. I think with the Internet, people can stay plugged in. I've just got to balance it all, because this illness isn't going to go away. It's a chronic illness. It's not curable at the moment, so I am going to be in and out of hospitals every other week for the rest of my life. So I am going to have to just balance that out with whatever rock 'n' roll I can do. And I want to do as much as I can.

I appreciate you being so honest about what you have been through.
I just think it helps other people. There are other people out there that aren't as lucky as me. So if they can find out about my story and they can draw their own strength and direction from it then that …

Definitely. With _Under Attack_—the album sounds great by the way.
Thanks.

Under Attack just sounds like you went in the studio with the express purpose of recording a certain number of songs. It sounds great, the mixing and everything. What was it like completing that record for you?
When we started, we actually went in to make a different kind of record. It partly had carried over from the previous album, _In the Poppyfields,_ and the songs from that session that got us our deal with EMI. There was a certain amount of pressure that we had to cut those songs. But when we got in the studio and we started playing, we knew we wanted to make a different kind of record. We wanted it to be a collective band record. In the past, in the history of the Alarm, my hand's been in all the songwriting. Individually or a part or whatever, but most songs sprung from the Mike Peters well, if you like, and they still do. I usually would finish a song off before the band played it. So I'd take it into rehearsal as a finished piece, and I'd have very formed ideas of what I wanted everybody to play. I'd be telling the guitarist how to play, the bass player, the drummer, and then we

would go from there. We'd have a virtual arrangement before it was tweaked a little bit. But this time I didn't want to do that. This time I wanted to go in and have a looser form to the songs, so I'd go in with just the verse waiting for the chorus—to see where the chorus wanted to go once we got some music under the verse, and let the lyrics come while we were singing, and let James and Craig [Adams] and Steve [Grantley] add their own personalities. I wasn't trying to say "the drums have to go this way." Let Steve hear what I was playing and say, "Yeah, let's make it faster or let's make it slower, let's do it this way. Whatever way you wanted to do it." Because all the guys in the band have contributed some great pieces of music in the past in their own groups, with the Sisters of Mercy from Craig and the Mission or James in the Cult. They have helped with those bands, and I thought since we have been playing together for a long time that it was important that everyone had their say in this record. I felt we could get more out of it as a band rather than being a band that was just interpreting the songs of Mike Peters. It was a bit more of a scary record to make for me, because I had no mind picture of what I thought the record would be at the end. It was kind of like riding a bucking horse and having to control it. But it was really exciting because of that. Things were happening spontaneously. There was a lot of excitement in the room when we were making it, and I think that is what comes across in the record as well. It was pretty much recorded live. We didn't want to try and do too much overdubbing or add too much production. I kind of felt [that] was something that maybe we got a bit too bogged down in in the past. We had to concentrate on our performances and getting as much out of the instrumentation that we had at our fingertips without over-layering too many ideas. So when we started recording the song for real, we actually had a really good arrangement that we'd worked out together and that was the basis of the whole album.

So it was more you coming in with some ideas and letting the band kind of form them rather than having an idea of what everybody should play?

Yeah, I never brought a song in that had lyrics or anything like that. I might have brought in a verse and the chorus, but just like, "It's called 'Cease and Desist,' and I've got no lyrics for it. I've got an idea for a title and that's about it." And then we'd just add to it as it went along. It was exciting. I remember even playing it for the first time for the band, and it's always a nervous process, because whenever you're playing a song for the first time, you never really know if it's any good or anything to anyone until you play it to somebody else. And even just in the act of me playing it to Craig and James and Steve, I'd add something to it right on the spot that I had no idea I was going to do until I got to that moment. They said, "Oh, that's a good bit." "Oh, wow. I just put that in because I didn't know where to go next." So just putting myself into that position, it put me on edge a bit as a songwriter again as well. I wasn't playing it as comfortably or sitting at home and rounding the edges off of the song as an arranger and the writer because I'd learned how to do all those things over the years. I was putting myself back into the position like we were when the band first started and you would sort of walk in with part of an idea, but then you'd go home and finish it off. This time I just wanted to go in with all that raw excitement of "Here's a few chords that sound great, and here's a great riff. Where should we go, boys? Dream up the adventure again."

Did you feel like how Pete Townshend must have felt with Keith Moon and John Entwistle, because you never knew what you were going to get with those guys?
There is an element of that, yeah I think so. I think that's partly what made it exciting for us, is that you go down into a song and then Steve would start playing something on the drums and you'd [say] "Wow, we'll go with that," and then that became the next part of the song, or James [Stevenson] would take something off on the solo or Craig would hold back on a bass note instead of following the chords like we were doing. "Wow what was that?" I think if I'd looked back at myself and criticized myself, I would say I probably got a little bit too controlling over the years, and so it became a

little bit one-dimensional at times, possibly, in terms of not so much the songwriting, but in terms of the way the music would be arranged around it. There was not enough room for the musicians sometimes, and sometimes that spawns a spontaneous moment that is at the heart of all great rock 'n' roll. There wasn't that space for that moment to happen. I wanted to make sure we had that space in this record, and I think we found it. We threw out tons of bits of music that we thought, "That's too predictable. That's not exciting enough." There was one day in particular where I think we used about three ideas that I had come up with and thought, "None of these are working" and I'm thinking "What's gonna happen here?" and I ran out into the garden and dug through my tape and just found a little bit, piled in, and off we go and it was one of the songs that made it onto the album. I think "Superchannel" came out of a moment like that. You had to really think quickly because everyone was waiting on an idea to start. It just put me on my toes again, which is good.

Do you see yourself as being more critical as you get older about what you do musically than you were when you were twenty-five?
I think you can do, but with this one I decided to not to be. You have to be critical to find out where you're going wrong sometimes, and yet you have to be—I'm not sure critical is the right word for the next thing, but you have to always be putting your music into context and seeing if it's working with your audience or with the outside world or not. And I felt when we started making this record—something we learned a little bit from Steve Brown when we did the *Poppyfields* re-records for the last album with him, he, as a producer, came up to us and said, "Look lads, I think you have a tendency to play things a bit slower than they should be. Just because you're getting old, you're more aware of tempos and you're more aware of how music sits and plays." And he said, "I think you need to speed things up again and forget about all that stuff and make it sound young and exciting." And he was right, because when we re-recorded "45 RPM" with him, we sped it up from the one we'd

221 | P a g e

recorded on the *Poppyfields* bond [A series of albums. –Ed.], which is only a bit slower, but it does make a difference. And I think when we were coming into this record, with every bit of music, we pushed it all as fast as we could. Some of it beyond the speed that was right, and then we learned a lot of things from that. Even when we look back on our old albums, like *Declaration* and that—even the slow songs on *Declaration* are quite fast.

I did an acoustic tour in April, which I think was a big part of getting me in the mindset for this record. I felt like when I started on that tour, I'd got out of the habit of listening to new music. I'd bought iPods and all that kind of stuff—that was the year that we're in, and I'd loaded it up with all my CDs and put it on random and it was great listening to the Who and Zeppelin and the Beatles and the Stones and the Clash and the Pistols and INXS—whoever pops up when you play it—but I felt like for a year or two I was wandering around just with the iPod in the car or on planes and I was listening to old music all the time. It was like listening to my own version of classic radio. I just felt like I had stopped buying brand-new albums. So when I went out on this tour, I think it was about thirty dates across the UK in April, I made a pact with myself to go and buy a brand-new album every single day by somebody I'd never heard of. And so I went in the shop every day, and I started off with an album by Bloc Party. I bought the Kaiser Chiefs and the Futureheads and all sorts of albums—Bravery—all these bands at the time, Kasabian—the list went on. It was really interesting for me, because at first I was listening to the albums and thinking, "Whoa, what's this?" I bought Bloc Party. I played it about twenty times in the first day. And by the second day I had listened to it maybe twenty-five times, [and] I was thinking, "This is a great album. I'm really getting into it." When I was young, I had the time to listen to records in that way. I could spend a week listening to an album in my bedroom, because I didn't have to go to work and things like that. And nowadays I have got so many things on the go, I don't have time to give something that much time. Because you are always working on your own albums, which are demanding. I really learned a lot from listening to all these bands, and the one thing that came to mind is everything is quite fast and up-tempo, and I really like that. I thought, "Yeah, maybe that has gone out in my own music. So let's make this album up and fast and raw and exciting. Make it like a young band. Make it with only what we've got."

We have rediscovered our enthusiasm on this record, and I think because of it, all the fans are re-discovering their own enthusiasm for the Alarm as well. I think we've reminded ourselves what brought a lot of people into the band, and I think it's done the same for the fans. So everyone's been rejuvenated through this record. The future looks great for the band. The now is happening, and you can't ask for any more than that. We don't really care about how many records we sell or how big it goes in the charts. The most important thing for us was to make a great record that we could stand by on stage, and that's why we felt confident going on at SXSW and opening up with seven brand-new tracks, because we knew they were as good as anything in the history of the band anyway, so it didn't matter. And when we used to come to America in '83, everything was a brand-new song then, and we still won people over. I think sometimes you can get a bit too saddled with the history of the band, and then there is no room for the newness to come through. So it's worked out great. We played a week ago last Saturday in Glasgow before I had my last treatment, and I have to say it was possibly one of the best gigs we've ever played in the history of the Alarm. It was amazing. It was like the old days, but so brand new. We started off with "Superchannel," and it was one for one all the way through the night. A new song, an old one, a new song, an old one. We played ten off the album and ten from the history of the band, right up to "45 RPM" and "In the Poppyfields." And then we added a few more songs—I think we played about twenty-eight songs in the end, but it was a fantastic night and an electric atmosphere, loads of people there. The biggest show we've played in Glasgow since the

'80s, and it just meant everything to us that we're getting it. It feels like we were in a new band again.

I noticed with "Raindown," you have that really beautiful harmony part in the vocals and then in the end it goes a cappella—how long did it take to nail that in the studio?
Probably as long as it took Queen to nail "Bohemian Rhapsody."

Well, they were using analog tape, and I have heard that the tape got really thin by the time they ...
Put it this way. When we recorded the *Poppyfields* album— we actually did record it on the same tape machine that was used to record "Bohemian Rhapsody," believe it or not, but not this one. So I can't lay claim to that, but yes, it was George Williams who was helping with the production. He was the engineer from the studio we went to after we'd cut most of it in the Doghouse. He's a really good musical ear and very good arranger, and he really helped us with the harmony structure. When we get going, the four of us, we're actually all good singers in our own way, especially Steve Grantley, the drummer. He doesn't like to sing live because he puts so much into his playing, but he has got a fantastic voice in the top range, and it's something we wanted to bring more out on this record. In the last few years, especially the *Poppyfields* album, I've tended to do a lot of the backing vocals myself on top of myself, a bit like the way Bowie does it. You just get it really close and tight. But this time, it was a conscious decision that we'd sing the backing vocals as a band like we do live, but build on them. It's tradition in the Alarm, with the original lineup, when we put a lot in the background vocals and were creative in that area, and I think possibly over the recent years, because that was such a big thing in the old lineup of the band that I tended to do it myself to make sure it sounded like the Alarm. But this time we thought, "We've been working together a long time. Let's find the blend in our own voices, in the four of us, and "Raindown" came out because we found such great harmonies in it, with George

helping us to find the right notes and things and to interpret ideas.

There were a lot of harmonies that I had in mind amongst ourselves, but George—they fit like the way George Martin worked with the Beatles. He's just able to help you stack it up so you can come up with something as beautiful as that without anything getting in the way, and he had the musical knowledge so you can write it down on paper, almost, whereas with us it's always instinctive and helps us create that beautiful end to the track. Whether we can do it all live or not—we play it live, but we don't do it quite the same way live. We have bottled out of it a little bit, because we haven't got Steve's voice live in the same way we have in the studio. So we do it slightly different, but we might demand that we have to learn how to do it.

Do you have any personal favorites on the new record—anything that means more to you than something else, maybe?
I like the whole thing as a piece, as a whole. I like the lyric to "This is the Way We Are," the last track on the album. That speaks to me. I like "It's Alright/It's OK"—just because it's very simple and direct. "Without A Fight" means a lot to me; much more to me now than it did when it was actually written, just because of what's happening to me. So to be able to go out and sing that song every night, in light of the circumstances I find myself in—I'm glad I'm going out doing that and not singing "you are the deceiver" or something, if you know what I mean. To be able to sing that in these circumstances is a powerful thing, and I think that it communicates to a lot of the audience out there as well. They all want to sing that song with me, and they don't want to give up without a fight either.

That's got to be a great feeling, when you play that song and you see people getting into it.
They go for it straightaway. The first time we played it at the Gathering—we played it the fourth song in at the Gathering.

Now we're playing it more down the end of the set, but then it was the first time we played it live, and all the new songs just felt like you didn't have to try to sell them to people right from the word go. Even when we were recording them or rehearsing them up as a band, we were all imagining ourselves playing these live in front of all the fans, saying, "Yeah, this is where we're going to come in and they're going to get this straight away because it's built on all those great things that made the Alarm good in the first place." All the excitement that made "68 Guns" good or "Strength" or "Spirit of '76"—we had all those kind of things in this record. It's weird, it's got a lot in common with the old—what made the Alarm good, and so we knew we had a good place to start with the fans on this album.

As far as playing in the U.S., are there plans to do a small tour here?
I can't say yet until I know—the plan is for us to possibly come in May, which we are trying to confirm at the moment, to play in New York, and then it's possible that we could be coming in June to do something on either coast but we won't really know the details for perhaps another week. Hopefully we should have something, but whether we can do a full tour yet, I don't really know. I'm not sure if I can get the time out from the hospitals and all that to do that sort of thing, but we'll have to just look at it when it comes up. Let's get the album out and see. Get myself into remission first, and then we can look at a tour.

The last question I have for you—I saw VH1's *Bands Reunited.* What was that like, doing the Alarm episode?
It was good. It sort of put a bit of closure on the past for all of us, I think—you know for the band, the original lineup, the fans. On the day, Craig, Steve and James were all at the gig, and they helped. They helped set up the equipment for the old guys. Craig was really helping to get Eddie back in the swing of playing his bass. It was almost like a bit of handing over, and I think because it was filmed, shown on TV, I [don't] think anyone felt like they missed out on seeing the

Alarm reunion. For us, as Nig, Mike, Eddie and Dave from the '80s, it was great to play once more and say, "Yeah, we can do it." It's not something that we want to do every night on a regular basis, but I'm glad we did it because it puts a good feeling for us. It wasn't a difficult situation with bad feeling and all that kind of thing. So it was good to put a closure on all that and say, "Yeah, that was great, and we had a great time." I think it was also good for the fans, because they saw the original one last time and thought, "Yeah, it was really good, but do I want to go and see the originals every night—probably not. Nice to see them, but I'd rather remember it how it was and let's get on with the future with the Alarm as it is today." "45 RPM" came not long after that and now here comes *Under Attack*. I think if we'd gone back to the original lineup then, it would have meant a lifetime of greatest hits, which is a bit like a jail sentence, I think. I think people would have got bored of that very quickly, and because of what had happened in the twelve years or whatever it was between Brixton Academy and doing the *Bands Reunited*—I think we'd have found it very difficult to find creative common ground to take the band forward with. Even after we'd been together in rehearsal for a short time, you could see why we'd grown apart. It was fairly obvious, and so I think it was good to leave it alone. Dave's played with us since, and we all speak, and it's all good, and everyone's happy with the way the Alarm continues [to] this day. So I think it was a great thing to do, and it's been something that the fans have been able to enjoy, and I think it's helped to sort of set us free for the future.

Do you wind up keeping in more frequent touch with those guys since the episode?
Not really, no. I speak to Eddie here and there. Dave comes on every so often and then again with Nig he lives out in San Francisco—Nig and Eddie have got careers and jobs that have nothing to do with rock 'n' roll, and they're very happy doing it, and I don't think they want to give those jobs up. Dave pursues his music in his own way, but he doesn't want to do what I do, and I don't want to do what he does. He is

doing a bit of acting now, and he seems happy. I think everyone is. I think that's what *Bands Reunited* reminded us all, that when we were together at the end of the Alarm in the '80s, we were all unhappy. Everyone's been in touch with my illness, obviously, and they're all concerned and I have been keeping them in touch with my progress, and it's good. I don't think we want to rock the boat anymore. We've got a good relationship, and if the opportunity presented that we could play again then we probably all would, for fun, but not in terms of going out and trying to be serious about it and making a brand-new album. I don't think anyone would want to go back to that.

Well, Mike, I really appreciate you doing this. I wanted to let you know that there are lots of people here in the U.S. praying for your recovery.
Thanks Chris, that's great. I can feel it. Thanks to everyone out there for getting behind me. Hopefully we can come out and share some dates with you all in the future.

I hope the recovery continues, and hopefully the record does well when it comes out here.
Thanks Chris.

BEN GIBBARD

Monday, January 11, 2010
Article: *Boulder Weekly* (January 21, 2010)

I tend to get addicted to things fairly quickly, musical and otherwise. Put a pizza in front of me and I will consume the entire pie—it may not be that same day, but the devouring will occur more quickly than it should for any normal person. The strange aspect of this food scenario is that I dropped over forty pounds several years ago, and part of this had to do with a commitment to exercise and a concentration on portion control—before I may have consumed the entire pie that night; now it takes a couple of days.

During the late 1990s while living in Nashville, I would often lunch at a place called Pizza Perfect. While the pizza wasn't perfect, it was pretty darn good. There was a guy who worked there who looked like he stepped straight off the streets of Brooklyn circa 1977, with shoulder-length black hair—he could have been an extra on *Welcome Back, Kotter* or a stand-in for one of the Ramones. Pizza places hold strange memories for me, I guess.

These visits to the Nashville pizza parlor happened long before I got myself into shape. I would get the lunch special, which consisted of a couple of slices. I would take several napkins and use them to absorb the grease on the top of each slice. For some reason, I thought this was the healthy way to go—years later I discovered this really does very little good. Here I was consuming well over a thousand calories and a hundred grams of carbohydrates, and I innocently thought that sopping up a little bit of liquid fat off what I was eating would actually amount to something significant.

Pizza wasn't my only addiction. There was diet cola. Ah, the lovely, dark, calorie-free drink that fizzed and bubbled, whose spray would gently hit my face when put on ice. Well, it's a nice description, but I would drink up to six cans of the stuff each day. The drink would call my name like a crack addict to the glass pipe's sinister company, and I would open a can regardless of whether I was actually thirsty or truly desired it. I've realized that I have this constant need to pour liquids down my throat. Perhaps it's a psychological aberration of sorts.

Eventually, I realized I was drinking a bit too much of the no-carb concoction and needed to stop. Too much of anything is not good—and addiction is not something to embrace. I decided to quit cold turkey and I did, without any drug-like effects. My friend and former Crash Orchid/Able Archer band mate Mike had the same kind of diet cola addiction, and he had a much more difficult time kicking the "habit." I've since gone back to a little bit of diet cola here and there, but nothing like what I used to consume. Club soda, sometimes with low-sodium V8 added, has somewhat taken its place. There are a couple of nice things about V8—it has tons of potassium and vitamin C, very few calories for a juice and significantly less carbs then many other juices. And it has a kick to it if you go for the Spicy Hot version.

And, of course, diet cola wasn't the only beverage I craved like no tomorrow—there was also light beer. It's not surprising, with my constant psychological need for liquids, that one would have to replace another, and when I "quit" diet cola, I started drinking more light beer. It started with a love of Coors Light, which at some point switched to Miller Lite. At first, I wouldn't make the switch from Coors to Miller. I remember going to see the Colorado Rockies play with a girl I was dating and she wanted to order a Miller Lite instead of a Coors Light. I was aghast. "Coors Light is so much better! I don't like the taste of Miller Lite." She gave me a look like I was stupid and in need of a lobotomy. "No," she said with a deprecating laugh aimed pointedly in my direction, "Miller Lite is much better." I caved in but was still a Coors man at that point. To this day, whenever the words "I'll have a delicious Coors Light" escape my lips into earshot range of an attentive bartender, my buddy Will laughs. After all, it is still his beer of choice, while mine has changed over the last several years to the light beer I used to dread, Miller Lite.

The appealing thing about light beer is that you can enjoy a few without feeling bloated and without getting hammered. If I were to do the same with a craft beer or domestic regular beer, the alcohol amount would make me feel as if I had devoured a decent-sized meal.

Then there's coffee—well, that's the same as the other beverages I've mentioned. As I write this, I've already had four cups and have only been around the coffee pot for three hours. Did I get this from my late Uncle Chuck? He'd brew coffee at all hours and probably consumed two pots a day. He was a fantastic, kind-hearted man and I miss him.

Music is as addictive as pizza, diet cola and light beer for me—I love it and enjoy it immensely. When I discover a new artist that strikes my fancy, that band or solo artist becomes the focal point of my musical listening time, which mostly occurs via iPod while working out or during my drives to and from work. Sadly enough, I don't hear many new artists that I wind up embracing. Most new artists fail to grab my ears with their tunes or are making albums that seem to lack the quality of the stuff I remember from my formative years. Maybe I'm just getting older and doing what every music fan does from the age before—insists the music he or she grew up with is better than the material "the kids" are listening to now.

Some artists make it through the filters I've created, and Death Cab for Cutie was one of those that escaped through the pin-sized holes in my musical net. Chad, my bandmate in Breathing Eve, Crash Orchid and Able Archer who once kindly helped me fashion a cardboard box to ship an eighty-pound Otari reel-to-reel multi-track tape machine introduced me to Death Cab. When we were roommates living in a house that doubled as the recording studio and rehearsal space for Crash Orchid, Chad received a DVD as part of a magazine deal. It featured videos by Black Rebel Motorcycle Club, Death Cab for Cutie and others. Death Cab had recently released the spectacular, haunting, and powerful *Transatlanticism*, and the DVD contained a video for "The

Sound of Settling." Chad, seated on his green vintage mini-sectional, called to me while I was in the kitchen cooking something. "Hey, Chris, I think you'll like this band." So I walked into the living room and, sure enough, I did, in fact, like what I heard. It had that Beatlesque pop edge I've been drawn to since infancy when visions of my dad's reel-to-reel tape machine floated around inside my head.

Soon, I found myself at Twist & Shout in Denver (when it was located at Alameda and Logan) and purchased *Transatlanticism*. I devoured the record like a fat kid downing a thirty-two-ounce sugar-laden soda. From the start of "The New Year" through the end of "A Lack of Color," I was taken on a ride of emotional, catchy rock with the right amount of atmosphere. Eventually, I went back to Twist & Shout and purchased most, if not all of, the band's previous albums. I was obsessed with listening to those discs and hadn't had that kind of reaction to a band since the Samples and Vigilantes of Love.

While in the midst of my new Death Cab addiction, I flew to Prague for a vacation with my longtime friend Chris. The Washington-based band became the musical soundtrack. The city was beautiful, modern and interesting. Everywhere I'd turn, there would be a beautiful woman who looked like Cameron Diaz. I'm surprised I didn't develop a severe neck injury or come back with a wife.

Throughout our travels in the Czech Republic, Poland and England on that trip, Death Cab's music provided a sonic escape when mutual disputes arose or I needed to retreat into my own world for a while or just sit back and relax.

Of course, as a music writer, I wanted to interview vocalist/guitarist Ben Gibbard and that was something that swirled around inside my head even more so after my trip. I thought about it as a few more years progressed. Here was a modern songwriter that I enjoyed and whose discs didn't get old on the ears. His tunes had helped keep me sane at times during an international vacation and had stayed in my CD player through several failed romantic relationships and a handful of minor life crises. It seemed like such an unattainable goal to interview him, however. Death Cab for

Cutie was an extremely popular band and had recently signed to Atlantic Records. I also wasn't writing much at the time, and when I did author articles, they were for smaller publications.

But my time to interview Mr. Gibbard came—albeit five years after my Prague trip. I had greatly increased my journalistic output and would sometimes write under a pseudonym, "Adam Trask"—a name lifted directly from Steinbeck's *East of Eden*, my favorite novel of all time.

The scenario to interview Ben Gibbard couldn't have been better. He had recently recorded a soundtrack, along with Americana music legend Jay Farrar, for the documentary *One Fast Move or I'm Gone: Kerouac's Big Sur,* which was centered on Jack Kerouac's powerful novel. A music business acquaintance worked in the Death Cab fold, and I approached him asking for advice on how to get an interview with Ben. He kindly put me in touch with Death Cab's management, who, in turn, kindly made an introduction to a publicity executive at Atlantic Records. I got the interview, and a renewed relationship with Atlantic ensued.

The Atlantic-arranged phone conversation with Ben Gibbard happened without any issues whatsoever, except maybe a rescheduling. He could not have been nicer. I realized how much I had in common with him, and that made the conversation flow well. He was into literature and film and around the same age as me—he did not come across any differently than somebody you'd meet at a holiday party while drinking a cocktail and eating yogurt-covered pretzels. He was able to reflect upon Kerouac's influence and also look at his own career and life in a way that provided for great quotes.

Writing the article was tough, as I did not want to screw it up. I did have some fun, though. The piece, of course, revolved around Kerouac—considered one of the fathers of the Beat movement—and I remembered an episode of *Leave It to Beaver* where Wally is transformed into a beatnik and starts to embrace that culture, much to Ward and June's dismay and Beaver's usual open-mouthed innocence. The beatniks in that show wore French berets and listened to live jazz—and also, if my memory serves me correctly, crossed their legs in female fashion. Since I like to find humor whenever I can, I thought it would be funny to start my story with that reflection.

Gibbard and Farrar played the Boulder Theater on Tuesday, January 26, 2010. I was joined by my friend Eric, who had provided a soundtrack of laughter when I got trapped inside the Samples' tour bus bathroom several years prior. The show itself was executed well and was remarkably different than a Death Cab performance, as it leaned heavily in the album's decidedly Americana direction. The lap steel player, Mark Spencer of Son Volt, was mind-blowing with his mastery of the instrument. Nick Harmer, Death Cab bassist and genius with bass melodies, provided the low end. I interviewed him a few years later when Death Cab was about to play Red Rocks and he, like Ben, was extremely friendly, reflective, and down-to-earth.

I kept running into a friend of my pal Greg's at the Boulder Theater show. I swear I kept calling this guy "Franklin" instead of his real name. The first time, I cried out, "Hey Franklin! Fantastic show, eh?" He corrected me with the name thing, smiled and said, "Yeah, Chris, it is a great show. I love these guys." But "Franklin" he remained for the rest of the night. It might be my imagination, but I am almost sure he started avoiding me after the third or fourth encounter as "Franklin." This wasn't the first, and certainly not the last, time I've forgotten a name. Just recently, at a party, I ran into a girl I had met a few times. I couldn't remember her name, so I decided to try "Gwendolyn." She gave me a dirty look.

****

What led to your involvement with the disc and the documentary?
About two and a half years ago, I got contacted through management by the producers of the film, and they asked me to be a part of this, to be one of the talking heads in the documentary, but also that they were working on this record, and Jay Farrar was writing all of the songs, and he was taking

the text from *Big Sur*. I was very much interested. At the time it was being sketched as, "It's going to be a lot of guest vocalists"—this person, that person. I was like, "Oh yeah, that sounds good. I'll go down with them and just record vocals and play a little guitar on a tune or something like that. Yeah, that'll be fun." And I got down to San Francisco and it's just me—me and Jay. We spent a couple days recording down in San Francisco, and those sessions were a bit strange because they were also filming them for a behind-the-scenes documentary or documentary documentary—didn't really know at the time. We really enjoyed working with each other. We were [both] very connected to the source material, so we decided to push forward and try to finish the record, just the two of us.

What was your reaction when you heard the completed record?
I really liked it. We'd been working together—we spent a little bit of time recording in San Francisco, but then I went down to St. Louis and we recorded a bunch more material. Jay came to L.A. and recorded a tune with me—I'd been monitoring the process while we were making the record. There wasn't anything that really jumped out at me about the record once it was finally finished other than the fact that it's something that I really enjoyed and I'm really glad to be a part of, because not only do I love the source material, but I also just love Jay's songs, and it was a lot of fun to make a record with him.

Do you have any favorite songs on the record?
Of the ones I sing, I really like "Willamine," because that was the first thing we recorded. We were in the studio relatively early in the day. We had really only hung out for maybe an hour or two total before we went in there to do that song. The basics of that track are Jay on piano and me on guitar and vocal, and those three elements are totally live. So the basis of the song is live, and I think in that song you can hear how the rhythm sways a little bit back and forth as we're trying to figure out how to play with each other. I just think

the vocal turned out really well since I was intrepid about how to go about singing this tune and also learning at the same time. So I really like how that turned out. I also really like "Breathe Our Iodine" on that record, because it's just Jay. I added a vocal or something like that, but it's just a really minimal, cool arrangement. I'm quite a fan of that tune as well.

What was recording the record like? You had mentioned something about spending three days on it.
We spent three days in San Francisco recording basics of what the record would turn into. When I went down to San Francisco to meet Jay, I was under the impression that there was going to be a backing band. It was a matter of going in and just singing a couple of tunes and strumming an acoustic guitar. But here it ends up being just Jay and I. So those first three days of recording were just Jay and I in a recording studio with our acoustic guitars. There was a piano in there, and some shakers and noisemakers, but no drum kit, no bass amp, nothing like that.

So we took those basic tracks and went to Jay's place in St. Louis and spent five or six days. I played drums on a bunch of the stuff that didn't have drums, and we re-recorded a couple tunes from the ground up. Mark Spencer, who plays in Son Volt and who's been playing with our live band, played a lot of lap steel and piano and bass. We all co-produced and arranged a lot of the tunes. And from there we were able to send a lot of the stuff off to be mixed, and Jay and I recorded the song "One Fast Move" ["One Fast Move or I'm Gone." -Ed.] in L.A. I guess it would be about a year ago, a little over a year ago, here in L.A. I guess on paper, it wasn't a lot of recording time, but that was spread over the course of—I guess we started in June of 2007 and then I guess the last recording we made for the record was January of 2009. We were e-mailing and sharing ideas, but the record didn't take two years to make. We only got together three times in two years to do the record.

What is the live show like? I'm assuming there's a full backup band. What has that experience been like?

It's been really fun. We've got Nick [Harmer] from Death Cab playing bass, and Jon Wurster, from Superchunk and Mountain Goats, and he's playing drums, and Mark Spencer is playing guitar and lap steel and some organ and stuff like that, so the live band has been really fun. I mean, we're obviously playing the record, but also we've augmented the set with some of Jay and I's more deep cuts, solo songs, there are some covers and stuff like that. So yeah, it's been fun. We did a week of these shows in October when the record came out. I, as much as Jay, was probably a little nervous about what people were going to expect from the show. We weren't sure if it was going to be a lot of people who were primarily fans of Jay's or mine coming expecting to see a Ben Gibbard solo show and then a Jay Farrar solo show or some weird combination, but for the most part, people who came to the shows, at least the first time, seemed to understand what the shows were about and also [were] really open to the fact that they were hearing a lot of new material. It was a lot of fun for me, as I'm sure it was for Jay. I guess I can't speak for him, but I think it's fair to say after me playing a set of similar material for over ten years and Jay going on twenty now, the opportunity to go out and play an hour to an hour and half, and it's all stuff you don't get to play, is really refreshing at this point in my career as a musician.

Oh, sure. You guys [Death Cab for Cutie] have had a grueling tour schedule since the Atlantic deal and even before that. So just being able to do this has to be somewhat relaxing, I would think.

Yeah, it's fun. Nick obviously plays in Death Cab, but it's nice to spend a little bit of time seeing how other people work. This is a quote-unquote "tour," but it's a week and a half long. We're flying from show to show. It's in no way a grueling trip, and it's fun. It's fun because it's new and it's not a fifteen-month campaign. We're enjoying ourselves. I'm looking forward to these shows coming up.

Tell me about your first experience with Kerouac's work. How did you discover him?

I was in college in Bellingham, Washington, and I believe I was between eighteen or nineteen or so and I was on this path, as many people are in their lives at that age. You're not really sure what you want to do with yourself. I was studying to be a scientist. I figured out that's what I wanted to do. And at some point I had this roommate—in fact, Nick [Harmer, Death Cab's bassist] was my roommate in college. He was an English major and had this big stack of books on the shelf and he asked, "Have you read *On the Road*?" I was like, "No, I haven't read this actually."

It's everybody's first book for most people who obviously like Kerouac. And I just fell in love with it. I don't mean to sound overly dramatic or anything like that, but in reading that book and going on a huge Kerouac kick where I just dove into every book I could find in used bookstores around Bellingham, it really set me on a particular path in life. I've been able to live a healthy version of that life as a touring musician for the last ten, twelve years or something like that. Just being on the road and traveling, having friends spread out all over the country, you get to swoop in for one day and "See ya," and then you're on the way to a new city. I really fell in love with the notion of that life, and it certainly helped push me out the door onto our first tours and allowed me to really enjoy that period of the band as that being the background.

What was your reaction after reading *Big Sur* for the first time? That's quite a different book than *On the Road*. *On the Road* has the highlights and *Big Sur* seems to be almost the downward spiral.

Yeah, when I started reading those books, I just read them all as quickly as I could get my hands on them, but when I read *Big Sur*, and I say this not as some—I'm not saying this because we just did a record on *Big Sur*; *On the Road*, that's like the *Sgt. Pepper* of the Kerouac canon. That's the one that everybody knows. Everybody thinks that that's the best one.

But *Big Sur*, that was my favorite when I read it. It was just so dark and it was so honest. Kerouac, throughout all of his work, has always been very honest and very heartfelt in every way. But what he chose to share with everybody in that book was really powerful to me at the time and still is. But I think even at a young age, I remember reading that book and thinking, "Oh yeah, the road has to end at some point. This is what happens when you continue on this path and you don't look back and you don't stop for a second and recognize that you can't live your life like this all the time."

Sure.
This is a way to live your life for a period of time, but if you don't heed the warning signs along the way, this is one of the potential outcomes of your life. And I think the way he was able to write about that—there's a number of passages in that book that talk about the shame of the hangover, you know, when you wake up after a night of serious drinking and you don't know what you did or what you said and you have that feeling as you're going through the withdrawals of just utter despair. He wrote about those so eloquently and in a way that if you ever had experienced that before, you immediately recognize it. You're just like, "Whoa, he totally captured that perfectly. This is what it feels like to be in that position."

You yourself, as a public figure and as an artist, do you find any commonalities with some of what he talks about in *Big Sur*? There's parts in there where he talks about success after *On the Road* and having to deal with that.
Not really. I think that one of the nice things about being a musician is that you kind of get to have your cake and eat it too. I'm sure that I probably pass more people on the street who maybe have one of my songs on their iPod then actually know what I look like. I sometimes feel people's eyes on me in public, but it's really not that often. It's not to an extent that I feel like I could relate to Kerouac and what he was going through. What he was going through was on a national scale and at a time when there really wasn't a playbook for

dealing with success. And certainly not for somebody who spent the majority of his time alone and when he decided he wanted to venture out into the world, he could go to a series of dive bars and bookstores and places like that, and all of a sudden those places that used to be his haunts, they're just overrun with the people who're there to see him and want to get a peek at him and they want the Jack Kerouac experience. I'm thankful that I can't really relate to that.

I'm sure I can't imagine what that would even be like. Well, Ben, I definitely appreciate you taking the time to do this and I wish you guys the best on the tour.
Thanks a lot.

Thanks again. I really appreciate it.
Yeah, no problem. It was nice talking to you.

RAY DAVIES

Monday, February 8, 2010
Article: *Boulder Weekly* (March 18, 2010)

I remember the crudely crafted letters—"The Kinks"—spray-painted on a light pole near the baseball field at the Freeman-Centennial School in Norfolk, Massachusetts. It was 1982. I was a second-grader at the Freeman part of the school complex. I had a fantastic teacher, Mrs. Pizzi, who was an actress and saw my creative potential. I also joined the Norfolk Youth Lions "Tan Tigers" soccer team at the gentle prodding of my dad: "Come on, Chris. You'll enjoy soccer." And I did. I was the resident goalie for most of the season, occasionally branching out to a defensive position. I think we won two games the entire season, but the spirit and camaraderie were there. We weren't even depressed when we had our final gathering with our coach, Mr. Merrill, at an area McDonald's—not in Norfolk, of course. We didn't have fast-food restaurants there.

But seeing the band's name painted in black on the post at my school got me thinking. I was prone to daydreaming anyway. I tried to imagine who would have deflowered that virgin post with the rock band's name. I figured it was probably one of the flannel-, leather-jacket or pullover-wearing cigarette smokers who spit a lot while waiting for the school bus and often gave me dirty looks. It had to have been them. I didn't think much more about the Kinks until V66, Boston's free music video station, launched as the mid-'80s were quickly approaching.

The UHF channel was a huge learning experience for me. My dad and I would often discuss music based on what I had seen and heard on the station. In fact, he had to correct me when I suggested Led Zeppelin was an American band and that the group I had called Deed Purple was actually Deep

Purple. Simple, but important, historical facts. But the truth is, I would probably never have been as interested in these bands had it not been for the combination of television and music—and we didn't have cable, so MTV was out of the question.

It was on V66 that I again encountered the Kinks—in the form of a video for the veteran British band's 1984 single "Do It Again." The song was catchy and energetic, and the video was fun to watch. I think I probably viewed the video twenty or twenty-five times while eating potato chips and drinking Hershey's syrup-laden chocolate milk during my after-school afternoons.

My dad and I were riding in our red Subaru station wagon one day, probably heading to the hardware store or the town dump to drop off our trash. "Sunny Afternoon" happened to come on the radio, and my dad turned to me and said, "That's the Kinks." "Really?" I asked. After all, it sounded nothing like the band that recorded "Do It Again." I remember hearing something about sailing and a yacht and thinking, "No, this is not good. Where are the power chords and loud drumming? Enough about yachts and enough about sailing."

Sadly, it would be years before I would delve into the band any further than "Do It Again" and the *Word of Mouth* album from which the song came. I blame this on a best-of compilation I picked up that, in my opinion, didn't do the band justice and failed to capture the power of their recorded catalog. The disc made me conclude that "Do It Again" had been an exception and not the norm. However, I eventually developed a full appreciation for the Kinks—including the magic of "Sunny Afternoon" with all its talk of sailing and yachts—and for Ray Davies himself, the creative genius behind the band—albeit years later.

My reintroduction to the talents of Davies (and thus the music of the Kinks) occurred courtesy of *Paste* magazine and the fantastic listening stations in Denver's Twist & Shout store. *Paste* had a heightened level of writing talent, and its album reviews mattered. When *Paste* praised the veteran British artist's just-released 2006 solo offering, *Other People's Lives,* and Twist & Shout had the disc at a listening station, I took the opportunity to put on a pair of low-profile stereo headphones and press play on the Nakamichi disc changer and my life changed. This was the type of material I would have expected from the writer of "Do It Again." Thank you, *Paste*, for the recommendation, and thank you, Paul Epstein for providing the listening opportunity in your store.

Soon after falling in love with *Other People's Lives*, I stuck my feet in the deep waters of the Kinks' back catalog. It started with a purchase of *Something Else By the Kinks*, the band's 1967 full-length, purchased at a Borders bookstore for under ten dollars. I was mesmerized by "Afternoon Tea" and quickly realized why "Waterloo Sunset" was a classic.

I decided to make an investment and over the course of the next several months, bought most of the band's catalog and didn't listen too much else. I purchased a Kinks T-shirt and firmly displayed my appreciation for the group. In fact, I wore the shirt while checking into a flight from Berlin back to Denver with my girlfriend at the conclusion of a too-short vacation. The German airline worker behind the counter said, "Oh, the Kinks. I love them. What's your favorite album?" My girlfriend looked at me as if it was some secret customs question meant to pick out fraudulent travelers. I replied, with a big smile and without much hesitation, "*Schoolboys in Disgrace*," the band's 1975 masterpiece. The airline employee looked at me, smiled, and said, "Wow! You must have been quite young when that came out!"

Ray Davies, with *Something Else By the Kinks*, *Schoolboys in Disgrace*, and "Do It Again" as a few small examples, is one of the most talented and prolific entertainers in the history of pop music. He will forever be remembered for "You Really Got Me," the timeless 1964 hit he recorded with the band he led for decades. Beyond his songwriting and frontman capabilities for the Kinks and solo artist work, Davies also produced the majority of the Kinks material, undertook film and television projects, wrote three books—*X-Ray: The Unauthorized Autobiography*, *Waterloo Sunset: Stories*, and *Americana: The Kinks, the Riff, the Road: The Story*. He's involved himself in a heaping amount of creative endeavors that would make artists half his age gasp with exhaustion.

In 2009, Davies released *The Kinks Choral Collection*, a disc he recorded with the Crouch End Festival Chorus along with his backup band. Songs from his celebrated and lengthy career were recorded with the sixty-five-piece vocal ensemble. The following year, he released *See My Friends*, an album of past tunes recorded with artists like Mumford and Sons, Billy Corgan, Bon Jovi, Bruce Springsteen and the late Alex Chilton—an interesting endeavor for sure.

When I discovered that Davies was coming to Denver in March of 2010, I quickly (and frantically) called every publicist I knew, attempting to obtain an interview. I carefully prepared my questions like I hadn't done since interviewing Rush guitarist Alex Lifeson eight years prior. I had seen Davies perform at Denver's historic Paramount Theater on July 6, 2006, and I wasn't going to sit idly by again and let a possible interview opportunity, however slim the chances, pass me by.

Davies proved to be incredibly personable and insightful, full of good humor and laughter. He politely answered all of my questions and even the questions about a Kinks reunion (something I was a bit nervous about—how many times has *that* been asked over the years?). When I was done with the phone interview, I exited my car, walked back into my day-job office building and sat at my desk. I was prepared for a barrage of customer service complaints, but I still managed to smile. I felt like I had met someone, however briefly, who truly was a gentleman and a musical genius; someone who deserved the accolades he had received.

Ray's show on the twentieth of March at Denver's Ogden Theater was electrifying, if you can use that term for an acoustic set. He played guitar and sang, accompanied by guitarist Bill Shandley. It was a performance full of startlingly powerful tunes, filled with energy. When Davies' opening act, the 88, came out and joined him on a slew of classic Kinks material, it was like it probably would have been forty years ago in a sweaty, smoke-filled British club. Sure, age has set in, but Davies proved to the appreciative crowd that he was in tip-top form and provided the full house with a show they will never forget.

****

How's Boulder?
Boulder's great! It's snowing, but it's great.

Oh, boy.

A lot like the scenario of "Postcard from London." Lots of snow right now.
I've played there before, and I enjoy it. It's a great place.

I appreciate you doing this. I just have some questions on the choral record and a few other questions for you.
OK.

Your songs naturally lend themselves to choral interpretation because you've always had strong melodies and harmonies. What was it like for you narrowing down the songs that you wanted to put on the record?
We had examined the tunes that had interesting harmonic structures. And, of course, the record company wanted certain songs, and the choir wanted certain songs, and it was down to the melody. Interestingly enough, these dates I'm doing are a two-man acoustic show. It's just me and Bill Shanley playing acoustic songs in Denver. We're doing a song called "See My Friends," which on the choral album was a cappella voices and no instruments. But the original instrumentation was both Bill and myself playing an acoustic version, so all the tonality and harmonic influences stem from that version. So when we play it in Boulder, what you'll be hearing [is] the original harmonic structure, if you like, to the choral record.

Oh, wow! That should be interesting. When you were working on that record, do you have a memorable experience that sticks out most from the recording?
Yeah. Listening to sixty people sing "You Really Got Me." That was fun, but the gig that sticks in my mind from the last year

was Glastonbury. It was a two-man show, like we're doing in Boulder, so it's Bill and I, and we got down to Glastonbury, and there are twenty-thousand people there, and we thought, "Oh, what are we going to do?" We went on, and something magical happened. There's a lot of dynamics and interesting diversity [that] can come out of two players, and Bill is a very talented accompanist. Each show is a surprise because we hit on something new every night.

Do you enjoy doing the more intimate two-person shows versus the full band?
I don't think I have a preference either way. I'm looking forward to this because we're just going through the repertoire today, learning songs, and Bill said, "You know, I had a song of yours on an album and it was in a movie, and I haven't heard you play it," and I thought, "Well, I haven't played that song before." So we're gonna do it, simply because it came about from the two-man experience. Sometimes you get the less obvious songs [that] come through when it's in a more intimate setting.

Oh, sure. Now what song was that that you're going to put in the set?
Ah, do you want me to tell you?

Do you want it to be a surprise?
It was an obscure song that was in a film, a European film called *The American Friend,* called "Nothin' In the World Can Stop Me Worryin' 'Bout That Girl." It was a Wim Wenders film. So we're going to try and do that. I've never played it since I recorded it with the Kinks. So that comes out of doing these smaller, intimate shows.

Back about forty-five years ago, you said in a bio on an album sleeve that you're "a collection of loose ends," that you don't want to be a pop star and you think this is just a part of your life that will come to an end. What does it feel like to still be doing this after forty-five years?

I'm still waiting for it to happen. I'm waiting for it to get started and I'm waiting for it to come to an end. But it's just one of those things. I never intended on being a songwriter. I wanted to just play in a band—everyone in art school wanted to play in a band. And I just played along on cover tracks; my brother did the lead singing. Then we needed a single, you know, something original, because the stuff they were giving us to record were like rejects from the Beatles or Rolling Stones sound-alikes. And I had this song, "You Really Got Me," I'd written when I played in a blues band, and when it came out, people said, "We've never heard anything quite like it before," and it was, in its time, revolutionary. You just don't know how these things evolve. That was the fifth song I ever wrote. So here I am all these songs later, and today I discovered one I had forgotten about. It's quite an interesting journey.

Do you ever forget any of the lyrics?
I'm ashamed to say that once I forgot the lyrics to the second verse of "Waterloo Sunset," to my everlasting shame. But I won't do it this time.

You've always injected sarcasm and satire into a lot of your songs. When you're writing songs, is that something that comes naturally for you?
Yeah. I think the best kind of satire is, you know, you're going to throw a pie in somebody's face, you always get hit with the pie yourself. That's the secret of satire. People know that the pie's gonna hit somebody, and when it hits yourself, I think that's the true essence of real satire. It's not to make other people the brunt of it; it's got to pay off on you as well. To me, that's the funniest kind of comedy.

Sure, sure—kind of like the lyrics to "Do It Again"—what you were doing in that song.
Yeah, exactly. Exactly.

I know that you have a few children. Have any of your children pursued music?

My daughter Natalie's got a band. She's got a drummer and a piano player and she sings, and it's quite interesting music. I think they've all tried from time to time, but they decide to do it as part of their life and they start growing up and they leave it behind.

Do you give them advice about music?
I try to. I wrote a song called "The Hard Way." It's a punk song and I wrote it for my [daughter]. [Not Natalie, but another daughter. –Ed.]. She was not barely a teenager at the time, and they turned it down, and it went on a Kinks album instead. It's strange how different music appeals to people, different age groups.

I loved the "Postcard from London" single. How did the idea for that come about?
That came about from a project I'm writing called *Olympic Land*. [I'm not sure of the exact spelling. -Ed.] It's about the London Olympics and what effect it's going to have on the city. And that was a song written about somebody that had left the country, found a new world—probably Australia or New Zealand—and they pick up this postcard thinking they've got a new life and everybody likes the new world, and it evokes a memory, just maybe a romance, you know, an affair or something, and the message on the postcard seems to give them hope, and just for that moment they share that bond from something thousands of miles away. I think those sorts of things are important. I've got a twelve-year-old daughter, and she did real good in her English reports—tests at school, and I wrote her a longhand letter and sent it instead of sending an e-mail, and it just started off, "Well done in your classes. Remember, this is the way people used to write."

That brings up an interesting point. I know way back when you wrote "20th Century Man," you talked a little bit about technology in that song. Do you think technology has done more damage or more good?

In many ways, it's made everything more accessible, but I'm encountering so many techno-casualties at the moment—people who can't get off. They open their e-mail and they sort of go into freefall. They've got no time to live their lives. Some people are what I call "techno-casualties." So there's an element of that building up in the world.

Ray, what are your future plans? I know that, unfortunately, the *Come Dancing* tour was canceled.
Yeah, that's been put back because of technical difficulties, but the next project I'm doing hopefully will be staging this musical by the end of next year. It's a big show to mount. I'm doing a collaborations album at the moment with other artists that I'm really excited about. I've already done a track with Bon Jovi.

Oh, wow.
[I'm doing a] track with Bruce Springsteen, and we're all really excited about it.

Is that all Kinks and solo material of yours?
Yeah, yeah. And I think I might be collaborating on a few new ideas with people too.

Wow! Now I know that you've been asked this a lot: What's the latest on a possible Kinks reunion? Has that kind of been shelved for now?
Well, no. I've put some tracks down with Mick Avory on the drums, and they sound real good, so it's a question of when Dave [Davies, Ray's brother and Kinks guitarist] wants to come on board. You know, Dave did a lot of late guitar overdubs. He used to come do his part later on, so it's nothing new. I'd really like to see it happen, but in a dignified way.

Sure, sure.
Yeah. And we'll have to have new music, as well as just playing the old stuff.

How is Dave doing? I know that he had some health issues for a long time.
He had some health issues. My advice to Dave is to go slow, take your time and the machinery, his machinery—his arms, you know, just make your hands work the best way they can for you. It's your artillery.

I just have one more question for you. I know your time is kind of short. Now, your backup band on the tour is the 88?
Yeah.

So they're going to play, and then you come out and do an acoustic set with your guitar player and then they come out and back you on a bunch of songs?
Ah, we might do that. We'll see what songs we both know.

All right, Ray, well I definitely appreciate you taking the time to do this.
My pleasure.

Have a great tour.
Thank you, man.

CROWDED HOUSE
(NEIL FINN)

Sometime in late August or early September 2010
Article: *Westword* (September 9, 2010)

When I first interviewed Neil Finn, of Crowded House fame, in January of 2003, I was more than a little excited. Any time I have the opportunity to speak with a songwriter I truly appreciate, I'm always keen on hearing the artist speak and trying to get at the heart of their personality, craft and what influences they bring to their work. Back in 2003, a cheery, friendly Neil got on the phone, said he was happy to meet me, and gave me a great interview full of good humor and insight. During that phone conversation, he also stated that there were no plans for a Crowded House reunion. In the years since that interview, which centered around Finn's *One All* album, Paul Hester, Crowded House's original drummer passed away. With the addition of new drummer Matt Sherrod, the band was reborn and reactivated, to much fan applause.

While Finn was working as a solo artist, years prior to the Crowded House reunion, I started to really investigate the band's work. I had enjoyed Finn's first solo effort, *Try Whistling This*, but never to the extent I would have wished. However, when the Virgin Megastore in Denver carried Finn's *One Nil* album as an import, I snatched it up, paying something like twenty-four dollars for a copy. I relished in the songs and the performances. This was Neil Finn back to his songwriting prowess.

I remember flying out to the Chicago area to visit my brother soon after buying *One Nil*. While spending the night on his couch in pitch-black darkness, I pressed the play button on my portable CD player and started to realize just how good the disc sounded. *One Nil*—and, later, its North American counterpart, *One All*—became soundtracks for that period of my life where I was really struggling. It was extremely difficult for me to plug in and meet people. I would go to church from time to time, but I didn't like the singles group there. My work friends were fun to hang out with, but I was craving something more. My roommate Tim was a great guy and a long-term friend, but you can only spend so much time with one person. And there was my weight issue. I had gained a significant amount of body fat since being reduced to a desk job upon my move back to Denver. Let's just say it was hard to meet women, and probably a lot of that was fueled by my piss-poor self-image. But during the time that *One Nil* and *One All* were significant parts of my ear food, things started to change slowly. I moved to Denver proper and became roommates with Chad, the guitar player in the band we had just formed, Crash Orchid. I was finally putting my two hundred and fifty dollar treadmill to use and seeing the results. I was eating better, and I finally was at a place where my self-confidence around the opposite sex went from horrible to tolerable. I also got involved with a new church and was meeting people and developed a nice social circle of friends and events to attend.

Five years later, Finn's music was still in heavy rotation on my iPod when a regrouped Crowded House released a reunion record, *Time on Earth* and toured in its support. I was able to catch that show and was incredibly glad I did so, but I didn't pursue an interview—I was taking a break from writing at the time. Later, in 2010, a follow-up disc, *Intriguer,* was released and U.S. tour dates were announced, including a stop at Denver's Fillmore Auditorium. I landed the following interview and was able to write a short piece for *Westword,* but I did not get to see the performance. I had a good reason, though: I was off trekking around Eastern Europe by train. When Crowded House went on stage in Denver, my buddy Jon and I were trying to figure out how to get off a graffiti-covered platform that led nowhere and jump on some sort of public transportation to take us to our hotel in Budapest, Hungary.

****

How is New Zealand?

New Zealand is awesome. We just got back for a short break between two legs of the American tour, so it's a bit of tease, in a way, being home, because we can't really settle, and we're off again next week, but that's OK. We're enjoying the tour anyway.

That's great. Now my first question for you is what has the rebirth and continuance of Crowded House been like for you?

Well, it's been engaging and absorbing, and I'm really enjoying it. I guess that's as much as I could have hoped for from it. I think that this time around we are slightly different in terms of our focus on what's important and able therefore to enjoy it, particularly the shows. There's a very strong connection of a community of people who've been coming to see us or had come to see us in the past and are coming to see us again, and it feels good and soulful and real, you know?

That's great. By the way, the new record, *Intriguer*, is great. What were you feeling when you first heard the completed record?

I was pleased with the fact that it sounded like a cohesive whole, even though there's a lot of variety on the record. It sounds like a band. We put it together in rehearsal rooms and on stages and in the studio, and everybody was involved from the get-go, so yeah, I'm really happy with that sense of itself. It's [got] a strong sense of character, I think.

Yeah, definitely. Now, for you, what is it like to still be recording and touring after all these years with Split Enz, early Crowded House, your solo material—what's that like to still be doing that?

It's a great blessing to be able to play music now for the good part of thirty years, and I feel there's every likelihood it will continue until I'm too old to pick up a guitar. So it's a really great continuum, and I'm really grateful for it. It seems like there's enough people to take an interest in whatever I'm up to that I can go and play anywhere, and the records spread out and they have great, mysterious lives, so I'm really appreciative.

I love the song "Falling Dove" off the new record. It has that trademark intensity that you seem to bring with your vocals and guitar playing. What is the songwriting process like for you?
It's a mystery, really. The days that you can't write, you can't remember how you ever did. But it's just a matter of dreaming away with an instrument in your hand until you get something that makes you feel something, you know? If it makes you feel something, it's the beginning of a song. Obviously songs tend to deal with empathy, and people relate to them. They make them into something too, sometimes not even the same thing, but a song can seem very sad to some people and to others uplifting or captivating.

Do you typically come up with words or music first?
Well, never just the words. On the odd, very rare occasion, just the words, but generally speaking, I'll get the melody and some chords and hopefully a few central lines; key lines, and then I'll flesh it out. And every now and again you get the whole lot at once, so that's always a good sign if that happens.

Sure. Are there things in particular that are inspiring you these days when you are writing songs; different topics—things like that?
Not really. I mean, not in particular that I could quarantine. I think you just take stuff in, it gets rearranged in the brain and comes out in quite random ways for me. I trust my subconscious. In many ways, when I'm actually writing words down or getting things done, often not even really aware of what the words are getting at, and depending when I look at them and ponder them, I finally go, "Oh, yeah. I know where that's coming from." Then you can find the connections, parts and threads; follow those directions.

What's it like having Liam following in your footsteps?
I'm very proud of what he's done. He's a very competent musician and a [Unclear. –Ed.] performer. And he's got his own spin on things. So yeah, I'm really proud of him.

Do you ever give him advice from things you've gone through as a musician?
I think sometimes when we talk I can give him a little comfort here or there about dilemmas he's facing that he shares with every Roger on the planet, and then he can give me advice sometimes. It's a good two-way street.

Years ago when I talked to you, you mentioned that sometimes when you're in the grocery store with your wife, you'll sometimes hear your song and not realize it's you. Does that still happen?
Well it does, yeah. For some reason, I do seem to not have a very good radar for my own music. It often sounds really annoying to me. I just get a slight—it's familiarity, but I haven't quite caught on that it's me. You know, I've had that happen a few times.

Is that more when they remove the lyrics and it's just the music?
That's even more confusing; of course, if it's bouncing around in the supermarket or something and then you don't hear it in a normal way. So if you're not concentrating, you're thinking about something else, it's overly familiar or something, you know?

After all that you've done over the years, is there anything that stands out as a triumph that you've had as an artist that you always look at and you're proud of that moment or achievement?
There's not one thing. I think any time you do a really great show, that takes over as your most recent favorite moment. I cannot really say there's one defining moment for me. There's been a series of really good things, and there's been a

few hard times here and there, as well, but music is quite an extraordinary thing; it takes you a lot of places.

What are your future plans right now? Do you have anything lined up that you're working on?
I'm working on a lot of things at the moment, actually, [that] I'll be unfolding next year. I'm playing drums on the next thing I'm doing. That's a change.

Are you going to be doing something with Tim again?
That'll come at some point, I'm sure. I'm not sure when that would happen, but I'm sure we'll roll that out again.

Neil, I just wanted to thank you again for doing this. Definitely appreciate you taking the time. What time is it there, anyway?
It's just on eleven in the morning, so it's eleven twenty or something.

Oh, wow. Okay. Well, I wish you the best of luck with the tour and I look forward to seeing you when you come through Denver.
Yeah, I'm looking forward to getting to Denver, as always. It's always been a good place for us.

Yeah, you told me a story about how they didn't have tea and toast at a hotel when you were here one time.
Yeah, I remember that. The guy wouldn't do toast, but he'd do a toasted sandwich. But he wouldn't do toast. It was a kind of small irritation of the day. I didn't do a JetBlue flight attendant, set off the fire alarms or anything.

Grab a couple of cans of beer and slide off the plane.
And slide down the chute? No. If only.

Thanks again, Neil. Have a great day.
Thanks, man.

THE POSIES
(JON AUER)

Thursday, October 28, 2010
Article: *Boulder Weekly* (November - December 2010)

My affection for power pop was birthed, as I've mentioned throughout these pages, when my dad used to play the Beatles' "White Album" in the basement of our house in Blacksburg, Virginia. I was barely able to walk or talk. I remember watching the reels spin on the reel-to-reel tape player and even the smell of the aged recording tape as it inched its way across the playback heads. I would sit there on the red shag carpet, often with a fire in the fireplace blazing away, taking in every note and work of melodic genius.

I fought my love of the Beatles for years. When I was a preteen and even well into my teenage years, I didn't really think much of them. I was a metal guy and also into college rock like U2 and the Alarm, but I stayed away from the Fab Four for some reason.

During my junior year of high school, however, my dad bought tickets for my brother and me to see Paul McCartney with him at the University of Colorado in Boulder. I was awestruck. This was one of the first times I had been to a show that large. A few years prior, my buddy Rob and I had seen the Stones play for free at the now-demolished and redeveloped Sullivan Stadium in Foxboro, Massachusetts, as his dad worked for a company that supplied ice to the food vendors. We were able to go in during Living Colour's sound check (they were opening that tour), and I remember members of the band or road crew seeing us watching and saying something like, "How are you guys doing?" from the stage. Living Colour proved to be amazing during that live performance, and the Stones were the entertaining, legendary rockers that they still are to this day. I was fairly stoned from the secondhand smoke that covered the stadium in a cloud-like haze. I didn't know any better. I'm sure I thought it was my allergies or fatigue or something of the sort. Scents invaded my nostrils I had never encountered before—some that I have yet to meet again, and I've been to a lot of concerts since.

Anyway, McCartney was amazing during his CU gig. He had a crack band, including guitarist Hamish Stuart. A musical seed was planted inside my head. I walked away mesmerized.

I wouldn't think about McCartney or the Beatles much again until a couple of years later, when I was in my freshman or sophomore year of college, and my parents took me, my brother and my grandmother to see *Phantom of the Opera* at the Buell Theatre in downtown Denver. After the show, we went to the old Pablo's location nearby and had coffee. The Beatles' *Revolver* happened to be playing in the background. The sounds of "I'm Only Sleeping" mesmerized me. I went out and bought *Revolver* the next week. Of course, I had heard the album before—my dad had a vinyl copy—but it didn't resonate with me at the time. It would be another several years before I would fully realize the impact the Beatles' music had on me. But this new appreciation for the band definitely helped push me a little further into developing my love for power pop.

When I moved to Nashville in '97, fresh out of college, I had a job (internship, not paid) working as a publicist for Absolute Records, a small label owned by former Prince and the Revolution guitarist Dez Dickerson. Dez was an amazing musician and signed some notable talent, including the band Believable Picnic. Believable Picnic's singer and guitarist was Jade Hanson, whose brother, Joel Hanson, was known for singing and playing guitar in popular Christian band PFR. PFR and Believable Picnic essentially were power-pop bands.

I happened to be around the Absolute office one day, probably throwing away junk faxes, and my coworker Mark was speaking with Jade. Somehow the subject of the band Jellyfish came up. I asked, "Oh, is that a rap band or something?" Maybe I was thinking of Fishbone. I'm still not sure on that one. I was quickly corrected after a bit of laughter. "You've never heard of Jellyfish, Chris?" Jade asked.

"No," I responded. "Well, I'm going to let you borrow both their discs," he replied.

He loaned me both Jellyfish records, *Bellybutton* and *Spilt Milk,* and I was hooked. The albums did not leave the stereo of my old Acura Integra for months. The sun would soak the black coupe with no air conditioning to compensate. I would sweat, and the seatbelt would leave giant marks diagonally across my shirts, but I was getting my daily Jellyfish fix. My fascination with them and with power pop in general lasted for a long time and eventually led to my discovery of the Posies.

Somewhere I saw a list of the most influential power-pop records, and it included the Posies' *Frosting on the Beater.* I went out and bought a used copy at one of the record stores that was around at the time. It might still be around, but, as of this date, those are a dying breed. Such a shame.

The disc drew me in. First and foremost, the drumming was frenetic, loud and creative with an abundance of energy and skill. Then there were the songs. These were not timid pop rock tunes, but full of loud guitars and great vocal harmonies and hooks to match the other elements. I could even hear some King's X nuances that had me even more fascinated.

Realizing how satisfied I was with *Frosting on the Beater,* I had no qualms about requesting a copy of *Every Kind of Light* from the label publicist when it came out in '95. I couldn't get into the disc—it was too different from *Frosting.* I did go see the band at Denver's Larimer Lounge after *Every Kind of Light* was released and remember thinking it was a good show but not as stellar as I had hoped—maybe it was the sound mix. Soon after, I purchased the band's sophomore record, *Dear 23,* and, like *Every Kind of Light,* it didn't resonate with me. Then I decided to purchase *Amazing Disgrace,* the fourth album and the one that followed *Frosting.* Like the other discs, I couldn't get into it. Many people have enjoyed those records tremendously, however.

Five years later, the band would release *Blood/Candy.* I was skeptical. After all, I had only really gravitated toward one Posies record, and it had been released long ago. I also found out the band would play the Bluebird Theater in Denver. Regardless of my skepticism, I wanted to interview Ken Stringfellow or Jon Auer, the two guys who are the nucleus of the Posies. I pitched the idea to the *Boulder Weekly*. My editor went for it, and soon I was in possession of *Blood/Candy*. I cranked my stereo receiver and pushed play, and as the first songs unveiled themselves, all my hesitation took a backseat. This album was brilliant, full of strong material and enough harmonies, melodies and tasty hooks to make the most puritan of power-pop fans smack their hands together with glee.

I interviewed Ken and Jon separately on the same day, back to back, by cell phone from my car during my lunch period at work. Unfortunately, the battery in my Sony MiniDisc kept acting up during Jon's interview (the first one of the two), so by the time Ken and I started talking, the power completely went out and I had to capture his quotes on paper.

Ken and Jon were very kind and full of good information. They played a great show at the Bluebird that was everything you would have expected from songwriters and musicians of their caliber. It was interesting to hear how they recorded parts of *Blood/Candy* in hotel rooms and different locales, sometimes when band members were thousands of miles away from each other in completely different countries. During my interview with Ken, he compared the whole thing to driving blind in a snowstorm—something he once did on the East Coast to make a show.

I hung out at the concert with my friend Ashlea-Ann, who worked at the Bluebird at the time, and my music-loving friends Randy and Josh. We had a fantastic time with good conversation and pints of IPA.

A couple years later, Randy and I would find ourselves seated in Moe's BBQ in Englewood, Colorado watching Ken Stringfellow perform. It was a true solo show and Ken spent a good part of the show playing in the small crowd of twenty or so folks. It was a night that will always be remembered.

****

CHRIS CALLAWAY

I know that you and Ken have had a partnership for over two and a half decades. How did you guys meet?
We met at a music store in this small town called Bellingham, Washington, that we both grew up in, about ninety miles north of Seattle. When I was twelve, I was kind of the hotshot guy who played guitar all the time around town, you know what I mean? And I would hang out at a music shop every day after school, and eventually my reputation spread far and wide through the small town of Bellingham. Ken was in another band with someone else who had heard about me, and they needed a lead guitar player. So one day this guy comes down to the music store, or these two guys do, and this one guy does all the talking and asks if I'd like to be in a band because they heard I was a hotshot guitar player. I was like, "Who is this guy?" and I look behind him and there was this other guy who wasn't saying anything, very shy, and that was Ken. Little did I know that meeting would lead to as many years as you just laid on me there of togetherness. So it started very spontaneously and almost accidentally, really. We spent a lot of time in bands together, and those bands ended up falling apart, and we always kind of gravitated toward each other. I had this little recording studio in my house when I was growing up, because my father is a musician, and we would spend our weekends there after school working on—basically making mini records together, not really knowing that we were kind of practicing for our careers, in a weird way. So yeah, that's how we met; very early, and after a couple years it was a very intense and concentrated relationship. We kind of called it a day at the end of the '90s with the Posies, and then we kind of worked our way back into each other's fields of gravity around 2000, and ever since then we've been doing the Posies when we feel like it, pretty much, and not ever because we're forced to do it, but because we enjoy it. We're certainly not making millions doing the Posies, so there has to be a level of enjoyment and satisfaction that comes from things other than finding monetary rewards. I guess I'm just trying to say that we enjoy doing it when we want to do it, and that's the best way to do it.

What's the funniest story you have about Ken [Stringfellow]?
This isn't fair. You're pulling out the big guns now.

Well, I'm going to ask him the same thing about you, so I figure I should be able to get some good stuff.
You know what you've got to do? You've got to write down this e-mail. Write down my e-mail. [Jon provides his e-mail address. –Ed.] And then send me an e-mail. I'm going to need a little more time to get the really good one, but I'll send you something really good.

All right, great. That sounds good.
I'm doing interviews like every ten or fifteen minutes, so something's not springing to mind right now. [There are] just too many good things. If you drop me a line, I'll get back to you.

Why five years since the last record? I know you guys are involved in a myriad of other things.
There just never is enough time in the day to get done everything you need to get done, basically. We both do a lot and we travel a lot and we have solo careers … [My battery died here so there is a gap in the recording. –Ed.] … clocks and realize that if we didn't give it some serious thought, it might be a really long time before there'd be a chance to even make another Posies record. So we just kind of went for it, and I'm really glad that we did. I must say, we barely pulled it off in time. We were right up to the eleventh hour with it, but it all worked out in the end, and here we are now.

You recorded the majority of the record in Spain. Why Spain?
Spain is a place that we've been going to since 1993. We kind of have a love affair with the Spanish people and the lifestyle, and it's a place that has continually supported us, too. I've already been there twice this year, and I think I've averaged two or three visits a year since 1993, so it's a very comfortable place for us. Yet we'd never actually made a full-

length record there. We'd done a little recording, made a live record there, but we'd heard of this really cool, funky residential studio in the south of Spain that Ken and I both eventually visited and checked out; a studio of this guy named Paco Loco, and he's kind of a legendary Spanish music figure. And we were sold on it once we visited the place. The idea of just sequestering ourselves together in this studio for a couple of weeks just seemed really appealing. All we did was wake up, make music, eat, sleep and repeat. The studio door was twenty feet away from the door of where we were sleeping, and it just made everything very streamlined and a lot of fun too. It's kind of hard to not have a good time in Spain, and the red wine is quite excellent there as well, so that certainly figures into the equation with us.

How did you wind up hooking up with Brendan Benson?
You know about the whole passing of Alex Chilton this year? He was with Big Star. One of the things that we had to fulfill after Alex passed was we still had a couple shows that were booked as Big Star. We decided the best option out of all the options we could have followed was to actually still play the shows, but maybe turn them into tributes of sorts. So we turned the South by Southwest show we had into a tribute with a lot of guests, and then the final show was the show in Memphis at a place called the Levitt Shell, which is a very historical place in Memphis. It's where Elvis first played. It's this amazing, old outdoor theater and park. Really cool, with these crazy lights. If you go Google it or YouTube it and look for some of the YouTube videos, you'll see what I'm talking about. But Brendan's name came up as a possible person to be a guest and to perform songs with us. Jody Stephens, the drummer from Big Star, had already met and hung out with Brendan a bit. We called him, and he showed up, and he was great. We hit it off very well—so much so that when we discussed touring this fall, it just kind of came up that maybe we should do this tour together. And, you probably know this, Ken and I are going to be half his band, basically, as well. In fact, I will be rehearsing Brendan Benson songs when I get off the phone with you. I've got my work cut out for me. It has

the potential to be a one-big-happy-family kind of vibe on this trip. We shall see.

How do you decide who sings what?
Pretty much we write individually, and so if one of us wrote it, we sing it. It's pretty simple. There's no great mystery there; pretty cut and dry, really.

BRUCE COCKBURN

Sometime in late April or early May 2011
Article: *Boulder Weekly* (May 19, 2011)

There are some artists you don't mind interviewing multiple times, as they are fascinating, well-spoken people who ebb and flow with insight, humor and friendliness. Canadian musicians I've had the pleasure of speaking to over the telephone seem to sparkle with these qualities that endear them to me as a music journalist.

Back in college, I had the privilege of attending a performance by a talented (and largely underappreciated) Christian pop group, who shall remain nameless, at the annual Cornerstone Festival in Illinois. The guys displayed a mastery of their instruments, and they held my attention the entire time. The music itself was pop but progressive, with some nods to Rush, and also had great hooks and harmonies.

I wound up meeting the two main band members a year or two later at the yearly GMA Week in Nashville and really enjoyed getting to know them a little bit, even if it was only for ten or fifteen minutes. I didn't have the opportunity to speak to them again until after I graduated from college, had lived in Nashville, then moved back to Colorado and started writing articles again. Early on in my rejuvenated freelance journalism career, a publication had asked me to write a piece on the same band based on a disc they had just released on a nationally distributed label.

The interview was expansive—and humorously expensive. Back then, landline international calls were ridiculously pricy, and this was not only an international call, but an international party call. It wound up costing seventy dollars or so. I called one of the two main guys, then called the other, and we had a great discussion. The conversation itself was laden with humor at times—they jokingly labeled a friend of mine a stalker and discussed how he even had a custom-made T-shirt displaying the name of their former band. They also discussed what I thought was a fictitious holiday. Later on, a quick Internet search would prove me incorrect.

"Chris, do you know what holiday it is in Canada right now?" one of the guys asked. It sounded like a serious "let me catch you up on the customs and holidays of your northern neighbor" question, and the tone betrayed nothing of the comical. And, of course, I had to answer. "No, what holiday is it?" There was a brief pause. "It's National Masturbation Month." I may have had tears running down my face due to the amount of laughter, but I had to ask a question of my own and I did it brazenly, "Are you guys celebrating?" I think we all lost it at that point.

Appropriate? Certainly not. However, I'm used to being inappropriate. As I've gotten older, I've retired much of my immaturity while still continuing to find ways to enjoy myself and remain somewhat inappropriate at times. There's only so much time you have to laugh. As a youngster, I used to liberate gas in absolute silence from my dress pants-covered rear end during church services while sitting next to my mom. The looks I received from her could have killed a Green Giant—the mascot of one of the companies that issued the very products probably responsible for this bit of inappropriateness. I'm sure the family friends surrounding us in the nearby pews knew what was going on, but they never said anything. I hope they have forgotten.

Later on, I would interview another Canadian musician whose songs I enjoyed immensely, the legendary Bruce Cockburn. He didn't mention any national holidays, but he was still friendly and full of good humor. He also possessed a mastery of the guitar like few musicians I've heard. The first time I interviewed Bruce, I had a great experience and my respect for him was solidified even more. A second interview happened a couple of years later, the article running in a defunct Colorado magazine.

After several years, I had the opportunity to speak with Bruce for a third time. I wanted to find out what had changed in his life. It was 2011, and he had released a number of albums since (including a live acoustic disc that truly displays his amazing guitar chops). He was touring behind his new release, *Small Source of Comfort*, so an interview opportunity was there. I had delved deep into Bruce's catalog during the eleven years since my first conversation with him, so I had a lot of solid, informed questions. I also had grown to respect him even more as a musician and songwriter.

True North, the label Bruce has long recorded for in Canada, had secured its own distribution in the U.S., so I dealt directly with a publicist there and set up a phone interview. Bruce, as before, was friendly, accommodating and full of wit and humor. He was heart-on-the-sleeve honest about his life, his career and the songs on *Small Source of Comfort*. He even mentioned his grandkids. I still—and I mentioned this in the interview itself—don't see Cockburn as a grandfather. He's the epitome of cool as an outspoken activist, talented lyricist, gifted songwriter and world-renowned guitar player—and he's still cranking out great material. *Small Source of Comfort* features some of his best work in a good while. But, really, are there any parameters on grandfather imagery?

Unfortunately, I didn't make it to either of Cockburn's area shows during the tour. I wish I had.

****

I had to laugh when I read the liner notes, when you talked about what type of record you were going to make, where it was going to be electric and noisy. I got really excited, and then I read the next line that it didn't turn out that way. Did you wrestle with maybe trying to get in an isolated spot to do that type of record?
No. I guess I could have forced the issue, but it didn't seem like a good idea. Basically, through that period of time, my girlfriend moved to New York, lived there for five years and then moved back to San Francisco, where she had been living before that. So I was spending a lot of time in Brooklyn. I guess I could have, [if I] had really put my mind to it, gone out and rented some studio space or something, but that's

not how I work, really. If I'd have been at my house, I could have cranked everything up and it probably would have been that kind of album, but I just can't really pursue that sort of stuff. It's not really new for me to be loud and electric. I did that in the sixties, but to develop a kind of approach to songwriting and using that sort of vibe requires some work, and it just wasn't in the cards.

Well, *The Charity of Night*—I know you had some dissonance on that, going back to that record more recently: "Strange Waters," things like that, and even "Get Up Jonah" had a little bit of that reverberation type thing. Do you think your next record may be more in that direction, or you haven't planned that far ahead?
I haven't planned anything except the touring that we're doing, but it could. It will depend on the circumstances that I'm in. If I lived a solitary existence, of course there would be no issues. I would just go do whatever it was I wanted to do, but when you are close with people you kind of have to be close with people or you will stop being close with people. That becomes the priority, at least in terms of location, and I don't think I'm going to be able to pursue the noise thing in the immediate future. For me, the big issue wasn't so much about the noise as about improvisation and creating a more improvisational approach to songwriting, which, in theory, I should be able to do with any kind of music, but it's a tricky one for me, because when I start writing something, I want to write the whole thing. That's what I've always done. I write a guitar part that fits the melody that fits a set of lyrics, and it's a whole composition—sometimes with a little bit of room for improvising, but not as much as what I was imagining it might go to, so we'll see. I don't know. No promises.

Well, it sounded great anyway. I just thought it was funny that you wrote that and the next paragraph is like, "But it didn't turn out that way."
Yeah, right.

I love the song "Call Me Rose." It's just a great melody and structure, and I love the liner note that said, "What would it take to rehabilitate the soul of Richard Nixon?" And you have the line in the song, "I'm back here learning what it is to be poor/to have no power but the strength to endure." It's very "deny yourself" oriented, very universal. What was it like writing that song?

It wasn't like anything. It was a little bit of work, but mostly it was unlike anything else in that I woke up and the whole song was there in my head. That's never quite happened in exactly that way before. I've had something close to it. Maybe it was something about living in Montreal, where I was at the time, because the other song that comes to mind that was a bit like that was "Open," but there it was more logical. I had an idea about "Open," and then I just started cataloging the sounds and sights that were right around as I woke up in bed, right, so you can hear the bells—the cathedral bells—from outside and noises from people and whatever. But this was totally different from that. For one thing, it's not in my voice. I'm singing in third person; I'm adopting a third-person voice for this song, and I very rarely, if ever, have done that. I think the only other time I can remember doing that was when I was writing "Goin' Down the Road" for the movie, that title. So it was weird from that point of view, like, where did that first line come from? I don't know. My theory is that it had to do with some deep psychological issues around power and me, but expressed through language that was provided by Bush. There's some sort of association there, but I was not really clear on what it is.

What was it like recording the record? Was there a different approach to it this time around? I know you worked with Colin again, and I know you've had a longstanding relationship with him.

It wasn't so different. There were perhaps minor but significant differences though. One is that we recorded in a residential studio in Ontario owned by a band called the Tragically Hip. It's in a former inn, I think—an old stone building that kind of looks like a farmhouse but it wasn't. It

REEL TO REAL BY REEL

was something else. But a nice atmosphere to record in and a residential situation. My house happens to be quite close to that, just a ten-minute drive away, but everybody else came in from wherever they came from. Jenny Scheinman from New York and some of the folks from Toronto, Colin up from Nashville, and they all stayed there and it created a fantastic atmosphere of camaraderie and unity and fun around the whole thing. It was very relaxed, and nobody was going anywhere. Nobody had to rush anywhere. You just sort of roll out of bed, get fed and then you'd start recording. And it was fun. Jenny had her little boy with her and her boyfriend. It was just like a little family scene—well, like a big family scene. That was kind of different for me, but in other respects, we follow the same approach that we have when I've worked with Colin before, which is basically to put a band together and go in the studio and record. You learn the songs as you go and get live performances of them, basically, and then work with those to add whatever or fix whatever as needed.

You mentioned someone's little boy coming into the studio. I know you at least have one daughter. Have any of your children gone into music, and, if so, what type of advice have you given them?
No. I have one daughter, and she has two kids of her own, so they're too young to be getting advice from the likes of me. She sang in a punk band briefly, my daughter did, but she's an anthropologist. She's in the process of pursuing a Ph.D. in anthropology right now. I don't have much advice to offer in that regard either. It's a kind of university experience that I didn't have at all. I went to music school for a couple years, but it was a different atmosphere than what she's experiencing.

What's being a grandfather like for you? I can't picture you—and not in a bad way, but you're Bruce Cockburn, you write songs. You're a songwriter. You address important topics of the day. What's being a grandfather like for you?

Well, it's a bit more long-distance than I would prefer it to be, because they live in Montreal, and I'm hardly ever even at my house, never mind in Montreal. But my daughter did field work last year for more than half [Unclear. -Ed.] she was in Bolivia. She was working with farm people on some aspect of their lives, or aspects of their lives, and she had her youngest kid with her, who turned one right after they got there. He's going to be two at the end of April. That little boy had experienced his—I mean, a third of his life, he'd lived in Bolivia by the time I got down there, in the September of that year. So I went down and had a good visit with them and got to hang with that grandchild. The older one—there's one who's seven now—or is about to turn seven, I guess, and I'm more familiar with her because she's been around longer. I don't really wish for anything different from what I've got, more or less, but if I were to wish for something different, it might be a little more time in one spot so that those guys could see more of me.

I know that you do a lot of traveling. Do you have a trip planned next, and do you bring a journal when you go?
I'm no good at keeping journals. I go with good intentions, but I never write anything unless I have a song idea. Occasionally little bits of description or images that jump out from somewhere, and those will go in the notebook. And the other part of the question: No, I don't have anything like that planned right now because right now it's all about touring, through the summer, anyway, and probably into next year. This tour with the band lasts into early June, and then I'll be doing mostly solo stuff after that. That includes some U.S. dates and some Italian dates and I'm not sure what else yet.

With the tour that you are going to embark on pretty soon—you said that is going to have a full band?
Well, it's a mini-band, and we're about a week into it actually, now, and it's been going extremely well. The band is Gary Craig and Jenny Scheinman, both of whom are on the album, and so it's guitar, violin and drums. And Jenny and I sing. "Drums," loosely, because there's no actual standard drum

kit. It's a modified kit that Gary made out of interesting-sounding drums of various kinds, and then there's a lot of other percussion instruments that get used in the show as well. It's very musical and it's a little bit folky because there's no bass player and you can hear what the guitar is doing on the bottom end and stuff like that.

Are you going to bring along your Surfcaster? [This is an electric guitar made by Charvel that Cockburn used when I saw him live years prior to this interview -Ed.]
No, I'm not using that one. That would have been that other album that we were talking about earlier. There's only one tune—the one tune that's on the album with electric guitar is the only electric guitar piece that we're doing. That's "Comets of Kandahar," and that's on the National Resolectric.

I think you used that on "Wake Up Jonah" and some other songs off _The Charity of Night_, didn't you?
Certainly on "Get Up Jonah," yeah. I think actually—let me think now—I can't even remember what's on those albums now. That one and _Breakfast in New Orleans, Dinner in Timbuktu_, I get them mixed up a bit, but anyway, that guitar does appear on those two albums, for sure.

You've been doing this for a long time, recording under your solo name since, I think, 1970. What's it like to be doing this for so long?
Long! It's weird, because sometimes it feels like I've been doing this a really long time, and other times it just feels like I'm barely getting started and it was yesterday, you know. I guess that's just the way it is for everybody who reaches a certain age. The shape of your life assumes a different perspective when you start approaching the end of it, even though we don't really know. The day after you're born could be the end of it, but we don't think about that until you have to, and of course once you start getting older you have to. Your friends start dying, or you're having crises, at least, and you have to notice that. So it changes the perspective on things, but if I went back and tried to remember all the things

that happened over those years, I don't know if I'd like to do that. There'd be [some] neat stuff in there, there'd be some things that were great from the point of view of creating songs out of the angst that they produced, but I'd rather live with the songs than the memories of some of the stuff that happened, of course. That's probably like everybody else, too.

But it was cathartic. You got everything out in the songs—probably a lot of it. So if you were to look back at your songs, I'm sure you can identify different things at different periods of your life.
Absolutely. It's like looking through a photo album.

I know as a person of faith, a person with a relationship with God, I know that's greatly influenced your songwriting. Are there any convictions through that that you're currently feeling that may make their way into songs?
Well, the ongoing quest for—what's the word—a direct line of communication, I suppose, of some kind. That continues to inform a lot of what I do and certainly to be a lot of what my life is based around. I don't think I take on any specific issues of faith or questing or whatever, but several of the songs do touch on that—"Boundless" being the most obvious. The term "boundless" is a translation of "En Sof," which is the Cabalistic name for God. The thing I like about that is that there's absolutely no definition in there. The only thing you know is you don't know. That God is there, but we can't ascertain any more than that, and then, of course, in their frame of reference, there's all sorts of activity between God and humans through angels and whatever—other avenues. I haven't studied the Cabala particularly, but I like that image of God—or the lack of image of God—and so "Boundless" is a lot about looking for the sense of contact with that. I think having done—I don't want to say "gone through," because I don't know that it's through—but having used the Christian approach to that divinity contact for a couple of decades, I guess I gradually have drifted—I'm not sure if it's away from it or not, but I've drifted away from any sort of orthodoxy

around that, anyway, and into looking for the way in which the Divine touches me, or touches any of us, and how to feel that on a more ongoing basis than I do. So I don't know what to call that; that's a long-winded answer to your question.

"Called Me Back," I thought, was a great song, and it kind of reminded me how technology has changed things and not necessarily for the better. What's your take on that? You said right before the song, "Everybody is too damn busy these days."
Yeah, you know, it just was funny because it's based on a real episode, of course, which has been repeated a thousandfold by other people in my life. You call somebody, try and get a hold of them, and they don't call you back and they don't call you back, and you call them again, and they don't call you back, and eventually they do, or there's some communication, but in the end there's usually a good reason why the response wasn't there. It just seems like such a common thing, and it's annoying, and it's like, "I should write a song about that—this one particular time that it happened," and so I did. I'm thinking it's a humorous song because, of course, everybody lives through this kind of crap, and everybody would get it, you know? It's the kind of topic that's not really worth a serious song at all, but it's just one of those little cartoons, I guess, of life.

And the music matches that, by the way. It just kind of has that cartoonish flow to it, which is good.
Yeah, it's so much fun. Jenny Scheinman went all primitive and played like she hardly could play, and it's fantastic; it's exactly right for the song. But it was so, I thought, very brave of her to just step out and play like that—like in such a beginner's style, you know, all shaky and everything. Gary and I got into some funny percussion stuff in there and he does some of the vibes too.

I was going to say, if you ever decided to play "Silver Wheels" live, it would be great to kind of combine that

with "Iris of the World," because they're both kind of driving songs, you know, similar themes.
Yeah, yeah, yeah—true. Although "Silver Wheels" is a bit more Ginsberg-influenced, apocalyptic, but they are kind of companion pieces. Sure.

I just thought that was interesting, because that was the first thing, when I heard "Iris of the World," wow, this thematically, in certain aspects, it sounds a lot like "Silver Wheels." Anyway, Bruce, I really appreciate you doing this and I hope the tour goes well and I look forward to seeing you when you come to Boulder.
I look forward to it too.

Okay, no problem. Have a great day.
Thanks for your interest.

BILL MALLONEE

previously unpublished
June 2, 2013 and June 20, 2013 (by e-mail)

As this book has made abundantly clear, growing up, discovering, appreciating, playing and finally writing about music entered into the category of obsession for me long ago. It started with my dad playing the Beatles' "White Album" and Chicago's "25 or 6 to 4" on his reel-to-reel tape machine when I was an infant and toddler. I then graduated, much as I'm ashamed to admit it, to a love of Waylon Jennings' "Theme from *The Dukes of Hazzard* (Good Ol' Boys)," a 45 I played on, of all things, a Sears kids' record player covered with graphics that made the device look like the seat of a pair of jeans. There's a bad joke in there somewhere, but I'll refrain for now. It's my thirty-ninth birthday as I'm drafting this. Beer and good food is what's on my mind—both items will be consumed in just a few hours, but I digress. How the mind wanders from the task at hand!

Following my days with the jeans-seat record player, there was an introduction to cassettes and a lot of time spent listening to albums like Van Halen's *1984*, Tears for Fears' *Songs from the Big Chair*, Phil Collins' *No Jacket Required* and plenty of U2. Then there was a Fisher boombox, Christian rock like Rick Cua, Steve Camp and Steve Taylor, and cool things like when radio station WBCN in Boston broadcast an entire U2 show. It must have been from the *War* or *Unforgettable Fire* era, but I recorded the whole thing and played it over and over. Then I became enamored of Stryper and other Christian metal bands—and about this time I also received my first CD player, a JVC model that cost around a hundred and fifty bucks at Lechmere in Framingham, Massachusetts. I realized how cool it was that I no longer had to worry about the decreasing quality of an album's sound when you played it over and over like you did with cassettes, along with the fear of an inadequate player eating the tape. I don't know how many times I had to repair a cassette by carefully taping it back together with the skill of a surgeon. It's no wonder my eyesight started deteriorating at thirteen. I did get really good at cutting up and applying microscopic pieces of tape to mechanically-chewed cassettes, though. Is this a marketable skill? Then there was the considerable amount of time consumed by reeling tape back into cassette casings. My parents had a Subaru station wagon with a horrible aftermarket tape deck that my dad installed, and it consistently devoured certain cassettes. It was fine for most duplicated tapes that didn't cost ten or eleven bucks. But let's say Chris purchases U2's *Boy*, plays it in the car, then has to spend twenty minutes fishing a yard of unraveled tape out of the tape deck while sitting in the driver's seat and trying to see into the pitch-black, tape-playing abyss. Ah, those were the days!

Aside from all their disadvantages, however, cassettes had CDs beat with one simple, unarguable functionality—you could record on them. Recordable CDs wouldn't become available until some eleven years later, and even then it took an advanced knowledge of computer programming to make them work. It was a task best left for those who spent lots of time online, in an apartment scattered with dirty dishes and the air conditioning cranked to meat-freezing levels.

CDs were so cool, though. I remember holding and examining one for the first time, realizing that it was plastic, not metal. And the sound was fantastic. I'd take RCA cables (usually yellow and black or yellow and white ends), plug them into the back of the Fisher boom box (with removable speakers!), set the selection switch to AUX, and I had pristine sound. I simply struck a track button and could go from song to song, or use the rewind or fast-forward buttons and get to certain parts of songs. Gone were the minutes spent getting to a certain tune on a cassette or cueing up to the composition you wanted to put on a mix tape. It was almost *instantaneous*.

277 | P a g e

Honesty in music was important to me early on. This would later show through in many of the choices I made regarding artists I covered in the pages of the *Boulder Weekly*, along with the questions I asked. Growing up, I had spent hours and hours alone listening to the Alarm and U2, two bands that wore their hearts on their sleeves in the lyrical realm and delivered their melodic songs with unbridled passion. I later grew to appreciate bands like Counting Crows and King's X for their earnestness and honesty. I discovered the Samples and was blown away by the candidness of feelings expressed by frontman Sean Kelly. The music fit the words so perfectly, and I would spend hours during lonely college weekend afternoons and nights listening to albums like *The Last Drag* and *Outpost*, trying to play along with Andy Sheldon's melodic, often syncopated bass parts on my purple Peavey Dynabass (hey, it was dark purple, so it looked black! My choices were limited—two basses that I loved, a really old ESP and a cherry-red Peavey Patriot, had been stolen out of my car a year or two prior).

And then there was one of the greatest musical discoveries of all, which also happened while I was in college—Vigilantes of Love. I had first heard of Vigilantes' front man Bill Mallonee in Christian rock publications, and Dan Russell, someone I respected in the industry, was managing him. The first V.O.L. record I listened to was *Blister Soul*. While I liked the idea of the band, I wasn't sold on the disc. About a year later, however, my opinion of the band would change irrevocably when I digested a V.O.L. sampler I had been given and heard Bill's masterpiece "Welcome to Struggleville" for the first time. I was hooked, and I continued to inject V.O.L. into my musical veins. The following fall semester, I interviewed Bill for a college project, and a friendship began that has continued to his very day.

Bill has remained someone I respect and admire as a songwriter, performer and person. He's had his ups and downs, retired V.O.L. (soon after the overlooked, beautiful pop disc *Summershine* was released—an album I played over and over continuously for weeks upon its release—my roommate Tim and I couldn't get enough) and began a solo career. He currently tours with wife Muriah as a two-piece and plays as many house concerts, coffeehouses and small bars and sometimes churches as he can each year. He's very DIY (like Mike Peters of the Alarm) and amazes me with his energy and preponderance of releasing song after song, EP after EP and album after album.

He shines with what I love about music—humor, honesty, learned lyric writing with a heightened amount of intelligence, a lack of fear, and a desire to ask questions and try to experience a relationship with the Almighty. He, like me, has gotten to a place where the past is the past, you look toward the future, lick your wounds and are thankful for the days you have. It was only fitting that Bill should be the final interview for this book.

Initially, I decided to ask Bill some of the same questions I asked him during an interview for a *Boulder Weekly* piece in 2000 (included earlier in this book) and add some additional questions if time permitted. I decided instead to take one of his answers from that interview and formulate it into the first question, which became, paraphrased, "Do you still consider yourself a confessional writer?" The focus then became his career and his thoughts about his long foray into the music world.

Even better, during a phone conversation when trying to determine an interview time, Bill described how he'd prefer to respond to the questions by e-mail. He stated that his answers would be more focused, and he knew it would save a lot of time spent in transcription. He was certainly correct and knew the laborious nature of that little-known facet of journalism—recorded interviews take a huge amount of time to put on paper. Most of the interviews in this book took two to five hours each to transcribe. I did hire someone to handle that task for many of them, but I still had to go back and make edits and research names and places. Listening back to the recordings and editing accordingly takes almost as long as doing the actual transcriptions. So I was very thankful to Bill for taking that piece away from me for this last interview.

This time-saving aspect couldn't have come at a better time. A few months prior to my conversation with Bill regarding the final interview, I had made a tough decision and decided to sell the house I had owned for eight-and-a-half years. There was still a lot of stress with transitioning myself into becoming a renter again and having a roommate. But I had to be an adult and admit that the time had come for a change. The truth be told, I couldn't justify continuing to pay my mortgage. My current full-time job wouldn't truly allow me the continued expense of living larger than I could afford. I also knew if I remained in my house, it would be difficult to have a roommate. I tried that once. It lasted two months. The house was filled with the possessions I valued and it was "my" space. So the lengthy process of prepping and listing my house began.

I sold most of my furniture, including a seven-foot long black leather couch that looked as if you could lie on it and confess your innermost conflicts and emotional constipation to a psychologist, and some of the artwork I had accumulated and didn't want to move. I dragged countless items to my parents' house to store in their garage (then later moved most of them to a storage unit). I went as far as selling my elliptical machine and sixty-pound rubber floor mat and joined a gym. It was extremely cathartic in a way to get rid of a lot of items I had become attached to over the years, but there was also a sense of loss and a bit of an identity crisis. I was Chris, the guy who owned his own place. I could have people over whenever I wanted to. I could go home and be left alone whenever I desired. I could have dates over and mix martinis without interruption. Now everything had shifted; I didn't know what would be next. I'm grateful to the Lord that He brought about a good living situation in the same general area. It made moving easy. My buddy Tim (not my college roommate Tim), always a generous soul with his time, helped me move the furniture I had left in about an hour—that's loading and unloading. I had the U-Haul for about two hours and drove it only eight miles.

My house, during the selling-of-furniture process and especially after the Saturday with the U-Haul, morphed into a big empty room with an air mattress in the middle of the living/dining room. Every day, more items would be gone and eventually it was just an old pub high-top table where I continued to work on this book, some items in the fridge and my clothes. I'd walk around and clap my hands, hearing a deep echo, when before there was too much stuff that would deaden the sound. I'd sometimes pace around the house and wonder if selling was a good idea, but I kept reminding myself that it needed to be done.

Then the final day in my home came. It was Friday, May 31. I was up very early, diligently piling final items into my car and cleaning. That afternoon, I would give possession over to the new owners at the closing. I was already enveloped in a blanket of stress. At seven fifteen a.m. I had received an e-mail message from my realtor that I didn't discover until a follow-up text message popped up on my phone. It simply read, "Chris, could you scan or take a picture of your driver's license and send it over?" This was not the type of message one wanted to receive the same day his or her closing was to take place. Apparently due to a misspelling of my last name, the buyer's lender wanted legal verification of the spelling of my last name. I took the photo and quickly sent it, and the stress had begun.

Then another e-mail a short time later, "Chris, could you sign this attached document showing the spelling of your name?" Sure. No problem. Then yet another message about signing one more document that confirmed the document I had just signed.

But, folks, it didn't end there. As I'm almost ready to lock up and leave for the last time, another note across the screen of my iPhone. "Chris, the closing won't be at one, more like two. The loan company doesn't have the final figures to the title company." "OK, no big deal," I thought. I took the high road and decided to remain as calm as possible. I had to get out of there, though, and I started driving in the direction of my realtor's office, where the closing was to take place. I was hungry by that time, and settled on a Safeway store after I had located my realtor's office. I knew I could easily get a cheap deli sandwich there.

I walked out of the Safeway with the sandwich and a generic diet cola and went to my car, turned on the air conditioning, listened to a comedy station and vegged out, thinking it would just be a couple of hours. I'd check my phone every so often, as my realtor was going to let me know when the time had been changed. I would receive updates every so often and, before I knew it, I had been in that parking lot for over two hours. I drove around a bit a couple different times to alleviate my growing frustration, fear and boredom. Each time the text or e-mail would say, "We are still waiting for the lender to send over the final numbers." There was very little they could do.

Finally, after praying, cursing, and letting my thoughts swirl for the afternoon, it was down to the wire—the car clock read five p.m., and I knew that my closing that day was in jeopardy. I found Ironworks, a brewpub I hadn't been to since 1999 when I first joined the band Breathing Eve and we'd practice over at a house in Lakewood where Chad (also in Crash Orchid and Able Archer) and one of the other band members, Jeremy, lived. It was kind of nostalgic and kind of apropos to the occasion. I quickly washed down a couple of beers, realized I had last been at this pub at another time of serious change in my life, and then got the e-mail I hoped I'd get: "Chris, how fast can you get to the title office?"

I left the title company's building at about eight that night but at least everything went smoothly once we were there. My realtor was very apologetic but, again, it wasn't his fault. Such is life and business proceedings.

This book is all about my moving from one place to another and things that happened while I was there, and it's about the music and people who left an indelible mark on me. It's about musicians speaking, largely unedited, about their past, their future, and their craft. It's about the Bill Mallonees, the Ray Davieses, the Mike Peterses, the Bruce Cockburns, the Ben Gibbards, etc., all communicating as musicians do, sharing their talents and gifts with the world. It's about people and the humor and seriousness of life, along with a celebration of well-crafted art. It's about asking questions (sometimes too many).

Thank you for reading. It's been thirty-nine interesting years as I write this—maybe another year or two before you read it, but, again, thanks. And thank you once more to all the people and musicians who have colored my life and weaved themselves and their art through it; without whom this book would have never been written.

****

Right before *Audible Sigh* came out on Compass, you described yourself as a "confessional" writer. Do you feel this still holds true? How has your perspective changed?
Hard to assess it all after fifty-plus records, Chris. I'm still writing fifty songs a year and releasing records. I don't even think about the audience, really. I say this with no vitriol: I've always been denied access to whatever "inner circle" of hipness or coolness got an artist to blow up and become a household word. My endeavor has been about me being me. I've never written with an audience in mind. I've simply written as the songs keep coming, tried to get better at my craft and playing, recorded tons of records and toured like crazy all over these twenty-two years. Hopefully what one hears is something called "authenticity." I guess by "confessional," I mean less "tabloid-personal" and more of an "everyman" kind of stance. We live in similar skin, and that has to be the reference point for any art to connect with others. The notion of what defines a "hero" is something I've delved into in recent years. We all have the chance to be such on any given day and at any given moment. I think my songs are me "working it out" in an existential world.

How do you view your musical career now, versus when you first started? Anything you would do differently or avoid altogether?
It has much to do with the superstructure it was played out in. Vigilantes of Love was a cutting-edge band, I believe. I did write songs from a faith perspective, but there was never any agenda whatsoever in the music. I don't think some critics or audiences could grasp that. We tended to garner fans who were struggling with depression, grief, addictions or who were burned out on fear-driven religion. Me? I just wanted to

play my brand of rock 'n' roll. To my mind, we were an Americana rock band that could play to all nuances of that definition. You have to realize that all this was going down about the time of Uncle Tupelo's emergence. My reference points, artistically, were artists like Neil Young and the Byrds. But thematically? Lyrically? I think we were all our own. That being said, I think V.O.L. was embraced by folks who would describe themselves as thinking, evangelical Christians. In some way, Vigilantes of Love was branded as a Christian band in a day and age when such categorizations were a kiss of death. Maybe we were groundbreaking, since now it seems that many artists can discuss "bigger themes" without it branding them commercially. I hate to dwell on this stuff; it's bad energy. I trusted way too many people who had no idea what I was about as an artist, nor did they have the courage to say, "We can't do this job." They had good intentions, but no experience. I think I was duped. What that meant in practice was that, as an artist, I was constantly placing my fellow musician friends in peril by trusting these folks. Me? I was young, hungry, and writing seventy-five songs a year from like 1991 to 2002. The band was getting fantastic attention from national press from almost every quarter. I just wanted to write, play and perform with my bandmates. We were absolutely committed to the hard, grueling work of touring. My guys were heroes.

How has your faith changed over the course of your career?
Being a writer is a solitary kind of life. I need that form of loneliness to create, I guess. When it comes to faith, it's become more "desperate." So many of the early "non-negotiables" I hold a little more lightly. I think I've learned to live with the incongruities of life and even those in the Bible. One has to make room for wider, more compassionate views. But yeah, more desperate—by that I mean it's a do-or-die sort of arrangement. Believing in Christ's historic resurrection as proclaimed by the early Church is something of cataclysmic ramifications. That's a lot to take at face value, you know? And I do trust it as far as I am able. But at the end

of the day, I suspect you just start talking to Him. Really, that's all there is to it. Talk and live a life that isn't driven by fear and hate. I bring nothing to the equation, and if God so desires a relationship with me, then I must confess, I have no idea why or why He/She seems absent from the world much of the time. Those are things I've wrestled with in songs since the mid-'90s. I read scripture a lot. The world aches. People ache. I ask God to show Him/Herself in my life so I might perceive that woundedness and bring a little good to those around me. My faith has been a paring-down of what's essential and what works for me. I don't mean that in the selfish sense, either. There's a lot in the whole religious enterprise that seems driven by fear, arrogance and hate. I've no use for any of it, even if that means abandoning something that on the surface is doctrinally correct. The whole notion of the Church has been pretty elusive for me. How it showed up, what the early apostles claimed for it, how it evolved, and even the claims it's made for itself over the centuries is something I give less attention to. I have to live in the here and now. At the end of the day, one can only bring a wayward, fickle heart—and ask for mercy and grace. There's a quote from Paul Tillich: "Accept your acceptance. The courage to be is the courage to accept oneself in spite of being unacceptable."

How do you come up with material? Any cures for writer's block? A nice IPA or a walk in the desert?
Walks in the desert and IPAs are quite nice, but they rarely "inspire" the songs. After twenty-two years of it, I wish I knew how to dissect it a bit, but I don't. I do feel like it is a gift, even a communication sometimes from elsewhere. You tap into it and ride it. It's why I often come up with seven to eight verses for every song. Honestly? I usually just pick up a guitar and something shows up. Lyrics and music. All there. I try to never overthink it. I know that sounds all too easy. Seriously? It usually is. One chord, one melody, one little technical movement or an idea leads to another. Song's done. Sure, some of it is trusting one's gut. But that also assumes that you've schooled your instincts, you know? I don't edit

my processes or what comes of it very much at all. Muriah saw some show recently on savants. After seeing it, she wondered if there might not be some element of that in the way my brain works, in the way I write. I dunno, really. I love the nuances of feeling that emerge while I'm engaged in it. It feels very salvific, saving, sometimes even cleansing. It's all very personal. A nomenclature I've made just for myself. It's still very drenched in the Americana mindset. It's not a trance state or anything like that, but there is definitely a certain place I go to to bring a song to birth. I used to write on tours a lot when it was a full band. These days, with just Muriah and I doing the folk-duo thing, I get to lay back, look at the scenery and talk with the missus. Then, when I get home, it's not uncommon to write six to seven songs in a week That's why I started doing the WPA EP releases, recorded lovingly on four tracks. It's too many songs to hammer out in a studio with a full band, although I would love for each one of them to get that kind of attention. Still, the intimate quality and immediacy of the WPA series (there are at least eighteen EPs now) is something many fans have said they prefer over the "bigger" sounding studio albums.

Did Josh or Joe [Bill's sons. –Ed.] ever pursue music? What would your thoughts be if either of them was to choose music as a vocation?
They both love music. Can't live without it. Joe is self-taught on mandolin and likes to smack a set of drums once in a spell. At this point I think they've seen just how brutal and uncertain the whole music biz is—I've spent the last six out of eight years in poverty. But who knows? I didn't start playing guitar and writing songs until I was thirty-one. I started on drums when I was twelve and played in lots of bands, so I knew lots about music, arrangements and how instruments work together.

Frederick Buechner is an amazing writer. How did you discover his work and how has that influenced you personally and professionally? Any other writers currently on your reading list?

I stumbled on Mr. Buechner's work in 1992, I think. We were on tour. Years of evangelical "buzz" language and the pithy little phrases and platitudes Christians seemed to use to communicate with each other had just burned me out. I would sit in Bible studies and think I was witnessing and participating in some strange play. It was a study in denial and unreality. I was bored to death. But Buechner introduced me to a view of the Bible and Jesus Christ—Scripture that was bracing, sober and above all life-affirming. He's an ordained Presbyterian minister, but don't hold that against him! The first book I read was *The Hungering Dark*, a collection of short essays on spiritual topics. Buechner has published over fifty books. I've read a good many of them. All beautiful and nurturing. His ability to expound the truths of time-worn (and often misapplied Scriptures) was electrifying to me. I've never met anyone who has read him who came away disappointed. His take on the universality of God's love is behind the scenes in all of my work.

If a time capsule was unearthed in a hundred years, what song of yours would you want featured and why?
Can't really answer that question. Not being evasive, but I love all of my children equally.

Future plans?
Love life, enjoy all of its glory and joys. Never give in to bitterness. Love all. Carry grace everywhere, since we've all been recipients of it. Bring some light to the world. The songs keep coming, so they get recorded. I'll release three to four EPs a year, plus a full-band studio recording every year. I know it's oversaturation, but the low-budget touring and home recordings are the only income I really have. And at fifty-plus albums over twenty-two years, I've sorta committed, you know? Me? I'm getting ready for oblivion. Shy of a miracle, nothing's really going to change. The "shakers and movers," the "inner circles," "gatekeepers" and "hipsters" have kept me outside for years. No, I don't think it's a conspiracy, but it's been near impossible to garner attention or get my records profiled. They can have their

game. I'm building a world. Politely, I say, "Fuck 'em." I never needed their permission to do or be the writer I am anyway. And deprivation makes for some great art, I think. I'm still here, so to speak, and it's all fan-driven. That's a beautiful thing. You get used to poverty and her sisters after a spell. Keep recording, playing, praying.

Note to self: "Don't die."

CPSIA information can be obtained
at www.ICGtesting.com
Printed in the USA
FSOW02n1023120215
5156FS